MARXISM
Last Refuge of the Bourgeoisie?

MARXISM

Last Refuge of the Bourgeoisie?

Paul Mattick
Edited by Paul Mattick, Jr.

M. E. SHARPE, INC.
Armonk, New York

THE MERLIN PRESS
London

© 1983 by M. E. Sharpe, Inc.
80 Business Park Drive, Armonk, New York 10504

Published in the United Kingdom by The Merlin Press, 3 Manchester Road, London, E. 14

Library of Congress Cataloging in Publication Data

Mattick, Paul, 1904-
    Marxism—last refuge of the bourgeoisie?

    Includes bibliographical references.
    1. Marx, Karl, 1818-1883. 2. Communism. 3. Communism and society.
4. Middle classes. 5. Marxian economics.
I. Mattick, Paul. II. Title.
HX39.5.M384 1983   335.4   83-620
ISBN 0-87332-233-9 U.S.
ISBN 0-87332-286-X U.S. paperback
ISBN 0850363071 UK
ISBN 085036308X UK paperback

Printed in the United States of America

Bourgeois class rule fights its last battle
under a false flag, under the flag of revolution itself.

ROSA LUXEMBURG

To the Memory of
Marinus van der Lubbe

Contents

Foreword

The present book, Paul Mattick's last writing, was unfinished at his death in February 1981. I have included, as a final chapter, an essay written in 1978 that summarizes the theme of the book. But it may still be useful to introduce these pages with a few words on the projected whole of which they were to be part.

On the manuscript title page Paul wrote, "A summing up/ A summon up." *Marxism—Last Refuge of the Bourgeoisie?* was to be a final statement of a lifetime's reflection on capitalist society and revolutionary opposition to it. Arguing that Marxism, as a *critique* of political economy, could be of service to the development of bourgeois theory and practice only if emptied of its essential content, Paul answers the question in his title with a clear No. For this reason the book is also a summons to action, since Marxism's comprehension of modern society—the only alternative so far to that society's failed attempts to understand itself—implies the necessity of active opposition to the system of wage labor in all its forms.

Marx's analysis of capitalist society was neither an economic nor a political theory. Instead, by showing that bourgeois politics is dominated by economic questions, and that the latter are only the ideological representation of social class relations, Marx demonstrated the limits inherent in both sets of categories, the political and the economic, for the explanation of social reality. The workers' movement against capitalism, he showed, would have to abolish both capital and the state, replacing "economics" and "politics" with the self-organization of the "free and associated producers."

Since Marx's time, however, the two aspects of his unified critique of politics and economics have been represented by differ-

ent individuals and political currents. The Stalinist Henryk Gross-
mann, for example, was the major figure in the rediscovery of
Marx's critique of economics, while Rosa Luxemburg, who understood this critique imperfectly, developed Marx's theory of the socialist movement as working-class self-organization. Paul Mattick
alone in our time recombined these strains into an analysis of the
many-sided process that constitutes the capitalist mode of production. Moreover, as the various organizational forms and ideological expressions of the Marxist movement have been part of
the unfolding of this mode of production, he saw that the Marxist
critique must be extended also to them.

This book, accordingly, was envisioned in four basic parts.
The first centers on a restatement of the fundamentals of the
Marxian critique of political economy, with special attention to
those aspects of Marx's theory—the labor-value analysis of price,
and the empirical validity of the theory—that have been the main
points at once of bourgeois attack and of Marxist writers' retreat
into bourgeois economic analysis. The second part traces the history of the main forms of the Marxist political movement, Social
Democracy and Bolshevism, to show how adoption of the structures of bourgeois politics has implied the abandonment of both
socialist practice and Marxian theory. A third section, unwritten,
would have explored recent attempts on the part of economists,
radical and otherwise, to overcome the ever more visible bankruptcy of their discipline by integrating elements of Marxism into
it. In *Marx and Keynes*[1] Paul had already shown the failure of an
earlier form of this attempt, in the realm of theory as well as in
that of political-economic policy. In the present work the argument was to be extended to "post-Keynesian," "neo-Ricardian,"
and "Marxist economic" theory. The final section of the book
would have returned to its starting point, the restatement of the
basic principles of Marxism, with an analysis of the meaning of socialist revolution at the present time. Here Paul intended to discuss
both forms of revolutionary action and the nature of the postrevolutionary social organization—a system of workers' councils—
implied by the abolition of wage labor and the state.

Unfortunately, there is no one person alive who could complete this book, or write a substitute for it—who has not just the
breadth of knowledge necessary but the irreplaceable personal experience of the twentieth-century working-class movement. But

one can hope that the increasingly apparent need for the abolition
of private-property capitalism in the "West" and of the party-state
system in the "East" will produce new generations of socialists
who will carry on the theoretical and practical struggle to which
Paul wished this book to summon us up.

Meanwhile, it has seemed to me immensely worthwhile to
publish the book, even in its unfinished state. Paul characteristically
wrote and rewrote, draft after draft. In this case, his conception of
the book changed after he had written the first part: what had be-
gun as a critique of post-Keynesian economics turned into a more
ambitious project. He continued writing, planning to rewrite the
work as a whole when he had completed a draft. In doing this he
would undoubtedly have changed it very much, not just stylistically,
but also by the rearrangement and even alteration of content.

The text here published is essentially the text Paul wrote. I
edited all his manuscripts from *Marx and Keynes* on. For the most
part this meant catching grammatical and semantic slips, although
I would also sometimes suggest rearrangements of material. I proceeded in the same fashion in editing this book, although in this
case Paul could not make the final decision on what suggested
changes to adopt. The second essay was much rearranged, to clarify
the course of the argument; the second half of the manuscript
was reorganized into a larger number of shorter essays.

This was the first book that Paul wished to dedicate. Marinus
van der Lubbe, the man who burned the Reichstag in early 1933,
was a member of the Dutch Group of International Communists.
In January 1934 Paul published an article exposing the Third International's attempts to portray van der Lubbe as a Nazi agent
even as the Nazis portrayed him as a Communist agent.[2] Van der
Lubbe, Paul wrote, "saw how fascism was developing in Germany
and how the labor parties did nothing to oppose it. . . . On the eve
of the fascists' seizure of political power the workers' leaders had
nothing to advise but the fraud of parliamentary activity. In protest against this swindle van der Lubbe set the Reichstag on fire, as
a sign that it was not voting but revolution that was needed. . . .
Van der Lubbe is no Nazi agent, but a class-conscious worker, to
whom the sympathies of the revolutionary proletariat are due."
One could hardly appeal to a revolutionary proletariat today. But
by invoking the memory of Marinus van der Lubbe, I believe, Paul
meant to remind us that at a moment like this, when capitalism is

making good on its promise of economic collapse, and threatens nuclear war and ecological catastrophe to boot, the limits of reform indicate the need both for a radical critique of the system's ideological bases and a revolutionary abolition of the realities they reflect.

PAUL MATTICK, JR.

MARXISM
AND
BOURGEOIS
ECONOMICS

Introduction

Insofar as the criticism of political economy represents a class, it can, according to Marx, "only represent that class whose vocation in history is the overthrow of the capitalist mode of production and the final abolition of all classes—the proletariat."[1] In Marx's view, political economy was the theoretical expression of the rising capitalist society, which found nothing contradictory in the specific class relations that made its own development possible. The *critique* of political economy focused exactly on the contradictions inherent in capital production in both theoretical and practical terms. The practical critique remained, at first, the actual struggle between labor and capital over wages and profits within the framework of capitalist production relations. But this struggle implied and expressed a definite developmental trend of capitalism, pointing in the direction of its eventual dissolution. To lay bare this trend was the function of the theoretical critique of political economy.

Just as the proletariat opposed the bourgeoisie, so Marx confronted bourgeois economic theory: not in order to develop it, or to improve it, but to destroy its apparent validity and, finally, with the abolition of capitalism, to overcome it altogether. Whereas the actual class struggle within capitalism was still "political economy," albeit from the standpoint of the working class, the critique of bourgeois theory anticipated the end of political economy and therewith the end of the society in which its criticism constitutes a necessary part of the proletarian fight for emancipation.

Marx's critique of political economy is both an immanent criticism of bourgeois economic theory, made by showing that there is no connection between that theory's assumptions and the conclusions drawn from them, and a fundamental criticism, which

3

maintains that by assuming its own economic relations to be natural and unchangeable the whole of bourgeois economic theory fails, and must fail, to comprehend its own society, thereby condemning itself to misapprehend its own development as well as to misconceive its state of being at any particular time. For Marx, bourgeois political economy was incapable of being the theory of its own practice and could serve only as an ideology to safeguard the social conditions of its existence.

With regard to the past, it was true of course that bourgeois economic theory was the expression of the bourgeoisie's own class struggle within and against feudal society, and to that extent was able to see in the development of production and the productivity of labor the vehicle for social change and the basis of capital accumulation. The classic labor theory of value emerged together with the rise of the bourgeoisie, which considered itself a progressive class because it fostered the increase of the wealth of nations. But with its consolidation as a new ruling class, the bourgeoisie found its early insight into the social labor process quite embarrassing, for it was now confronted by a working class that challenged capitalism on the strength of its own labor-based theory of production by demanding more, or all, of the social product. From then on it was for the bourgeoisie "no longer a question, whether this theorem or that was true, but whether it was useful to capital or harmful, expedient or inexpedient, politically dangerous or not. In place of disinterested enquirers, there were hired prize fighters; in place of genuine scientific research, the bad conscience and the evil intent of apologetic."[2]

Marx spoke thus of two different schools of political economy—the "classical," extending from Adam Smith to David Ricardo, and "vulgar economy," which saw its sole purpose in the justification of the capitalist *status quo*. Whereas there was a necessary connection between classical theory and Marx's critique of political economy, this congruity dissipated with the further development of bourgeois theory, to be totally lost with the rise of the subjective theory of value and the restriction of economics to the study of price and market relations. The connection between Marx and the classics does not, however, imply an identity between the bourgeois and the Marxian value concepts, but merely refers to the common recognition that it is labor that bestows value upon commodities. The classical theory was not just a weaker version of Marx's value theory, but a different theory altogether, because the classical value theory had failed "to solve the riddle of surplus value."[3]

Marx's theory of value and surplus value, implying the exploitation of labor by capital, could only find an antagonistic reception in bourgeois economics and was either totally ignored or "refuted" by a simultaneous disowning of classical economy in the shift from "political economy" to "economics"—a positive science that concerns itself exclusively with exchange relations, apart from any consideration of the social production relations on which they are based. This, of course, was as it should be, even though Marx himself voiced some disappointment over the meager response his work elicited among bourgeois economists. His economic writings, particularly *Capital*, became, in Friedrich Engels' rather inappropriate phrase, "the Bible of the working class," and as such found only derision in bourgeois economic doctrine. "Marxism"—another unfortunate expression—was recognized as the revolutionary ideology of the working class, which stood in unbridgeable opposition to the capitalist class and to the set of ideas justifying its existence.

How things have changed since then. Not only has capitalism undergone extensive modifications through its own development, which have found their reflections in bourgeois economic theory; Marxism, too, has altered its character in the course of the shifting fortunes of capitalist society. The successful expansion of capital and the amelioration of the conditions of the laboring class led to spreading doubt regarding the validity of Marx's critical theory. This doubt drew its strength not so much from an immanent criticism of this theory, as from its confrontation with an empirical reality that seemed to contradict Marx's expectations with respect to capitalism's future. Marxism became an increasingly more ambiguous doctrine, serving purposes different from those initially contemplated. This change was still in line with the Marxian conception that changes in material conditions will alter the consciousness of men, but this must now be applied to the reception of Marxism itself. It lost its revolutionary implications and became the false ideology of a nonrevolutionary practice.

The accommodation of socialist theory to the realities of the unfolding capitalist system was brought about through the incorporation of bourgeois economic ideas into the framework of Marxism. Until recently, however, there was no reciprocal response on the part of the bourgeoisie, for

> Marx was not merely the author of a scientific treatise, but also the great leader of the socialist movement. He was, therefore, a person whose conclusions were so unacceptable to economists that few of them had any will or patience to endeavor to profit by the aspects of his work which might have been serviceable to them. So that, as far as theoretical political economy is concerned, the influence of Marx was, for a time at least, almost altogether indefinite.[4]

This attitude was of an exemplary consistency—which cannot be said for the position taken by the proponents of "Marxist economics." As classical economy degenerated into vulgar economy, a type of "vulgar Marxism" arose which tried to avail itself of the "progress" being made in the "science of economics." The marginal utility theory seemed to be a closer approximation to actual price formation than was Marx's derivation of prices from labor-time values. The exchange of one theory for the other was deemed the more desirable because the marginal principle was not restricted to capitalistic exchange relations, but could be regarded as a universal and therefore neutral principle valid for all times and all societies. So there were, after all, "economic laws" that could be appreciated by friend and foe alike, thus breaking down the harsh dividing line between opposing social systems.

In contrast to Marx, modern "Marxists" tend to see in bourgeois economic theory more than just apologetics inasmuch as it also serves the practical needs of economic policy:

> If bourgeois economists objectively investigate some aspects of the economy and thereby determine the results of one or another policy, they perform a useful function for capital, quite aside from their simultaneous ideological defense of the system. Instead of merely pointing to the apologetic nature of bourgeois theory, Marxists should consider and evaluate its practical consequences and recognize the double function of the economists.[5]

This concession on the part of "Marxism" has found some reciprocation in the bourgeois camp. Attempts have been made to overcome the strict opposition of bourgeois economy to Marxism, in order to utilize some of the findings of the latter for the "enrichment" of bourgeois theory.

This two-pronged endeavor to reconcile, at least to some extent, the historical antagonism between Marxism and bourgeois economic theory reflected a crisis in Marxism as well as in bourgeois theory. While the crisis of Marxism is a long spun out affair, dating back to the turn of the century, the crisis in bourgeois theory came together with the Great Depression in the wake of the first world war, which demonstrated the falsity of neoclassical price and market theory. The latter, however, found some sort of resurrection through its Keynesian modifications. Although it had to be admitted that the assumed equilibrium mechanism of the market was not operative, it was now asserted that it could be made so with a little governmental help. The disequilibrium of insufficient demand could be straightened out by government-induced production for "public consumption," not only under static assumptions but also under conditions of economic growth, with appropriate monetary and fiscal policies.

According to the "neo-Keynesian synthesis," a market economy enriched by government planning would overcome capitalism's susceptibility to crisis and depression and allow, in principle, for a steady growth of capitalist production. The long economic upswing after World War II seemed to substantiate these expectations. But despite the continuing availability of governmental interventions, a new crisis followed this period of capital expansion, as it always had in the past. The clever "fine-tuning" of the economy and the "trade-off" between inflation and unemployment did not prevent a new economic decline, manifesting itself in growing unemployment, with, and despite, an increasing rate of inflation. The crisis and the means designed to cope with it proved to be equally detrimental to capital.

Apart from the fact that actual crisis conditions brought the crisis of bourgeois economic theory to a head, its long-standing impoverishment through its increasing formalization, via marginalism and general equilibrium theory, raised many doubts in the heads even of academic economists. The current questioning of all the assumptions of neoclassical theory and its Keynesian offspring has led to a half-hearted return to classical political economy, most forcefully represented by the so-called neo-Ricardians. Marx himself is frequently looked upon as a Ricardian economist and as such finds increasing favor among bourgeois theoreticians, who now attempt to integrate his "pioneer work" into their own specialty, the science of economics. Meanwhile, just as the return from economics to political economy is in some quarters adjudged a progressive step within the field of economic theory, so the adoption of some of the analytical methods evolved by bourgeois economics is hailed in the "Marxist" camp as pointing to important similarities with respect to the problems to be solved and the tools available for their solution in both capitalism and socialism, thus indicating that there are general economic laws valid for all societies.

Strange as it may seem, the new interest in Marxism in general and in "Marxist economics" in particular does not stem from a revived Marxist labor movement but pertains almost exclusively to the academic world, which is essentially the world of the middle class. An enormous outpouring of Marxist literature is occurring at a time when the labor movement—not to speak of the workers as a class—finds itself at the historically lowest ebb of its emancipatory aspirations. "Marxology" has become a new profession, and there are Marxist branches in "radical" economics and other social science disciplines. This academization of Marxism goes hand in hand with the adoption of the term "Marxism" by national and social movements that have not the remotest connection with the problems that were Marx's concern. All this may imply no more than a passing intellectual fad, but even as such it bears evidence of the twilight state of modern society, which is no longer the capitalism of old and, short of a proletarian revolution, cannot be transformed into socialism. Moreover, "Marxism" in its apparently "realized form" in the self-styled "socialist countries" seems to offer a way out of the present impasse, or at least, suggests the direction in which capitalism must move to solve its crisis problem without sacrificing its social-class or production relations.

The current preoccupation with Marxism on the part of social scientists and the "modernization" of Marxist theory has led to an amalgam of erroneous and contradictory interpretations that becloud more than clarify Marx's intentions and the implications of his theory for capitalist society. Before discussing the various endeavors to integrate Marxism into the body of bourgeois economic theory, or to accommodate the latter to the teachings of Marx, it is thus unavoidable—once again—to start with an exposition of Marx's critique of political economy and to elucidate its true content. Only then will it be possible to demonstrate the wide disparities between Marx's own position and the various misinterpretations it has found in the numerous attempts to bridge the contradiction between Marxism and bourgeois economic theory. Accordingly, what follows proceeds from a presentation of Marx's critique of political economy, in as short a form as possible, to a discussion of the different receptions it has found in socialist and bourgeois circles. It will then be possible to evaluate the present state of both bourgeois economics and Marxism, and their relation to one another, and to understand the reasons for their apparent predisposition to converge as a mere reflection of the general crisis of capitalist production.

Value
and
Price

Although classical economic theory had been able to recognize in labor the source of value, it was incapable of reconciling the production of surplus value with the exchange of equivalents required by the law of value. By failing to distinguish between labor and labor power, David Ricardo could not consistently apply the value concept in his investigations of the capitalist economy and its development. But then, Ricardo took capitalist society for granted; he was not so much concerned with the capitalist exploitation relations as with the distribution of the social product between the recipients of wages, profits, and rent, on which in his view the fortunes of capital accumulation depended. He saw the value of commodities as emerging out of the physical production process and not, as did Karl Marx, out of the specific social production relations of capitalism, which are what make a mere production process into a value-producing and value-expanding process.

Like Marx, Ricardo was little interested in the determination of particular market prices, but concerned himself with the broad aggregates of production and distribution as determined by the existing class relations. In his view, the value of labor equals its costs of production. Profits result from the difference between the amount of labor required to produce the workers' subsistence and the value of the total social product. The less the workers receive, the more the capitalists will get, and vice versa. In Ricardo's view, this division of the social product between labor and capital depends, on the one hand, on the value equivalent of the means of existence of the labor force and, on the other hand, on the competition of the workers for employment, as determined by the Malthusian law of population. The value of labor varies here not only with its cost of production but also with the state of supply and demand on the labor market. Similar inconsistencies were displayed in his distribution theory with respect to profit and rent, thereby disqualifying the value concept as the sole key for comprehending the capitalist world. Thus Ricardo was not able to detect the contradictions of capitalism in capitalist production itself, but found them in the progressive exhaustion of the soil, which, by raising the cost of production for labor, diminishes the profits of capital in favor of rent, thereby impeding the capitalist accumulation process.

While Marx fully appreciated Ricardo's acuity, he was nonetheless obliged to point to his inconsistencies, ambiguities, and confusions, not only in order to strengthen the coherence of the labor theory of value, but also to ask the hitherto unraised question of why there was value production, and a corresponding theory, in the first place. Marx noticed that the classical concept of value, although derived from capitalist exchange relations, was not restricted theoretically to these relations but was conceived as identifying a phenomenon valid throughout history. This may already be gathered from Adam Smith's definition of human nature as characterized by a "propensity to exchange," as well as by his illustration of the exchange of labor-time values in an "early and rude state of society" in which neither capital nor landed property exists. For Ricardo, too, this was "really the foundation of the exchangeable value of all things, excepting those which cannot be increased by human industry."[1] There is, however, no evidence that this rule of exchange actually prevailed in precapitalist times and the assumption that it did implies no more than the ascription of contemporary conditions to the past, or a reading of history with capitalist eyes.

Of course, the hypothetical labor-time exchange broke down as soon as capital and landed property entered the picture, giving rise to all the inconsistencies of classical value theory. Although Marx, too, started his value analysis with the exchange of equivalents, he did so not on the assumption that such an exchange is a real possibility, either in the present or the past, but as a methodological device for demonstrating that an exchange of labor-time equivalents presupposes the existence of the capital-labor relationship and the transformation of labor power into a commodity— that is, that the exchange of labor-time equivalents is nothing other than a means to the appropriation of surplus-value by capital.

It was necessary to deal with the phenomenon of value not only because it was the principle of bourgeois political economy, but also by reason of the fact that commodities can only be exchanged after they have been produced, and because the varying production times required for different commodities necessarily have some effect upon their relative values. As Marx remarked, "all economy is economy of time"; but labor time is one thing and labor-time value another. Commodities appear as values not because their production requires time but because they are commodities, produced for exchange, and are therefore in need of a common denominator regulating the exchange. The generalization of commodity production in capitalist society, including the commodification of labor power, demands a universal value equivalent to allow for the distribution of the social labor in accordance with the existing production or property relations between individual capitalists and between them and their workers.

Without these capitalist production relations it would still be necessary to consider labor time, so as to assure a rational social production capable of satisfying the needs and demands of the producers. But in the absence of class and therefore property relations, labor time would merely be a technical datum. It would not appear expressed as value in exchange, but as a direct notation in the material production process, which as such would leave the distribution of the social product indeterminate. In other words, labor time appears as labor-time value not because it is a necessary requirement of social production, but because this production is carried on under specifically capitalist relations of production.

Without attempting to recapitulate Marx's abstract value analysis of commodities and their exchange, it may be pointed out that though human labor creates value, it does not itself possess value, but acquires this character with the commencement of commodity production and its progressive generalization. In order to express the value of any particular commodity in terms of a certain quantity of human labor, this value must be represented by something other than the commodity itself. It must have an existence independent of the existence of the commodity as a thing of utility. As use values, commodities are qualitatively differentiated, just as the kinds of labor involved in their production are qualitatively distinct. But as exchange values, they are expressed in quantitative terms, as different quantities of undifferentiated labor. "Every product of labor," Marx wrote, "is, in all states of society, a use-value, but it is only at a definite historical epoch in a society's development that such a product becomes a commodity, viz., at the epoch when labor spent on the production of useful articles becomes expressed as one of the objective qualities of that article, i.e., as its value."[2]

The concept of value based on labor and seen as an objective quality of the commodity arises with the dominance of commodity production under the auspices of capitalist entrepreneurs and the availability of wage labor—in short, in a society where basic social relations take the form of relations between owners of commodities, either of capital goods or of labor power. These relations seem to arise naturally out of social production itself, whereas in reality their source is in the capitalist class and exploitation relations prevailing at this particular stage of the general development of the social powers of production. Social relations—which are, after all, relations between people—assume here the form of relations between commodities. Under these conditions,

> the labor of the individual asserts itself, as a part of the labor of society, only by means of the relations which the act of exchange establishes directly between the products, and indirectly, through them, between the producers. To the latter therefore, the relations connecting the labor of one individual with that of the rest appear, not as direct relations between the individuals at work, but as what they really are, material relations between persons and social relations between things.[3]

But so it is: a historical fact, which found theoretical expression in the labor theory of value. There is, then, no point in denying the theory's validity, even though it refers to no more than a social production system that can be "social" only via the specific capitalist exchange relations, by way of commodity production. Because exploitation is an integral part of this process, the class profiting from it will see in commodity exchange the regulator of social production, allocating social labor in the socially required proportions, as if guided by an "invisible hand." The "invisible hand" represents what Marx called the "fetishism of commodity production," the control of the producers by their own product and the subordination of social production, and therefore of social life in general, to the vicissitudes of market events.

In order to show that the value concept is itself a fetishistic category, Marx referred to a noncapitalistic mode of production that would also require the consideration of labor time, but without the need to express this fact as a value relationship between commodities, and in which the recognition of individual labor as a part of the total social labor could allow for conscious regulation of social production in accordance with the will of the associated producers. "Political economy," Marx wrote,

> has indeed analyzed, however incompletely, value and its magnitude, and has discovered what lies beneath these forms. But it has never once asked the question why labor is represented by the value of its product and labor time by the magnitude of that value. These formulae, which bear stamped upon them in unmistakable letters, that they belong to a state of society, in which the process of production has the mastery over man, instead of being controlled by him, such formulae appear to the bourgeois intellect to be as much a self-evident necessity imposed by nature as productive labor itself.[4]

The bourgeois labor theory of value represented an attempt both to understand and to justify the capitalist system of production. It looked for the ordering element in the general disorder of market events, and found it in the labor content of commodities, which determines their relative values and regulates their exchange. Without bothering themselves with the question of why the capitalist relations of production must take on the form of value relations between commodities, the bourgeois theoreticians held that varying market prices are merely temporary modifications of commodities' exchange values as determined by labor time. For them, the law of value allocates social labor via the supply and demand relations or, vice versa, the assumed equilibrium tendency of supply and demand implies an equilibrium in terms of labor-time quantities, or the automatic regulation of social production.

Not only in the bourgeois mind, but even in the Marxist camp, the labor theory of value, both in its classical and in its Marxist version, is often seen as an equilibrium mechanism, operating through the market, to bring about the distribution of the social labor required by the system as a whole.[5] In Marx's view, however, the working of the law of value or, what is the same, the lack of conscious regulation of social production, precludes any kind of equilibrium and "regulates" the capitalist economy "like an over-riding law of nature" only in the sense in which "the law of gravity asserts itself when a house falls about our ears."[6] In his view, the dynamics of capitalist production exclude an equilibrium situation with regard to the distribution of the social labor, or to any other aspect of the economy. What the law of value brings about are crisis conditions, which affect capitalist production as soon as its dynamic is impaired by a distribution of the social labor that hinders or prevents the expansion of capital.

To be sure, value production, being the production of surplus value, is not really an exchange between labor and capital, but the appropriation of part of the workers' product by the capitalist owners of the means of production. Although wages are paid for labor power, their commodity equivalents are produced by the workers, plus the commodity equivalent comprising the surplus value, or profits, of the capitalists. The wages merely determine the conditions under which the workers can produce both their own means of subsistence and the surplus product that falls to the capitalists. The capital-labor exchange is only apparent, for the means of production, as well as the capital advanced in the form of wages, are parts of already appropriated surplus value produced during earlier production cycles. This process found its historical starting point in the workers' divorce from the means of production—that is, in the primitive accumulation of capital—which first brought the modern wage worker into existence. The allocation of social labor is thus organized basically not really by exchange relations but by the social production relations. Like the law of value, "wage labor" and "capital" are fetishistic categories for capitalistic exploitation relations. But, again like "value," they are nonetheless names for real relations that determine the nature and development of capitalism.

To speak of the allocation of social labor by the law of value is to refer not to a general necessity, valid for all systems of production, but exclusively to the conditions of capitalist society. Thus it refers not to an allocation of labor that satisfies the regulatory requirements on social production for the various articles of utility on which social life depends, but to an allocation of labor on the basis of its division into labor and surplus labor, or value and surplus value, through the exchange relations represented by the exchange value of commodities. The allocation of social labor required to satisfy the actual needs of the population is merely incidental to its allocation for the production of exchange value. Although, generally, exchange values must also be use values, it is the first and not the second that determines whether goods will be produced or not. Capital, not producing anything at all, appropriates surplus value because of the exchange-value character of labor power, the size of which is determined by the division of labor into necessary and surplus labor, where necessary labor means that required for the production and reproduction of labor power. Thus it is the quantitative relationship between necessary and surplus labor that determines whether or not capitalist production is undertaken, and therewith also the allocation of the social labor under conditions of capital production.

No other social limits are set to the production of exchange value, as an abstract form of wealth, than those that hinder the expansion of surplus value, that is, the extent of the exploitability of labor power. Capitalists strive to appropriate the maximum of surplus value, of unpaid labor, simply because they are capitalists, quite apart from the circumstance that they are also in competition with other capitalists and are therefore compelled to expand their capital by increasing their appropriation of surplus value. Leaving the allocation of labor to the winds, to the "invisible hand," or to the law of value, the production of useful commodities is determined solely by their exchange value, that is, by their capacity to turn surplus value into additional capital. The allocation of social labor is thus determined by the expansion of capital, and the fact of accumulation indicates that the law of value distributes the social labor in accordance with the exploitation relations of capital production.

Capital accumulation is a dynamic process, implying continuous disequilibrium. The appropriation of surplus value and its expansion imply continuous changes in the productivity of labor and therewith in the value and exchange relations in general, as well as with regard to labor and capital. Only conceptually may the system be considered as stationary, should this be of help in comprehending its movements. Actually, there is no static situation: the system either expands or contracts; at no time can it be found in balance.

An increase in the productivity of labor means that more can be produced with less labor. The individual commodity labor-time value decreases with increasing productivity. But the larger quantity of commodities brought forth during the same amount of time previously needed for a smaller one compensates for the loss of labor-time value with respect to the single commodity. The same or a larger exchange value is now expressed in a larger quantity of use values. For the capitalists to be positively affected by an increase in the productivity of labor, the relationship between necessary and surplus labor must be altered. This can be brought about in two ways: either by lengthening the working-day, i.e., the increase of *absolute* surplus value, or through an increase of labor productivity, which reduces the value of labor power by reducing the value of the commodities in which it finds its expression. This increase of *relative* surplus value provides the capitalist rationale for the increase in the productivity of labor.

The twofold character of the commodity, as both a use value and an exchange value, allows for the fact of surplus value. While the workers receive the exchange value of their labor power, the capitalists get its use value, which includes its ability to produce surplus products beyond those containing the necessary labor. Capital accumulation implies a decrease of the value of labor power through its increasing productivity. But as all commodities, and not only those that constitute the commodity equivalent of necessary labor, are affected by the increasing productivity, an increase of production is not necessarily accompanied by an *equal* increase of exchange value. Value production is thus not only the instrument of its own expansion, but also a procedure that may lead to a relative decline of exchange value with respect to the physical expansion of production and the mass of commodities.

This contradictory movement, inherent in the two-sided nature of commodity production, compels the capitalists to always greater efforts in the appropriation of surplus value, for it is only by a relatively faster increase of surplus value that the decline of exchange value associated with the increasing productivity of labor can be countered. In an expanding system like capitalism, however, a greater mass of commodities may well yield an equivalent or greater mass of surplus value despite the commodities' declining exchange value. This decline exists then as a mere tendency, constantly counteracted by the expansion and extension of capital and therefore unnoticeable. Nonetheless, it provides a spur to the accumulation of capital independent of the compulsion of intercapitalist competition. In this way, the relative decline of ex-change value comes to the fore as an absolute growth of value and surplus value, or the accumulation of capital.

As the allocator of social labor in capitalism the law of value implies, first of all, a continuously changing division between necessary and surplus labor and, based on this division, continuous alterations in the exchange relations with regard to both the use-value aspect of commodities and their exchange-value content. But we must now point out that the law of value is not a natural law of the sort that govern physical phenomena, even though it asserts itself as if it were such a law, by seeming to operate outside of hu-man control. The law of value refers in fact to the *results* of a sys-tem of social production that, due to its peculiar social relations, does not and cannot concern itself with production as a social un-dertaking and finds its "regulation" only through the bondage of the commodities' exchange values to their use values.

Surplus value is appropriated in the form of commodities. These commodities, as well as those that satisfy the requirements of necessary labor, must have the quality of being of definite util-ity, even if this has to be quantitatively expressed in their ex-change value. The quantification of the qualitative differences be-tween different commodities, as well as between the various types of labor that produce them, is actually accomplished in the money form in which all value relations are expressed. All articles of util-ity find their exchange value and their commensurability in terms of money—the most abstract form of value, as well as its uni-versal equivalent. According to Marx,

> the fact that the exchange value of the commodity assumes an *inde-pendent existence* in money is itself the result of the process of ex-change, the development of the contradictions of use-value and ex-change-value embodied in the commodity, and of another no less im-portant contradiction embodied in it, namely, that the definite, partic-ular labor of the private individual must manifest itself as its opposite, as equal, necessary, general labor and, in this form, social labor. The representation of the commodity as money implies not only that the different magnitudes of commodity values are measured by expressing their values in the use-value of one exclusive commodity, but at the same time that they are expressed in a form in which they exist as the embodiment of *social labor*, that they are translatable at will into any use-value desired.[7]

The money form of value is the counterpart of abstract labor, that is, labor *per se*, without regard to its different qualifications. Of course, abstract labor does not really exist as such, independently of the types of concrete labor, just as the abstract money form of the commodities' exchange value does not negate their use-value aspects. In both cases, however, what is meaningless when looked upon from the physical side of production and exchange, is nonetheless true and cannot be otherwise in a capital-producing society. According to Marx, capitalism displays an actual tendency to turn concrete into abstract labor, by transforming skilled into unskilled, and specialized into general labor, or sheer labor power. Apart from this tendency, the difference between skilled and unskilled labor can be quantitatively expressed by counting skilled labor as multiplied simple labor, that is, as labor that produces in less time a given quantity of the value and surplus value incorporated in commodities. Actually, capitalist enterprises do not concern themselves with the individual qualifications of their labor forces; they do so only insofar as the physical process of production is concerned, but not for purposes of commercial calculations, which are based on their total wage bills, considered as costs of production. The wage bill measures the cost of a total labor time, regardless of the different individual contributions that enter into it and yield a quantity of commodities embodying the necessary and surplus labor time expended on their production. What is true for the single enterprise holds also for total social production, so that at any particular time the total social labor time equates with the total of produced commodities, no matter what the differentiations within the concrete labor process may be.

Social labor is necessarily abstract labor. Just as it is not the particular labor time applied by the individual producer, but the socially necessary labor time, that enters into the value determination of the commodity, so the product of any specific enterprise, in any of the different spheres of production, must be socially necessary, in order to be a part of value produciton. The *interdependence* of social production has become a fact of social existence, which subjects all separate producers to its necessity. Each capitalist produces only a part of the total social product, the market determining whether or not it is actually a part of the whole. It is then the totality of social production, or the whole of the labor time expended on the total mass of commodities, that determines whether and to what extent the individual producer is also a social producer and thereby enabled to partake of the social product.

The regulation of all individual producers by the capitalist requirements of social production is only another way of saying that it is the total mass of socially expended abstract labor time that sets limits to the different shares of surplus value falling to the individual capitalists. It is abstract labor time because it is not associated with any particular kind of production, but represents the sum total of all the different production processes subjected to the law of value or to the distribution of the total social labor which allows capitalism to exist and expand. As a sum total, it does not exist as concrete labor, but only as a conglomeration of all kinds of labor divorced from their peculiarities. It is abstract labor, moreover, because no conscious arrangements of social production actually exist; in fact, the social character of production has to assert itself, so to speak, behind the backs of the producers, through their products and the quantitative value relations between them.

Because every capitalist reckons his capital in money terms, he engages in production in order to increase it in terms of money. If he fails, he has not employed his capital capitalistically, that is, has not increased its value. Unaware of the actual use-value production requirements of social existence, capitalists strive for the maximum of exchange value, as the only criterion for success of their operations; if they do succeed in their endeavors, they have by that token also satisfied capitalistically determined social needs in terms of use values. If they do not succeed, their capital, insofar as it is not lost, must be differently engaged in order to function as capital. Thus it is the amassing of exchange value, or its universal equivalent, money, that serves as the allocator of social labor with regard to the use-value requirements of capital production. But it can perform this function only through the quantification of all qualitative relationships, that is, through the abstract money form of value and the transformation of individually concrete labor into socially abstract labor.

Because in the competitive money economy capitalists can only concern themselves with the maintenance and therefore the enlargement of their own capitals, social necessities must assert themselves in the face of—and indeed through—the lack of social consideration on the part of the individual producers. How are we to explain that, in the absence of any social consideration of the fragmented production process, there nonetheless exists a recognizable regularity and a definite developmental trend of capital production? In the classical bourgeois view, to recall, this is brought about through the competitive market mechanism, which tends toward the establishment of a supply and demand equilibrium in which market prices approximate the value of commodities. Since the production process is here regulated via the exchange process, it is only the latter that warrants theoretical consideration. The abstraction from the production process allows for abstraction from the social relations of production and therefore from commodity production as a process of surplus-value production.

In Marx's view, in contrast, it is only by abstracting from competition and market relations that it becomes possible to lay bare what regulates capitalism and determines its development. That is not to say that market competition has no regulatory functions, but only that these functions are in turn predetermined by occurrences in the sphere of production. Commodities are not produced solely for the purpose of exchange; rather, commodity exchange is instrumental in the extraction of surplus value, without which there would not be a capitalist market. Capitalist production means the division of the labor time of each and every commodity into necessary and surplus labor. On the assumption, which is also a possibility, that all commodities are exchanged, both the necessary and the surplus labor go through the market to their social destination—the first to meet the consumption needs of the workers, the second to meet those of the capitalists and their retainers and to be incorporated in the expansion of capital. This process presupposes an allocation of the social labor with regard to both use value and exchange value, which yields such proportional amounts of consumption goods and capital goods as a frictionless reproduction of capital, on either the same or an enlarged scale, requires.[8] This allocation of the social labor must be brought about through the uncoordinated activities of the diverse capital entities in their competitive pursuit of surplus value. And if it is brought about in some fashion, this is not due to any equilibrium tendencies stemming from the supply and demand relations, but is accomplished through shifts of labor-time relations at the point of production, as determined by the value and surplus-value relations of capital production. Because the production of commodities is subordinated to that of capital, the social allocation of labor is determined by the accumulation of capital. The regulatory element in capital production must then be looked for not in the market, but in the production of value and surplus value as determined by the capitalist relations of production.

The market exchange of commodities must lead to the accumulation of capital. If it does not serve this end, there exists no possibility for the exchangeability of all commodities, which is a necessary condition of the equation of supply and demand. With the consumption propensity of the workers restricted to the value of their labor power—that is, to the necessary part of the total social labor time—the whole of the surplus value, in its commodity form, would have to be consumed by the capitalists in order to assure the exchangeability of all that has been produced. This would imply a condition of simple reproduction, which, however, is foreign to capital. It is, then, the accumulating part of the surplus value that may allow for the exchangeability of all commodities and therewith for an apparent identity of supply and demand—an identity indicating not an equilibrium of production and consumption, however, but only a relationship between necessary and surplus labor assuring the enlarged reproduction of capital. Only this can provide a basis for the allocation of labor over the different spheres and branches of production. Thus it is always an allocation of labor resulting from the social relations of production and therefore from the value relations in which they find their fetishistic expression.

The actual capitalist production process is a matter of the production of commodities and their saleability on the market. It is the descendant of previous precapitalist processes of production, in which earlier generations managed some kind of coordination between their production and its marketability. The progressive "socialization" of production through the extension of the division of labor and the expansion of market relations did not prevent the individual producers from finding, by trial and error, some balance between the production and the exchange of their commodities. They would not for long overproduce and waste their time manufacturing unsaleable commodities, and they would, where possible, increase production should the demand for saleable goods grow. In this way, changing supply-and-demand relations undoubtedly affected the allocation of labor producing for the market, with labor time allotted in accordance with the specific requirements of the different products, and finding its reflection in their prices. The allocation of labor through market relations thus preceded capitalism and provided the starting point for the capitalist allocation of social labor via the law of value.

The allocation of social labor by way of the law of value is something other than its allocation through the supply and demand relations of the limited market. The latter was based on commodities' use values, produced by concrete labor, whereas the allocation of labor via the law of value rests upon exchange value and abstract labor. The so-called laws of the market of bourgeois theory, from Jean-Baptiste Say to almost the present day, were based on the idea that everyone produces in order to consume, that supply creates its own demand, and that the allocation of labor reflects no more than the extension of the social division of labor. And in early capitalism, due to the relative scarcity of capital and the still limited productivity of labor, the use-value aspects of production seemed indeed to dominate the exchange relations. But the extension of the capitalist mode of production and the expansion of capital implied a shift of emphasis from use value to exchange value. To be sure, just as the use values of the past had definite exchange value, so the dominance of exchange value cannot dispense with its embodiment in definite use values. But it is now their exchange value and its expansion that, in increasing measure, determines the character of use values and makes their production dependent on the accumulation of capital. That is to say, use values are only produced to the extent that their exchange value incorporates surplus value utilizable for the augmentation of the existing capital.

With surplus value the goal of production, the expansion of capital depends on an allocation of the social labor that assures the enlarged reproduction of the total social capital via the accumulation of individual capitals. It is the *interdependence* of the various production processes that demands the expansion of the total social capital to assure that of the separate capital entities. Total capital, however, is a fact without being a datum on which calculation might be based. It consists, of course, in the sum of all capitals existing at any particular time. It is enlarged through all the isolated attempts of the separate capitals to enlarge themselves, each finding support, but also a limit, in the expansion of other capitals. What is at the disposal of total capital is the total social surplus value, also an unknown but nonetheless a real quantity in the form of the commodity equivalent of surplus value expressed in money terms. There is no way of ascertaining the quantity of surplus value required to assure the enlarged reproduction of the system as a whole, on which the increase of the separate capital entities depends. The individual capitals can only try to increase their own profits by enlarging their production in anticipation of larger markets. They may or may not succeed; whether they do or do not is discovered in the sphere of circulation, although determined in that of production by the relationship between necessary and surplus labor required if the total capital is to accumulate.

It is in the same sense in which total capital is a fact without being a datum, and total surplus value a real but unknown quantity, that the law of value underlies market and price relations, even though neither value nor surplus value is a directly observable or measurable phenomenon. In classical theory, to recall, labor-time value, or "natural price," determines "the respective quantities of goods which shall be given in exchange for each other," even though there are "accidental and temporary deviations of the actual market prices of commodities from this, their primary and natural price."[9] In Ricardo's view, it was the changing supply-and-demand relations that led to these temporary deviations of price from value, but also "prevented the market prices from continuing for any length of time either much above, or much below their natural price," so that these deviations could be disregarded and price and value be treated as identical. This equation of value and price was carried over into neoclassical theory, albeit now expressed in subjective value terms. In Marx's theory, however, prices alone exist in the actual capitalist world, even though these prices find their *social determination* in value relations.

Although commodities do not reveal the quantities of necessary and surplus labor incorporated in them, their production testifies that labor and surplus labor have entered into their prices. Marx did not attempt to discover the labor-time content of commodities in their prices. For him, capitalist production is possible only on the basis of price relations, which differ from value relations but by that token verify the labor theory of value as the key for comprehending the real capitalist world, its price formations and its development. For Marx—as for the classical economists and for everyone else—only prices exist. As regards exchange relations, value, whether considered as of an objective or a subjective order, is not an empirically observable but an *explanatory* category. As such it does not cease to be a real phenomenon, but manifests itself not in its own terms but in terms of prices, precisely because capitalist society rests upon value relations. These value relations, with their source not in the physical production process but in the social relations under which it is carried on, will for that reason not be recognizable in the individual commodities, or in any particular sphere or branch of production, but only in the fact of capitalism's existence as a social system of production and in its expansion or contraction, as the case may be.

It is value and surplus value, not labor and surplus labor, that determine the formation of prices and their changes. These prices are not prices in a general unhistorical sense, as they are conceived by bourgeois economic theory, but prices specific to the capitalist mode of production. They are determined not by supply and demand, nor by physical needs and possibilities, but by the accumulation of the total social capital, which enforces a distribution of the total social surplus value through price relations, which, although not changing the labor-time content of the commodities, do alter their relative exchange values, in accordance with the surplus-value requirements of the system as a whole.

Price must deviate from value to allow for the existence and expansion of capital. However, "deviation of price from value" is a somewhat unfortunate expression, because, mixing explanatory and empirical terms, it appears to refer to an empirically verifiable process, while observable reality contains no values but only market prices. Nevertheless, there is no way of avoiding the value-price duality, if we wish to understand why prices are what they are and why they change. On the other hand, the "deviation" of price from value does not mean that the labor-time content of commodities can be deduced from their prices, in the sense that the former are merely concealed and the latter open to scrutiny. The value of commodities can only find expression in prices and does not exist outside of price relations.

Given that the value of the commodity can only appear in its price, which thereby ceases to measure its labor-time content, the labor theory of value seems indeed to be contradicted by the actual exchange process. While it remains true, of course, that price itself refers to labor-time quantities, price-regulated exchange is not the exchange of labor-time equivalents. Classical economy started with the obvious observation that commodities are produced by labor. It assumed that their relative values must be proportional to the labor time incorporated in them, only to find out that this was not so in reality. Marx started with the discrepancy between value and price, in order to find out why they deviate and whether or not this deviation made the labor theory of value redundant. It is true that Marx started as a Ricardian, but Smith and Ricardo had already raised the question of the difference between value and price and had unsuccessfully tried to accommodate this fact to the labor theory of value.

Adam Smith realized that under capitalist property relations the exchange value of commodities does not correspond with their labor time, for besides wages it included profit and rent. Ricardo noticed that the accumulation of capital occasions different proportions between fixed and circulating capital in different industries and different degrees of durability of the fixed capital, both of which preclude exchange relations based on labor-time values. Inconsistently, both Smith and Ricardo relegated the exchange of labor-time values to an earlier stage of society, "before much machinery or durable capital is used; . . . but after the introduction of these expensive and durable instruments, the commodities produced by the employment of equal capitals will be of very unequal value."[10] The principle of labor-time exchange was not applicable to industrial capitalism, or was applicable only with great modifications. The identity of value and price was a thing of the past and not true for capitalism.

Notwithstanding some ambiguous statements on Marx's part, which may be ascribed to the unfinished and provisional state of the manuscripts comprising the second and third volumes of *Capital*, and judging by the whole corpus of his work and its inner consistency, it is quite clear that for Marx value was a historical category, in the sense that it evolved with capitalist commodity production and is bound to disappear with the ending of capitalism. Still, Marx found it "quite appropriate to regard the value of commodities not only theoretically, but also historically, as existing prior to the prices of production."[11] From this, Friedrich Engels drew the conclusion that the law of value dominated all commodity exchange, from its earliest beginnings thousands of years ago, up to the fifteenth century, from which time forward the proportional labor-time exchange turned into disproportional exchange in terms of prices of production.[12] This of course would turn value into an ahistorical category, as it was for Smith and Ricardo. It would also relegate the value concept to the sphere of exchange, not to that of social production relations, and would falsely identify labor-time value with labor time as such.

Now it is obvious that commodities are produced by labor and that labor time must necessarily be considered in the formation of more or less regular exchange relations. What is produceable in one hour will not willingly be traded for a product requiring, say, five hours of labor. If one wishes to refer to this state of affairs as a "law of value," then, of course, it applies only to noncapitalistic situations, whereas it was Marx's intention to demonstrate the validity of this law for capitalist conditions. It would have only as much historical connection with value in capitalism as, for instance, the existence of money as a medium of exchange has with money as capital. Whether the mutual "rational" consideration of expended labor-time quantities in exchange was a historical fact, or a mere assumption on the part of classical theory, it has in either case no bearing upon the question Marx was concerned with—namely, how the law of value asserts itself in a society where there is no "rational" mutual consideration of the labor-time requirements of social production, but only the blind drive of individual producers to amass capital. It is therefore of no interest whether or not precapitalist exchange approximated an exchange of labor-time quantities, which, in any case, could not be the abstract labor-time value of Marx's theory, but only labor time in the classical sense, that is, as a unit of account for quantities of concrete labor time spent in the physical production process.

For Marx,

> price is not equal to value, therefore the value-determining element— labor time—cannot be the element in which prices are expressed, because labor time would then have to express itself simultaneously as the determining and the nondetermining element, as the equivalent and nonequivalent of itself. Because labor as the measure of value exists only as an ideal, it cannot serve as the matter of price comparisons. . . . The difference between price and value calls for values to be measured as prices on a different standard from their own.[13]

Value cannot find a measure in itself, but only in its price form. In the latter form, it finds its social determination, which overrules all the diverse labor-time values of commodities, as well as the difference between the kinds of labor required for their production. The "social" character of capital production comes to light not in value relations but in price relations.

Smith's and Ricardo's "early stage" of society, in which labor-time exchange is the "general rule," was a figment of their imaginations, for value exchange presupposes surplus value, that is, the commodity character of labor power and its dominance in social production—in brief, capitalist society. Evolving out of the emerging capitalist conditions, value theory could only be grasped as a theory of surplus value. But even though Adam Smith saw, at times, that profit and rent were deductions from the products of the laboring class, at other times he spoke of wages, profits, and rent as being component yet independent parts of exchange value. And though Ricardo insisted upon labor as the sole source of value, he could not square this with the unequal exchange that was actually taking place. This confusion agitated classical economy as the problem of the difference between "real" and "exchange" value. There was not only the distinction between use and exchange value, but also that between the latter and value as such. "Exchange value" referred to a commodity's purchasing power, while its real value consisted of the quantity of labor expended in its production. This difference was also expressed as one between relative and absolute value. It is from this state of the value theory, in which Marx found it, that he proceeded to clarify the reason for the divergence of price from value. Well aware of this discrepancy, Marx nonetheless begins by considering isolated value relations. It was, however, the consideration of price relations that led him to this analysis. Once this was done, it was possible to reverse the procedure—and to demonstrate the derivation of prices from value relations. This is in theory only; in reality there are always only prices, whose movements and their consequences with regard to capital accumulation reveal the regulatory value relations.

"Even if there were no chapter on value in *Capital*," Marx wrote to Kugelmann, "the analysis of the real relationships which I gave would contain the proof and demonstration of the real value relations. All that palaver about the necessity of proving the concept of value comes from complete ignorance both of the subject dealt with and of scientific method."[14] The real relationships appear of course as price relations, as the selling and buying of labor power; the prevalence of profit, interest, and rent; supply and demand; competition and an average rate of profit. But these relations constitute the phenomenal capitalist world and shed no light upon its inner connections and its particular dynamic. To discover these, a systematic analysis of the existing economic categories and of their interrelations is necessary, so as to distinguish between the essential and the derivative, between reality and appearance. This analysis could, in principle, start anywhere in the manifold capitalist world. Marx chose to begin with the commodity and its value character because his analysis of capital evolved out of the critique of classical value theory. He could just as well have started with the analysis of market prices, only to end up with value relations, as the fetishistic form of the capitalist relations of production.

The labor-time value of a commodity refers to socially necessary, not to individual, labor time. It manifests itself as market value and reflects a rough kind of social average productivity, from which individually produced values deviate. The variations between the particular conditions of production in different enterprises lead to value differences prior to price deviations due to changing market relations. The latter affect the oscillations of the individually produced values around the socially established market values, which then gain their final form as varying market prices, distinct from market values. Like value itself, the market value of any commodity does not exist as such but appears as a definite price, or price range. Insofar as prices are determined by market values, they emerge as a result of all the isolated strivings of capitalists to secure their profitability. The given prices, which serve as the capitalists' point of orientation, are established independently of their own individual activities and yet are the result of these very exertions establishing and altering the market values of commodities. In this way prices are altered by the changing productivity of labor (e.g., lowered with the increasing productivity of labor), which implies that the division between necessary and surplus labor (or, in capitalist terms, the relationship between wages, as a cost of production, and the market prices of the commodities) has been changed.

Because the market value in a particular sphere of production differs from individually produced values but dominates the exchange relations, it leads to different rates of profit for different enterprises operating under varying conditions of production. As all producers must sell the same type of goods at the same price, which reflects the market value, their profits vary. Instead of different prices, derived from heterogeneous values, there are roughly identical prices and different rates of profit. The social determination of value finds its expression in price competition through all the various attempts on the part of the individual capitalists to secure for themselves a rate of profit sufficient to stay in business, that is, to come close, to reach, or to surpass the rate of profit determined by the market value of commodities.

Assuming equal rates of exploitation in all enterprises in a particular sphere of production—an assumption that is at best only approximately true in reality—the different conditions of production, leading to different rates of profit, would signify differences in the "organic compositions" of the various capitals. This Marxian term refers to the relationship between constant and variable capital—between capital invested in means of production and capital invested in labor power—with respect both to value quantities and in a technical sense. As the rate of profit is "measured" on the total invested capital (that is, on constant and variable capital combined), and as only its variable part yields surplus value, a capital of high organic composition (that is, one with relatively more constant than variable capital) should yield a lower rate of profit than a capital in which these conditions are reversed. It is, then, not only the determination of any particular commodity's value by socially necessary labor time that leads to different rates of profit in a special sphere of production; the different conditions of general production, characterized by varying organic compositions of capital, differentiate the rates of profit even more. Whereas it is conceivable, and in some measure even true, that the conditions of production within a particular sphere of production are increasingly equalized by way of capital concentration, this equalization cannot be realized for totally different spheres of production, although here, too, the concentration of capitals yields a tendency in this direction—one held in check, however, by the use-value aspects of capital production.

The expansion of capital cannot free itself from its embodiment in use values, such as labor power, the various means and materials of production, and the countless utilities of the commodities brought forth. The material or physical side of production, which in its abstract side is the increase of exchange value, cannot be shed, but only bent to suit the accumulation needs of capital. Each sphere of production produces what is required of its particular commodities by the prevailing demand as determined by the expansion of capital and the system as a whole. Subordinated to exchange value, the necessary use-value requirements of capitalist production assert themselves through capitalist competition within and between the different spheres of production. In the search for the best profits, capital wanders from one sphere to another, and through these wanderings establishes a kind of socially average, or general, rate of profit. This general rate of profit is the average of all the average rates of profit in the different spheres of production. Of course

> the real profit deviates from the ideal average level, which is established only by a continuous process, a reaction, and this only takes place during long periods of circulation of capital. The rate of profit is in certain spheres higher in some years, while it is lower in succeeding years. Taking the years together, or taking a series of such evolutions, one could in *general* obtain the average profit. Thus it never appears as something given, but only as the average result of contradictory oscillations.[15]

But there can be no doubt that

> aside from unessential, accidental, and mutually compensating distinctions, a difference in the average rate of profit of the various lines of industry does not exist in reality, and could not exist without abolishing the entire system of capitalist production.[16]

Approaching this fact from the standpoint of value theory, the mechanics of this process consists in the establishment of market values in the separate spheres of production and in the equalization of the profit rates in all spheres of production through capital movements from one to another. Prices, corresponding to market values, represent the socially necessary labor time assigned to commodities by competition. These are the prices capitalists must pay for the commodities they buy and utilize in their own production process. They constitute their cost prices, the starting point for all their commercial calculations. The cost prices, however, are here considered as value relations before they become prices of production that contain the capitalist profit. In this form, cost prices do not exist in reality, because the elements of production are bought on the market, where the cost prices already include the realized profit. The cost prices must therefore be analytically deduced from the prices of production. This dissociation of the profit components from the labor-time components that constitute the capitalist expenditures for purposes of production require a *thought experiment* that separates the profit components from the value components of the prices of production. Considering society as a whole, it is not only possible, but quite realistic, to place the sum total of all cost prices on one side, and the sum total of profits on the other side, as the two components of the total labor-time value expanded in production. Looking at capitalism from this vantage point, it is clear that whatever the composition of the prices of production may be, all actual prices together cannot express anything else than the total value and surplus value of the commodities brought to the market. In this sense, according to Marx, "the fundamental law of capitalist competition which regulates the general rate of profit, and the prices determined by it, rests on the difference between the value and the cost-prices of commodities, and even on the resulting possibility to sell a commodity at a profit even below its value."[17]

In the real capitalist world, all that matters is a sales price that stands high enough above the cost price to allow an approximation of the general rate of profit. This rate is the point of orientation that determines the capitalists' reactions to market events. Differences in profit rates are noticed by comparing market prices with cost prices. In every sphere of production the average rate of profit determines the expansion of individual capitals, in the sense that a low profit rate will discourage further investments and even eliminate capitals of insufficient profitability. Capital will move to other spheres of production where the profit rates are comparatively higher, indicating the possibility of further profitable capital expansion. This is not a question of moving capital bodily, in the form of means of production, from one sphere to another (although it is not excluded that the same type of means of production may serve in the production of commodities belonging to another sphere), but of shifting new investments from less profitable to more profitable branches of production. This is the more easily accomplished because capital accumulation goes hand in hand with the development of the credit system. For "credit is the means by which the capital of the whole capitalist class is placed at the disposal of each sphere of production, not in proportion to the capital belonging to the capitalists in a given sphere but in proportion to their productive requirements."[18]

In Marx's own words:

> A decline in the rate of profit below the ideal average in any sphere, if prolonged, suffices to bring about a withdrawal of capital from this sphere, or to prevent the entry of the average amount of new capital into it. For it is the inflow of new, additional capital, even more than the redistribution of capital already invested, that equalizes the distribution of capital in the different spheres ... As soon as a [profit] difference becomes apparent in one way or another, then an outflow or inflow of capital from or to the particular spheres [begins]. Apart from the fact that this act of equalization requires time, the average profit in each sphere becomes evident only in the average profit rates obtained, for example, over a cycle of seven years, etc., according to the nature of the capital. Mere fluctuations *above* and *below* [the average rate of profit], if they do not exceed the average extent and do not assume extraordinary forms, are therefore not sufficient to bring about a transfer of capital, and in addition the transfer of fixed capital presents certain difficulties. Momentary booms can only have a limited effect, and are more likely to attract or repel additional capital than to bring about a redistribution of the capital invested in the different spheres.
>
> One can see that all this involves a very complex movement in which, on the one hand, the market-prices in each particular sphere, the relative cost-prices of the different commodities, the position with regard to demand and supply within each individual sphere, and, in addition, the speed of the equalization process, whether it is quicker or slower, depends on the particular organic composition of the different capitals (more fixed or circulating capital, for example) and on the particular nature of their commodities, that is, whether their nature as use-values facilitates rapid withdrawal from the market and the diminution or increase of supply, in accordance with the level of the market prices.[19]

Whatever the complexity of this process, the general rate of profit can only be understood with reference to the social value relations. These relations, however, are not something given, from which the general rate of profit can be deduced; on the contrary, the existence of a general rate of profit requires an explanation consistent with the actual material production process in its capitalist form and leads therewith necessarily to labor-time relations.

Without the value concept, the average rate of profit

> would be purely imaginary and untenable. The equalization of the sur-
> plus-value in different spheres of production does not affect the abso-
> lute size of the total surplus-value, but merely its *distribution* among
> the different spheres of production. The *determination of this surplus-
> value* itself, however, only arises out of the determination of value by
> labor-time. Without this, the average profit is the *average of nothing*,
> pure fancy. And it could then equally well be 1000 per cent or 10 per
> cent.[20]

On the other hand, the average rate of profit cannot be explained
directly in terms of value relations, but requires intermediary reference to capital competition, though competition itself can
neither increase nor decrease the given surplus value, but only affect its distribution.

Forgetting the value relations altogether and attending only
to market events, it is quite obvious that any particular capitalist
producing specific commodities in competition with other capitalists will expand his production as long as this yields him the customary profits. If the profit should decline consistently, he will
stop expanding his production, and the resulting lack of new investments, within the general framework of the expanding economy, will come to the fore as a relative decline in the production
of the commodities in which he specialized. Or, to look at it the
other way around, changes in the composition of the total social
capital in the course of its accumulation may reduce the demand
for his particular commodities or eliminate it altogether, in which
case this capitalist will experience his loss of profitability in a decline of the demand for his commodities, and he will either attempt
to gain a larger share of a diminishing market, at the expense of
other capitalists, or withdraw from this particular sphere of production. In either case, the production of commodities in which each
capitalist is engaged depends on processes beyond his comprehension, as determined by the allocative labor-time requirements of
the system as as a whole.

The system as a whole, to repeat, is nothing other than the
combined production of all capitalist enterprises: a mass of value
and surplus value, representing socially necessary labor-time quantities embodied in commodities. This mass of value and surplus
value is, at any moment, of a definite size, alterable only by either

the destruction or the expansion of capital. This mass sets the limits within which each capital can move and therefore to the enlargement of any particular capital. The viability of the system rests then upon a distribution of the total social surplus value that assures the expansion of the total capital in physical and in value terms. This distribution can only be exacted by way of capital competition, which, without concerning itself with the distribution of surplus value, effects its distribution nonetheless through the averaging of profit rates via the profit needs of the individual capitals.

How is the equalization of profit to form an average rate actually brought about? If commodities have been produced in excess of the effective demand as determined by the accumulation of the total social capital, part of the total social labor has been wasted. Some commodities represent a smaller quantity of abstract labor on the market than is actually incorporated in them. As some cannot be sold, and those that are sold yield a lower price, profits decline. The opposite takes place if the quantity of social labor employed in a certain sphere of production is not large enough to meet the social demand: prices and, with them, profits, will be higher than the average. This over- or underproduction with respect to social necessities, within the framework of capital production, is not a question of supply and demand, but finds its source in the expansion or contraction of the total social capital and the dislocating changes in the production processes connected therewith. These changes with regard to use-value requirements and the ability of use values to serve as carriers of exchange value first become visible in the circulation process, on the market, where they are experienced as supply and demand discrepancies affecting profit rates.

It is clear that these rearrangements of the expanding capital structure—which, on the one hand, grow out of the blind pursuit of profit and, on the other hand, force the capitalists to always new and equally blind efforts to maintain their profitability—cannot possibly constitute an even process that sets the average rate of profit at a point yielding an equilibrium of supply and demand. In any case, such an "equilibrium—that is, an allocation of the total social labor corresponding to the accumulation requirements of the total social capital—would not exist as an immediate reality at any particular time, but only as an average of very uneven capital movements over a number of years. The average rate of profit appears as a *tendency* to which all capitalists, at all times, are equally subjected. Nevertheless, capitalist competition, which brings this tendency about, does succeed, albeit in a very contradictory manner and with all kinds of losses, in effecting a continuous redistribution of the social capital.

Experience tells capitalists that profit rates cannot be set arbitrarily. They cannot do anything about the market prices which constitute their production costs: these are what they are, determined by the labor-time values and the average profit incorporated in them. Similarly, their own sales prices are circumscribed by the state of competition in their respective spheres of production. Their customary profit is the empirical expression of the average rate of profit. It is that profit the capitalist expects through the employment of his capital—be it large or small—in any kind of business activity. Should his capital turn over more slowly than other capitals, or his products be sold in near or more remote markets, in all cases, he counts on the customary profit on his investments and sets his prices accordingly.

> Every circumstance which renders one line of production profitable, and another less, is calculated as legitimate grounds for compensation, without requiring the ever renewed action of competition to demonstrate the justification of such claims. . . . All those claims for compensation, mutually advanced by the capitalists in the calculation of the prices of commodities of different lines of production, repeat in another way the idea that all capitalists are entitled, in proportion to the magnitude of their respective capitals, to equal shares of the common loot, the total surplus-value.[21]

As profit rates cannot be equalized in the production process, the average rate of profit can only be formed in the sphere of circulation, where differences in the rate of surplus value do not matter, for here it is the total surplus value, its mass, which finds its equal distribution among the individual capitals in the general rate of profit. The distribution of the total social surplus value in accordance with the necessities of capital production finds its market expression in the competitive supply and demand relations, the over- or underproduction in different spheres of production, their corrections, and the associated price relations, through which surplus value is transferred from one sphere of production to another. And thus, while each capitalist enterprise strives for the maximum of unpaid labor, its profits are not dependent upon the surplus value extracted from its own labor force, but determined by the amount of capital at its command and the average rate of profit. Of course, the magnitude of this rate depends on the total social surplus value on hand, and therefore on the degree of exploitation on a social scale, so that the capitalists' desire for the maximum of unpaid labor, though not affecting the averaging process of profit rates, determines their magnitude at any given time. Whereas the average rate of profit differentiates the surplus value produced by individual capitals from the profits they receive, the magnitude of the total social surplus value is the limit of the sum of parts into which it may be divided. It is here quite immaterial whether or not the entire surplus value is realized in terms of prices, which is actually never the case; but in "so far as the formation of prices is concerned, the sum of the average profit plus rent in their normal form can never be larger than the total surplus-value, although it may be smaller."[22]

In whatever complicated manner the movements of profit bring about the movements of capital, and the movements of the latter, in turn, movements in the rate of profit, in a ceaseless and intertwined process of production and exchange that can only be arrested and dissected in a purely conceptual way, in an attempt to isolate all the interconnected components that together constitute the social production and distribution process, one thing, at least, remains certain: no matter how the social mass of surplus value may be distributed among the capitalists, the mass of profit, or surplus value, cannot be anything but the total surplus value brought forth in the social production process.

To the concept of capital as a whole, and the explanation of the general rate of profit as the average of the profit rates of all the various capitals of different organic compositions, within and between all spheres of production, corresponds in practice the fact that each separate capital is but a part of the total social capital and is only distinguished from it, and from other individual capitals, by its particular magnitude. Because the organic compositions of different capitals differ, there arises a social average composition of capital, in which the relationships between constant and variable capital are such as to equate its surplus value with its profit; that is to say, its total surplus value yields a definite rate of profit corresponding with the socially average organic composition of capital. As noted before, Marx called capitals of "high" organic composition those that contain a larger percentage of constant and a smaller percentage of variable capital than is to be found in the social average composition of capital, and capitals of "low" composition those in which these relations are reversed. There may be capitals extant that have the same composition as the social average, which would yield the rate of profit determined by the social average composition of capital. Their prices of production, cost prices plus profits, would be equal, or at least approximately equal, to the value and surplus value contained in their commodities. In all other spheres of production, the surplus value would vary, but the profit rates would be the same, that is, correspond with the general rate of profit as derived from the average organic composition of the total social capital. Their prices of production would deviate from the value of their commodities without changing anything in the fact that the sum total of all prices of production for society as a whole would be equal to the sum total of the value and surplus value of the produced commodities. It is for this reason that Marx suggested looking upon capitalism as if it were one large stock company, and the various capitals, as far as their profits are concerned, as so many shareholders partaking in the company's profits in accordance with the number of shares in their possession:

> Every 100 of any invested capital, whatever may be its organic composition, draws as much profit during one year, or any other period of time, as fall to the share of every hundred of the total social capital during the same period. . . . That portion of the commodities which buys back the elements of capital consumed in the production of commodities, in other words, their cost-prices, depends on the investment of capital required in each particular sphere of production. But the other element of the price of commodities, the percentage of profit added to this cost-price, does not depend on the mass of profit produced by a certain capital during a definite time in its own sphere of production, but on the mass of profit allotted for any period to each capital in its capacity as an aliquot part of the total social capital invested in social production.[23]

The entanglements of social production are such as to exclude any attempt to trace the specific value content of commodities in their prices, or to deduce from their prices their specific value content. A disentanglement is only a theoretical possibility, a mental dissociation of what cannot be actually taken apart—the market prices from their market values, the cost prices from the prices of production, the value of labor power from its modification through the deviations of production prices from the value of the commodities that constitute variable capital. The theoretical attempt to penetrate the bewildering complexity of capitalist production is not only forced to adopt analytical procedures that cannot be duplicated in reality, but requires the construction of a model of capitalist production and distribution that is not identical with the directly observable capitalist system, but merely picks out the essential features on which the existence of the system depends. Apart from the fact that the data necessary for a strictly empirical study of the system are unobtainable, and the actually extant data are largely useless for the analysis of capitalist production, the very nature of the market economy and the price system precludes a realistic investigation even in terms of its own superficial categories.

If it were otherwise, if it were possible to recognize in the price relations the underlying value relations, this too would merely be an academic exercise of no practical consequences; for the capitalist system can only exist as a price system, even if it does find its unsolicited "regulation," its possibilities and limitations, in labor-time value relations. The law of value, which refers to general necessities that assert themselves blindly within the capitalist system of production and exchange, does not exist independently of price relations, as something with which the latter could be compared, but has its reality in the prices themselves, seen in the context of a social system of production as the production of capital. Thus there is no "law of value" as a concrete phenomenon; but there is a way of looking at capitalist society from the point of view of its inescapable necessities, and of recognizing that these necessities must be met by social labor and by the allocation of this labor in definite proportions, that is, by labor-time quantities, which have the form of labor-time values just because they are expressed in terms of prices.

Any concern with value relations as labor-time relations on the part of the bourgeoisie, and of all those satisfied with the capitalist system, would be a needless perversity. It was a luxury the classical economists could still allow themselves at that early stage of capitalist development, but one that became highly detrimental under more advanced conditions and the increasing polarization of class relations. Here it was a godsend that the price form of value covered up not only the exploitation relations at their base, but the value character of production itself. For in the price form, "the basis of the determination of value is removed from direct observation" and

> it is only natural that the capitalist should lose the meaning of the term value at this juncture. For he is not confronted with the total labor put into the production of commodities, but only with that portion of the total labor which he has paid for in the shape of the means of production, whether they be alive or dead, so that his profit appears to him as something outside of the immanent value of commodities. And now this conception is fully endorsed, fortified, and ossified by the fact that from his point of view of his particular sphere of production, the profit is not determined by the limits drawn from the formation of value within his own circle, but by outside influences.[24]

It was thus discretion as well as ignorance, and soon only ignorance, on the part of the capitalists that made them forget the real relations of production and exchange, and cling instead to their outward appearances on the market.

In reality the value of commodities is the magnitude that exists first, theoretically speaking, comprising the sum of the total wages, profits, and rent, quite apart from their relative quantities expressed in prices. These magnitudes are there also at the end of the analysis, if the system is looked upon, as it must be, in its totality, no matter how the surplus value is distributed among the capitalists via the "transformation" of values into prices of production. Thus, while it is not possible to relate the prices of individual commodities directly to their values, there can be no doubt that the total of prices represents nothing other than the value relations dominating capitalist society.

The Transformation Problem

At this point we might as well interrupt our outline of Marx's critique of political economy and attend to the so-called transformation problem, which agitated academic Marxism from time to time and only recently flared up again with special vehemence. Academic Marxism—pro and contra—is a phenomenon of the impact of Marxism upon the bourgeois world. The rise of socialist movements, the growing difficulties of capital production, the business cycle, class struggle, war and revolutions have induced the educated bourgeoisie to pay some attention to the critics of capitalism, not only in self-defense but also out of curiosity and sometimes even out of sympathy for the aspirations of the working class.

Especially Marxism, or "scientific socialism," was a challenge to the bourgeois social sciences and had to be met on theoretical grounds. This interest, to be sure, was not an overwhelming one, but an inescapable acknowledgement of the existence of Marxism, which remained a side-issue, but an issue nonetheless. Within the bourgeois social sciences economics is highly esteemed for being the only discipline supposedly approaching in its exactness that of the natural sciences. It is highly formalistic and thus inclined to concentrate its criticism and comments on the more esoteric aspects of Marx's theory, such as the reproduction schemata in the second volume of *Capital* and the "transformation" of values into prices of production as formulated by Marx.

The simplest way of challenging Marx's theory was the obvious one, by pointing to the apparent contradiction between the first and the third volume of *Capital*, where Marx has been seen as turning from an exclusive concern with value relations to concern with price relations. This simple way was chosen by Eugen von Böhm-Bawerk, who felt sure that Marx's transformation of values into prices was an *ad hoc* construction that could not bridge the contradiction. It is clear at once, however, that Böhm-Bawerk's assertion that "the theory of the average rate of profit and of the prices of production cannot be reconciled with the theory of value"[1] rests upon no more than his own inability to comprehend the Marxian theory of value and surplus value. Böhm-Bawerk assumed that Marx, like himself, "conceives the explanatory object of the law of value . . . as a question of the exchange relations between different separate commodities among each other."[2] In Böhm-Bawerk's view this is a question that cannot be answered by looking at the system as a whole, as Marx does, for then, in fact, it is not even a question but a simple tautology. Indeed,

> as every economist knows, commodities do eventually exchange with commodities—when one penetrates the disguise, due to the use of money. . . . The aggregate of commodities therefore is identical with the aggregate of the prices paid for them; or, the price of the whole national product is nothing else than the national produce itself. Under these circumstances, therefore, it is quite true that the total price paid for the entire national produce coincides exactly with the total amount of value or labor incorporated in it. But this tautological declaration denotes no increase of true knowledge, neither does it serve as a special test of the correctness of the alleged law that commodities exchange in proportion to the labor embodied in them.[3]

However, as we have seen in the preceding chapter, it was Marx's contention all along that commodities cannot be exchanged in proportion to the labor time embodied in them. He also held that the sum of the prices of the social total of products cannot be larger than the total value produced, but may be smaller —and no doubt is smaller—in reality. The equation of value and price for society as a whole is a theoretical assumption denoting perfect exchange relations, which do not exist in the real capitalist world. But even so, it remains true that the profits realized on the market are identical with the realized surplus value and that the realized prices of commodities are equal to the realized value and surplus value incorporated in them. We know too that for Marx the "explanatory object of the law of value" was not to be found in the simple exchange of commodities, but in commodity exchange under capitalist relations of production, in the specific allocation of social labor associated therewith, and in the circumscribed laws of motion of capital accumulation.

There is not much sense in dismantling Böhm-Bawerk's arguments against Marx's treatment of the value-price problem, for the simple reason that Böhm-Bawerk did not merely deny the cogency of Marx's procedure but the validity of the labor theory of value as well. If the latter is itself erroneous, nothing worthwhile can be derived from it. Böhm-Bawerk was an adherent of the psychological theory of value who would not admit that labor is the sole source of value, but saw in it, at best, an exchangeable good like others of equal relevance, such as the gifts of nature (or their scarcity) and the element of time, all of which, in his opinion, entered into the determination of price. If he is mentioned here, it is for the reason that he is the prototype of the bourgeois Marx-critic down to the present day, in general as well as with regard to the value-price problem in particular.

The critics of Marx's value-price "transformation" divide themselves into those who, like Böhm-Bawerk, deny its possibility outright, and those who find an investigation of its feasibility worthwhile. Ladislaus von Bortkiewicz stands in the same relation to the latter as Böhm-Bawerk does to the first. Bortkiewicz, too, was a bourgeois economist, an anti-Marxist, who approached the value-price problem as an intellectual puzzle, which, as such, deserved a solution. In distinction to Böhm-Bawerk, he maintained a soft spot for classical economy, especially for Ricardo, and therefore had some interest in the value-price problem.[4] This interest, at first dormant, was awakened by Tugan-Baranowsky's Marx critique, which, based on the reproduction schemata in the second volume of *Capital*, objected, among other things, to Marx's calculations regarding the establishment of an average rate of profit—which, in Tugan-Baranowsky's opinion, could be done much better without any recourse to Marx's value theory.[5] Although Bortkiewicz shared Michael Tugan-Baranowsky's marginal utility concepts, he thought it nevertheless "interesting to show that Marx erred, and in what way, without reversing his way of posing the problem."[6]

As already noted, Marx's reproduction schemata do not distinguish between values and prices; that is, they treat values as if they were prices. The reproduction schemata for which they were designed fulfill a *pedagogical* function—namely, to draw attention to the need for a certain proportionality between the different spheres of production, if the total social capital is to be reproduced. They do not claim to depict the real world of capitalism, but merely serve as an aid in its understanding. For this purpose it does not matter whether the relations of production and exchange are dressed in value or price terms. Only in the third volume of *Capital* does Marx deal with the "transformation" problem. Here he uses different diagrams to *illustrate* how the establishment of an average or general rate of profit changes values into prices.[7] The diagrams show that if a number of different spheres of production (five in Marx's example) constitute one total capital, the divergence of their individual profit rates, due to the different organic compositions of capital involved, takes the form of deviations of prices from values in the course of the establishment, through competition, of an average rate of profit, *without* altering the equivalence between total value and total price for the system as a whole.

Bortkiewicz, however, brought into this discussion Marx's division of the total social capital into two departments, taking it from the Volume II reproduction schemata, with one producing means of production and the other consumption goods. To suit his own calculations and simplifying assumptions, he added a third department, which under the rubric "luxuries," includes that part of total production which in his opinion does not enter into the determination of the general rate of profit. For our own purposes there is no need to replicate Bortkiewicz's system of equations and numerical examples, which are supposed to show that Marx's value-price transformation was erroneous "because it excludes the constant and variable capital from the transformation process, whereas the principle of the equal rate of profit, when it takes the place of the law of value in Marx's sense, must involve these elements."[8]

Bortkiewicz's own solution lies in extending, or completing, the transformation of values into prices throughout the system. The latter is treated as in a stationary state of simple reproduction. Equilibrium conditions cannot be maintained, he asserts, unless the constant and variable capital, left by Marx in their value form, are also transformed into prices of production. It must here be repeated, however, that although Marx left the constant and variable capital in their value forms, this has nothing to do with the assumed "equilibrium conditions" of either simple or expanded reproduction as dealt with in the second volume of *Capital*. The apparent "equilibrium" of Marx's reproduction schemata does not refer to the real world of price relations but is a methodological device that is supposed to mediate our understanding of these relations. "Aside from our ultimate purpose," Marx wrote in Volume II,

> it is quite necessary to view the process of reproduction in its fundamental simplicity, in order to get rid of all the obscuring interferences and dispose of the false subterfuges, which assume the semblance of scientific analysis, but which cannot be removed so long as the process of social reproduction is immediately analyzed in its concrete and complicated form.[9]

Actually,

> the fact is that the production of commodities in the general form of capitalist production implies the role which money is playing not only as a medium of circulation, but also as money-capital, and creates conditions peculiar for the normal transactions of exchange under this mode of production, and therefore peculiar for the normal rate of reproduction, whether it be on a simple or on an expanded scale. These conditions become so many causes of abnormal movements, implying the possibility of crises, since a balance is an accident under the conditions of this production.[10]

As the price form of value, dealt with in the third volume of *Capital*, is necessary for the analysis of the actual capitalist production and exchange process, the imaginary equilibrium conditions of the reproduction schemata in the second volume have no connection with the transformation problem. Furthermore, although approaching reality, Marx's treatment of the value-price problem is itself an explanatory model of the formation of a general rate of profit. The equality of value and price for society as a whole does not imply an equilibrium state, but indicates the identity of value and price under all economic conditions, in the sense that whatever the prices, their sum cannot exceed that of the actually produced value and surplus value. The injection of the notion of equilibrium into the value-price problem is due to the equilibrium concept of bourgeois economics and is not a requirement of Marxian theory. For Marx, moreover, the general rate of profit exists as a tendency over time, not as an actuality at any particular moment. The prices of production are not, at any given time, identical with the cost prices plus average profit, but deviate from this magnitude in one direction or the other; so that it is only through the dynamic of the system as a whole that value and price tendentially coincide.

Stating the quantity of constant and variable capital in price instead of in value terms, as Bortkiewicz recommended, would not yield their cost prices—that is, would not express the value of constant and variable capital—because cost prices, as we have seen, *actually* exist only as prices of production already containing the average profit. This holds true whether we deal with an individual capital or with the system as a whole. But for the latter it is at least possible to make a theoretical division between the cost price and the price of production of the total product, distinguishing the value of constant and variable capital and the mass of surplus value. It is the relationship between value and surplus value for the system as a whole that determines the magnitude of the general rate of profit, a relationship that would be needlessly beclouded if in Marx's transformation example the constant and variable capital were expressed in price terms. There is no point in shifting from value to price when dealing with the constant and variable capital, even though it is only in the price form that both appear in reality.

In Bortkiewicz's opinion, "Marx not only failed to indicate a valid way of determining the rate of profit on the given value and surplus-value relations; more, he was misled by his wrong construction of prices into an incorrect understanding of the factors on which the height of the profit rate in general depends."[11] Bortkiewicz adopts Ricardo's position that a change in the structure of production affecting only goods that do not enter into the consumption of the workers does not influence the rate of profit. On the assumption of simple reproduction, the supply of product from each of the three sectors must equal the demand for it, as this arises from the sum of income generated in the three departments. But the rate of profit, with a given rate of surplus value, depends entirely on the organic compositions of the capital invested in the two sectors producing either wage or capital goods, and not on that of Bortkiewicz's third sector, producing luxury goods and gold.

As a result, the average rate of profit does not lead to the equality of total value and total price, except under the condition that the organic composition of capital in the gold-producing industry is the same as that of the total capital. According to Marx, so Bortkiewicz relates, "with a given rate of surplus-value the only circumstance which affects the height of the rate of profit is whether the share of constant capital in total capital . . . is larger or smaller; and it would make no difference at all what differences existed between the organic compositions of the capital in the different spheres of production."[12] But as the rate of profit, according to Bortkiewicz, depends only on the rate of surplus value and the organic composition of capital invested in the departments I and II, the rate of profit on total capital is always smaller than the rate of surplus value, from which it follows that it is the general rate of profit, not the rate of surplus value, that accounts for the prices of production.

Bortkiewicz's "correction" of Marx's mistake consists, then, in the assertion that the equality of value and price depends on a particular relationship between the organic composition of total social capital and on that prevailing in the gold industry; total price, he thinks, can exceed total value or fall below it, depending on this relationship. On the assumption, for instance, that gold production requires a higher organic composition of capital than that which is characteristic for society as a whole, the price of gold would exceed its value. Because all commodities are expressed in terms of money prices, or gold, total price would be less than total value. Should the organic composition of capital in the gold industry be lower than for society as a whole, total price would exceed total value. Only in the special case where the organic composition of capital in the gold industry is the same as the social average organic composition of capital would total price and total value, total profit and total surplus value, coincide. And thus, while in general prices are not proportional to values, they may nonetheless be derived from value relations—which, though not vindicating Marx's transformation procedure, also does not impair Marx's contention that the rate of profit depends in general on the organic composition of the total social capital.

However, Marx's concept of total capital, to which the law of value applies, embraces all production, regardless of the different spheres of production in which it is carried on. Whatever the character of the various industries, all of them produce for the sake of surplus value, which falls to them, via competition and in terms of prices, in the form of the average rate of profit in accordance with the magnitude of their capitals. Prices of production are expressed in units of the money commodity (gold) because the latter is itself subjected to the law of value, that is, determined by socially necessary abstract labor time. It is therefore not possible to separate gold production from production in general and to deduce from the peculiarities of the gold industry the instrumentarium for calculating the divergence or convergence of value and price. Whatever the organic composition of the gold industry may be, it, like any other type of production, is overruled by the necessities of the system as a whole and thus by the law of value coming to the fore in price relations. The price of gold is therefore part and parcel of the total sum of prices, as it is of the total sum of value produced, for just as the prices of commodities are measured in terms of the price of gold, so does the latter find its measurement in its buying-power vis-à-vis all other commodities. A fall or rise of the price of gold finds its compensation in the rise or fall in the prices of other commodities without disturbing the equivalence between total value and total price.

Borkiewicz's "solution" of the value-price problem is a "technical solution," that is, a logical exercise, which attempts to test the inner consistency of a theory without regard to its empirical implications. It is a question of finding a mathematical solution for a mathematical problem, based on the concept of general equilibrium, which actually concerns no more than the supply-and-demand mechanism of the exchange process. The Bortkiewicz "solution" depends on the static situation of simple reproduction. It will not hold under conditions of expanded reproduction, when the capitalists of the third sector invest part of their profit in the departments producing wage and capital goods. It is perhaps for this reason that the transformation problem has played a rather minor role in Marxian theory, and found its locus of cultivation in bourgeois economics. The circulatory static conditions of simple reproduction bear a resemblance to bourgeois equilibrium theory—the main tool of bourgeois price theory. Marx's theory is thus approached as if it were a sort of Walrasian equilibrium theory, whether looked upon from the viewpoint of value or that of price, and presumably accessible to mathematical treatment. As capital by its nature is self-expanding, Bortkiewicz's "solution" has no connection with the real capitalist world. It remains a mere intellectual exercise, which may excite mathematically inclined economists but is no substitute for economic analysis, in which mathematics may serve for some purposes, as an aid to understanding, but never as a replica of real economic processes.

Just as Marx's reproduction schemata in the second volume of *Capital* do not claim to depict the concrete capitalist production and exchange process, so the transformation examples in the third volume do not profess to accomplish the impossible— namely, the actual transformation of definite values into definite prices—but serve merely as an instrument for the comprehension of the relations between values and prices. Not searching for an equilibrium in terms of prices, Marx's mixture of value and price relations suffices to illustrate the statement that prices and values will be altered through the competitive establishment of an average rate of profit. Whereas Marx's example of the transformation process has only an explanatory function, Bortkiewicz approaches the value relations as if they were actually ascertainable in price relations. Like Ricardo, he conceives of labor-time value in terms of physical commodity units, and not, like Marx, in terms of socially necessary abstract labor time. He therefore thinks it possible for analysis to proceed directly from technically determined observable production prices with a uniform rate of profit. But if this were so, there would be no need for value theory, for it would yield no more than can be found in price relations.

The concern with the "transformation problem" thus rests upon a profound misunderstanding of Marx's value concept. In Marx's conception there is no transformation, except as a mental construction based on the social production relations that underlie the actual price and market relations. Because the transformation of values into prices is a fact not of experience but of theory, the idea arose that the law of value is itself a mere fiction, though perhaps a necessary one, and not a real phenomenon. For Marx, however, the law of value is as real as capitalism itself, even though it manifests itself only in market and price relations. The fact that value relations are not observable does not imply that the *results* of the law are also unobservable, but only that they are experienced in other forms, in the various contradictions of capitalist production and in its crisis-ridden development.

There is, to repeat, no actual transformation of values into prices; there are always only prices, and the whole search for a mathematical transformation of one into the other is entirely superfluous. Still, to reiterate, if we start with price relations, the question immediately arises, what constitutes price? There are sellers who ask certain prices, and these sellers are also buyers who question the prices of other sellers. There must be a profit for capitalist sellers—a higher price for the commodities they sell than what their own production has cost them. Prices must be decomposed in order to be understood, although they do not need to be understood in order to function. The theoretical decomposition is hampered by the fact that the prices of production, which all buyers have to pay and all sellers ask, already include the capitalist profit. But it is obvious that each price must be composed of costs and profit, even though it appears as an indissoluble price of production containing both costs and profits. By mentally abstracting from the profit, one gets the cost prices. They are *real*, though not observable. By decomposing the cost prices, one comes to the *real* wages of the workers and to that part of capital that is used up in production and must be regained in selling the newly produced commodities. As only labor can produce surplus value, the profits in the prices of production are traced to their *real* source, to the unpaid labor of the workers.

It should be clear, of course, that a theoretical treatment of this process can never more than approximate reality. But it is not impaired thereby, so long as it concerns itself with the real basic structure of society. There is no doubt that the clear division between necessary and surplus labor in value terms does not exactly correspond with the division between them in terms of prices, because the prices of the consumption goods that fall to the workers are not equal to their values but to their prices of production, and enter as such in the value-determination of labor power as the price of labor power. But, although the workers buy only consumption goods, production of these goods is not separate from production in general. The price of labor power is expressed in commodity prices, which, as prices of production, incorporate, besides their value content, also a portion of the total surplus value. The price of labor power, like all prices, is thus composed of a mixture of value and profit. This commingling of value and surplus value does not prevent the division of the social product into necessary and surplus labor in the form of value and surplus value, for all that is here required is that wages be kept on a level securing the profitability and the accumulation of capital in price terms. In this manner, the profit content of the commodity prices that enter into the workers' consumption is appropriated by the capitalists through the price relations which play the attainable total surplus value into their hands. This of course implies the social struggles between labor and capital over wages and profits, which at times and to some extent may affect the level of profits as well as their distribution. In any case, our practical inability to reduce price to value, or value to price, cannot alter the fact that whatever the workers receive in terms of prices must be less than what they produce in terms of prices, and whatever falls to the capitalists in the form of profit must be extracted from the workers in the production process. A realistic analysis of prices and profits leads inescapably to value and surplus value.

According to Marx, the confusions of the classical economists with regard to value and price can be traced to their various attempts to abstract from the difference between surplus value and profit, in order to maintain the value concept, or to give up the latter altogether in favor of market prices. What was necessary, however, were further abstractions, so as to disclose the identity of value and price, of profit and surplus value, for society as a whole, in the value form of necessary and surplus labor, which underlies all other economic categories. As it is necessary to abstract from individual labor time to reach the socially determined abstract labor time, and to abstract from supply and demand to discover the market value behind the market price, so it is necessary to abstract from profit to reveal the value content in the cost prices beneath the prices of production and thus to lay bare the fundamental social production relations. Only then is it possible to comprehend the bewildering complexity of the capitalist world.

Marx did not especially concern himself with individual price determination, that is, with the relative prices of bourgeois "microeconomics," nor with the aggregates, such as national income, investment, and employment of the "macroeconomics" practiced by present-day equilibrium theory, whether static or dynamic. His concern was with the system as such, which rules out the artificial division into micro- and macroeconomics. It is the system as a whole that determines all prices in capitalism, even though their formation is left to the anarchic exchange relations. However, as the productivity of labor changes only slowly, the changes in the general price level are also slow in coming. This does not preclude more rapid changes in relative prices, due to the movements of capital and the profit disproportionalities that initiate these movements. The influence of value relations upon the movements of prices comes to the fore not so much in changing relative prices as in the changing general price level, wherein the various "abnormalities" of individual prices from the prices of production compensate one another without affecting the general price level determined by the changing productivity of labor and the accumulation of capital.

The distribution of the total social surplus value via the formation of the general rate of profit, as enforced by the system as a whole, not only overrides the different organic compositions of individual capitals, but also embraces the unproductive spheres of the capitalist system, such as merchant and banking capital, and that part of the total surplus value falling to monopolies or being absorbed through various forms of taxation. The general rate of profit is not all there is to the mechanics of the distribution of total surplus value, but is merely the first, decisive step in the process of price formation. The derivation of prices from value relations becomes increasingly more blurred through the wide dispersion of profits and finds its reflection in a practically impenetrable amalgam of price relations.

As there is no *practical* way to isolate value from surplus value, either with respect to the single commodity or for society as a whole, the derivation of price from value can only theoretically be deduced from the fact that the sum total of value and surplus value can be nothing but the sum total of prices, as well as from the corollary that whatever the distribution of profits may be, the profit itself cannot exceed the surplus value actually produced. In whatever complex manner the actual prices may come about, they cannot escape the boundaries set by the underlying value relations. This does not say much about relative prices. But this inability to pinpoint the value content of the single commodity in its price, Marxian theory shares with bourgeois price theory, which also is not able to account for the actually given price relations except by the imaginary textbook equilibrium of "pure theory," which can find no verification in actual price relations and is now in the process of being abandoned by bourgeois economics itself.

There is no need to consider the numerous attempts that have been made since Bortkiewicz either to prove or to disprove the validity of Marx's solution of the value-price problem. To repeat, for Marx there are no values that must be equated with their prices; there are only prices *derived* from, and circumscribed in their movements by, the value relations upon which the capitalist system rests. The recent rash of contributions to the "transformation problem" indicates not so much a serious concern with Marx's theory as a real disturbance in the minds of the economists. On the one hand, there is a loss of conviction in bourgeois price theory and, on the other hand, an urgent need to fortify this theory despite its failure as a realistic description of economic events. But the Marxian alternative is not open to bourgeois economists. In their search for a price theory more convincing than the standard theory of neoclassical economics, the Marxian alternative must first be set aside as a false, insufficient, or unnecessary approach to the price problem. To be sure, the defense of capitalism does not really require the concern they display with value and price, for its ideological value is quite limited; rather, this concern finds its explanation in the ongoing crisis of bourgeois economic theory. However, the debate around the value-price problem has taken a new turn.

It is now widely claimed that, whatever the difficulties involved in the transformation of value into price, the labor theory of value has its own virtue quite apart from price theory. It is said, for instance, that it is a necessary feature of the Marxian model

> that we have value equations and price equations as two separate systems. What is visible at the surface in the system of exchange relationships and price equations describes the system. Underlying the exchange relations are relations of production where the class division becomes manifest. A transformation from value to price and vice versa is essential for understanding the reality of the class divisions beneath the phenomenon of equality and free exchange under law. . . . [While] not a theory of relative prices or a theory of resource allocation, [the labor theory of value is essential as a theory] which brings out the influence of the class struggle in capitalism on the economic relationships of exchange.[13]

But even a superficial reading of *Capital* should make clear that Marx was developing not merely a theory of exploitation and class struggle and their effects upon exchange relations, but a theory of capitalist production and its developmental tendencies. Classical theory had already posited the class relations and the fact of exploitation. What Marx was concerned with were the immanent contradictions of value production, quite apart from the class struggle, even though these contradictions imply the appearance of class struggles specific to capitalism and even promise to bring the system to its end. Although the contradictions of capitalism are a feature of its underlying production relations, these relations appear in fetishistic form as value relations, and therefore as price relations, which, as they are identical with value relations for society as a whole, cannot be set against them. Since value is only a reality in its price form, it is not possible to have two sets of equations, one in value and the other in price terms. Moreover, the derivation of price from value is a one-way street; there is no way to reverse the procedure and go from price to value. The theoretical separation of value and price reveals, no doubt, the exploitative class relations, but also the derivation of price from value and therewith the value determination of resource allocation via the price relations. The price form of value merely affects the distribution of surplus value, but not the labor-time determination of the value of commodities, or their distribution in accordance with the allocation needs of capital production. The price relations do not make the exploitation relations less obvious, they merely dress them in different garb; instead of value and surplus value we have wage labor and capital expressed in terms of prices.

Meghnad Desai, for whom value theory has no other function than to unmask the hidden exploitation relations, suggests the need for two separate theories, one dealing with value, the other with price, and for a solution of the transformation problem that can accommodate "any quantitative empirical study seeking to understand the world in Marxian terms."[14] It will remain his secret, however, how this transformation can be accomplished, when, as he himself observes, the value relations are in principle "unobservable and unmeasurable" and the ascertainable price relations are far too misleading and unreliable to be counted as empirical evidence.

The separation of value theory from price theory seems to be common ground for many of the participants in the transformation controversy. Even Paul A. Samuelson recently felt obliged to recognize "two Walrasian systems" in Marx's theory—one in value terms, the other in price terms. Each may be justified, he says, but there is no bridge between them, no transformation of values into prices; we must choose either the one or the other. And of course, since value relations do not exist in reality, there is no point in elaborating Walrasian relations in terms of labor-time values, although this may bring out the fact of exploitation. But since the "exploitation hypothesis" may just as well be derived from a Walrasian system of price relations, the labor theory of value is redundant even as a theory of exploitation. According to Samuelson, "the tools of bourgeois analysis could have been used to discover and expound this notion of exploitation if only the economists had been motivated to use the tools for this purpose."[15]

But of course the economists were not so motivated, for in their minds the term "exploitation" is merely a misnomer for some objective necessities that face any economic system employing factors of production in addition to labor power. For them profit is no evidence of exploitation; to "give profit a bad name" is only to show a lack of sophistication. But even if one wants to use such foul language, there is no need to turn to Marx, as the alleged exploitation can be just as well defined in terms of bourgeois price theory. On this point, too, there seems to emerge a consensus among professional economists. If there is still some disagreement on Marx's intentions regarding the value-price transformation and on the merits of Marx's value theory in general, when it comes to profits and prices the value analysis is superseded by the better mathematical formulations of modern price theory. According to Michio Morishima, for instance, even though it is clear "that the long-run equilibrium rate of profit is possible if and only if the rate of 'exploitation' is positive," this proposition—which Morishima calls the "Fundamental Marxian Theorem"—"is completely independent of the concept of value. . . . Anyway, we may conceive of Marx without the theory of value, as long as we agree that the Fundamental Marxian Theorem is the core of his economic theory."[16] In this way, despite its analytical shortcomings, Marxism and the whole of classical economy may be reintegrated into the established science of economics and Marx's "pioneering work" recognized as an important contribution to this science.

It is clear that Marx, aiming as he did at the abolition of the price system, could not be deeply interested in a theory of relative prices. In William J. Baumol's opinion, "the value theory was never intended as a theory of prices," and in any case, Marx's "transformation was not from value into prices, but from surplus value into nonlabor income categories," such as profit, interest, and rent. For Marx, the transformation of value into price "was worth discussing only to reveal its irrelevance and to tear away the curtain it formed before our eyes, so that the basic truth about the production of surplus value could be reached."[17] Morishima seconds this interpretation by stating that "it is clear that the transformation problem has the aim of showing how 'the aggregate exploitation of labor on the part of the total social capital' is, in a capitalist economy, obscured by the distortion of prices from values; the other aim is to show how living labor can be the sole source of profit."[18]

But even if labor is the sole *socially* relevant source of production, and profit a deduction from the product of labor, Samuelson argues in reply to these points, one "cannot neglect the labor previously performed and embodied in raw materials and in equipment—i.e. 'dead' or indirect labor."[19] This "dead" labor happens to be the property of the capitalists, Samuelson points out, and is also a factor of production, adding to the value gained in the production process. Capitalist income, in the form of profit or interest, cannot be considered exploitation as long as it does not exceed the value of the capitalist contribution to production. The analysis of this factual situation, quite apart from the ethical issues it may raise, requires not a theory of value and surplus value but a general price theory operating on the undifferentiated national income.

It was perhaps unavoidable that the bourgeois economists' concern with the transformation problem should arouse a new interest in the subject matter in Marxist circles, leading, in some instances, to a revision of Marx's treatment of this issue. For both groups, this fresh interest in the transformation problem was a by-product of concern with the so-called neo-Ricardian approach to economic theory, which was itself a by-product of the crisis of bourgeois economic theory in its neoclassical form. Although the neo-Ricardians find ancestors in Dimitriev and Bortkiewicz, the current interest in the transformation problem is mostly due to the work of Piero Sraffa, even though the latter does not deal with it at all.[20] Most likely, Sraffa's intense concern with classical theory, as the editor of *The Works and Correspondence of David Ricardo*, led him to challenge the ruling marginalist conceptions by a return to Ricardo's preoccupations. Sraffa returned, however, not to Ricardo's labor theory of value but to his early attempt to

determine exchange relations and the rate of profit "directly between quantities of corn without any question of valuation,"[21] or,
in Sraffa's wording, by a consideration of the "production of commodities by means of commodities." As there is no value in the
Sraffa system, the issue of a transformation of values into prices
does not arise. Bypassing value relations, and referring to Marx not
at all, Sraffa concerns himself exclusively with the critique of the
conceptions of marginalism.

As a bourgeois economist, Sraffa joins his numerous colleagues in assuming the existence of a science of economics that
has relevance for all economic systems in the historical sense of
classical theory. His critique of marginalism remains within the
general conceptual field of bourgeois theorizing, and even of neoclassical theory, in which the notion of marginal utility refers to
nothing but the use-value aspects of commodity production as defined by consumer choices on the market. However, whereas neoclassical theory takes its starting point and seeks its validation in
the sphere of consumption, Sraffa finds it in the sphere of production, in which the exchange relations are regulated by wage and
profit relations.

Thus the crisis of bourgeois economic theory has led to its
modification in two directions. The major one was the belated
Keynesian recognition that Say's "law of the market," whether
stated in terms of an objective or in those of a subjective theory of
value, does not hold for the capitalist system, which tends toward
a permanent disequilibrium between its production and the effective demand. However, Keynes thought it not necessary to restore
the production-consumption equilibrium, i.e., to change the system, but rather to support it from outside, through government interventions that would bring effective demand in line with a scale
of production guaranteeing full employment. The other direction,
taken by Sraffa and the neo-Ricardians, assumes that effective demand depends on the distribution of the total social product as determined by the wage-profit relations. A way must then be found
to make possible a wage-profit ratio that would lead to a less crisis-
ridden capitalist development.

Sraffa's own work is offered as a mere "prelude" to a more
thorough examination of the distribution relations of commodity
production. As a prelude—and moreover, one that treats the
problems involved within the rarified realm of "pure theory"—it

is a preliminary undertaking for the clarification of economic concepts, quite apart from their possible confrontation with the actual capitalist world. This "pure theory" is dressed in use-value terms, in accord with the assumption that all relations of production and distribution are ultimately based on nothing but the material-technical conditions of production, which determine the structure and the functions of any economic system. Nevertheless, the collapse of Keynesian theory, as a result of the ineffectiveness of its policy recommendations, put neo-Ricardianism in the center of economic interest as a sort of refuge from the shambles in which bourgeois economic theory finds itself. And just as Keynesianism was to some extent able to influence some self-professed Marxists, neo-Ricardianism has done even better, because of its apparent return to considerations of social class relations and their effect upon the distribution of the social product.

We will deal here only with the reception Sraffa's work found among such professed Marxists as, for example, Mario Cogoy.[22] Sraffa's work convinced Cogoy that the transformation problem is of far greater complexity than Marx had imagined it to be. Although Sraffa's work does not deal with this issue, in Cogoy's opinion it nonetheless throws light upon the difficulties of Marx's transformation procedure. Among other things, Sraffa assailed the marginalist capital concept and the marginal determination of factor prices by constructing an alternative system of economic analysis that concerns itself exclusively with such properties "as do not depend on changes in the scale of production or in the proportions of 'factors'." In such a system "the marginal product of a factor (or alternately the marginal cost of a product) would not merely be hard to find—it just would not be there to be found."[23] In the light of Sraffa's construction, the notion of capital as an entity given and measurable independently of price formation cannot be sustained, because it itself is determined only after the profit and price relations are known. Cogoy convinced himself that this critique of the traditional capital concept also applies to Marx's capital theory because "capital cannot enter as a definite magnitude in the production process, since this magnitude can be established only after the determination of the relationship between wages and profits. The result of Sraffa's analysis destroys any and all concepts of capital as a magnitude existing *prior* to production and distribution."[24]

This would come as a great surprise to the capitalists, were they aware of the wondrous world of academic economics, for they do base their respective claims to the social surplus value on the size of their particular investments as measured by their market values. For the economics of the economists, capital may not be a definite magnitude to behold, but each capitalist knows quite well what his capital amounts to in money terms, and all capitals together constitute the monetary value of the total social capital, whether this is measurable or not. Originally, "capital" was identified with the physical means of production in the hands of the capitalists, along wtih the money "advanced" as wages to the workers. There was no problem with the concept of capital, and its accumulation expressed the growing value of capital in terms of money. This concept of capital prevails today—if not for the economists, at any rate for practicing capitalists. The goal of their production is a greater money capital, expressible in commodities of all descriptions, including means of production and labor power. The accumulation of capital is an extremely simple and transparent procedure, requiring no more than the existence of owners of capital and the wages system. The complexities begin with the distribution of the extracted surplus value. To understand this it is essential to distinguish the production of surplus value from its distribution, so as not to lose contact with the social production relations upon which the whole capitalist edifice rests. For this reason Marx's basic categories are "constant capital," "variable capital," and "surplus value." A capitalist system requires a definite relationship between these categories: the variable capital must yield sufficient surplus value to expand the total capital beyond its previous size in terms of money. Without this, there is no capitalist production.

Because of the complexities which the capital-producing system brings into the distribution of surplus value, the categories constant capital, variable capital, and surplus value lose their unambiguous meaning, for they are thoroughly intermixed within price relations. As Cogoy observes, "prices change not only because capitals of various magnitudes have to yield a uniform rate of profit, but also because these price changes alter the quantitative relationships between the different capitals. . . . Not only the prices change, but, because they do so, the magnitudes of different capitals fluctuate, which, again, influences the price relations."[25]

He concludes from this that the transformation problem cannot be solved on the assumption that the value relations between total capital and total surplus value are identifiable with the general rate of profit and that the transformation of values into prices must be accompanied by a simultaneous transformation of the value rate of profit into a price rate of profit. Cogoy must be reminded, first, that there is no such thing as a value rate of profit, but only a price rate of profit and, second, that no matter how price changes may alter the quantitative relationships between different capitals, and these again the price relations between different commodities, this cannot alter anything with respect to the concept and the reality of the total capital and total surplus value or, therefore, to the dependence of profits on the total surplus value.

Marx criticized the classical economists precisely because of their inability to recognize profit, interest, and rent as derivations from surplus value, which must be confronted as such with total capital if we are to understand its movements as well as the price relations bound up with it. This advance beyond classical economics Cogoy sees as Marx's "mistake," because it led to the false equation of total value with total price and total profit with total surplus value. For Cogoy, if total value equals total price, total profit could equate with total surplus value only if the product combinations in the profit category—with respect to quantities of the concrete labor time they embody—are the same as those in the total social product; this, however, is not the case. It is therefore not enough to know the mass of values entering and leaving the production process; it is also necessary to know the use-value combinations of each value unit that partakes in the formation of the price structure and of the rate of profit. Because this is so, "value is not the basis of price because the sum-total of all prices is equal to the sum of all values, but because the prices mediate an average rate of profit, which, though not identical with the value structure remains dependent on it."[26] It is thus necessary to give up the concept of capital as a definite given magnitude and to break it down into its various components with respect to both use value and exchange value.

Marx's mistake, Cogoy asserts, was to equate the sum of values and prices, of profits and surplus value, without bothering to investigate the interdependence of social production in terms of use values, or the technical conditions of production. He suggests a reformulation of the transformation problem that implies no less than an undoing of Marx's value theory, since it involves the replacement of abstract labor-time value by concrete labor-time relations defined in terms of the physical production process. Of course, this reformulation is not undertaken, but left to the future. But its implications are spelled out and prove to be so formidable as to warrant the certainty that it will never be endeavored.

Cogoy regards the traditional identification of value relations with the social production relations as an "empty phrase." People use this phrase, he says, to avoid making quantitative statements about value-price relations or about the organic composition of capital, under the pretense that this would be an unwarranted empiricism. But if, for reason of theory, the connection between the value and price level of analysis cannot be reconstructed in quantitative terms, then the whole transformation problem is only of methodological importance and the relations between the value-system and the price-system are equally irrelevant, whether one assumes that the price system does not require a value basis or that the value system suffices to explain the price mechanism. Cogoy believes that a way must be found to derive prices from values in a logically consistent system. In short, he assumes that there is an internal value structure of capitalist production and an external price structure, each existing in its own right, so to speak, and that it is only by a rigorous scientific analysis—an admittedly difficult task—that the quantitative value relations can be traced to quantitative price relations, in order to establish exactly what these relations imply for either value or price. But as value relations, to repeat, only exist as price relations, there is no way to conduct such comparative calculations. This condemns Cogoy to remain in the sphere of "pure theory" and to occupy himself with the playful construction of imaginary mathematical models in a search for the solution of a problem that does not exist.

It was of course as obvious to Marx as it is to Cogoy and the neo-Ricardians that the interdependencies of the capitalist economy, with respect to both value and surplus value, determine the movements of capital, profits, and wages, in an ever-shifting pattern, so that the system's basic determination by value relations asserts itself only in the course of capitalist development as an averaging of ceaseless deviations of price from value and profit from surplus value. If it were possible to arrest the developmental process and to distinguish the elements in the price structure representing the value of labor power from those referring to surplus value, the actual division between necessary and surplus labor in value terms would be revealed, whatever this may imply in terms of prices and profits. It is precisely because capital is not a given, but is a changing magnitude, that it is necessary to stick to the unchangeable relations of capital production, which prevail no matter what the effect of the movements of capital upon the price relations, and of the price relations upon the movements of capital, may happen to be. The concept of total capital excludes a division other than that into constant capital, variable capital, and surplus value. These categories include all spheres and branches of production, no matter what, or under what conditions, they may produce. The production of means of production is not differentiated from any other kind of production. All products, including labor power, are commodities of equal standing. They are equalized by the abstract money form of value and surplus value. Value exists, then, only as a social phenomenon, as an average of abstract labor-time relations with regard to the single commodity as well as the total social capital, for which the general rate of profit is determined in relation to the social average organic composition of capital.

What characterizes Marx's concept of value is its determination by exchange value, which overrules all use-value aspects of capitalist production. To be sure, the very existence of capitalist society depends on the production of use values and on their allocation through market relations in the pursuit of exchange value. Accomplished in one fashion or another through capitalist competition, as determined by the accumulation of capital, the social profit, or surplus value, is distributed in accordance with the magnitudes of the various capitals, which reflect, in their existence, the social allocation of labor. To bring this about, the general rate of profit must be *independent of any particular capital and its specific organic composition*, for it is only in this manner that the use-value requirements of capitalist production can be met.

The interdependency between the units involved in capitalist production determined by the use-value aspects of commodities *presupposes* the interdependence of production units established in terms of exchange-value. The technical relations of social production are a mere aspect of the value relations, as is expressed in Marx's concept of the organic composition of capital. The domination of exchange value precludes any determining role for the use-value character of commodities *outside* of the constraints of value production. The technically determined interdependencies of capital production, in other words, are subordinated to the interdependencies of the value relations, which determine capitalist development through their regulation of the accumulation of capital. It is the latter which determines the character of the technical relations, not vice versa, and with them the interdependencies of social production that come to the fore as use-value relations.

Because all production in all possible economic systems is the production of use values, this fact is totally meaningless with respect to the description and analysis of a specific economic system such as capitalism. For Marx, use value as such has no economic significance, except as the material basis of exchange value. Bourgeois economic theory asserts, of course, that there are general economic laws valid for all social systems, and thus feels enabled to see in capitalism only a special case of these general laws of economics. But these "general laws," which amount to the inescapable necessity for any system to reproduce itself, are just as meaningless as the fact that all production is the production of use values. In either case, the nature of capitalism as a historically specific form of social production is overlooked in favor of a pointless generalization of the obvious, namely, that all economic systems are subject to some natural necessities and thus share some similarities within their historical differentiations.

In capitalism, labor time appears as value and is determined by social necessity in a double sense, namely, with respect to both the time socially necessary for the production of any particular commodity, and the time required to produce the quantities of various commodities required for the enlarged reproduction of capital. Labor-time value is thus not identical with the actual labor time employed in production, but only with the *abstract* labor-time content of commodities considered products of the system as a whole. It is also only insofar as surplus value in the form of abstract labor-time value is produced that total surplus value equates with the total profit, and total value with total price. Unproductive labor—that is, labor not yielding surplus value—is not part of strictly capitalist production, whereas the labor time actually applied in society includes unproductive labor, which does not enter into the socially necessary labor time defining value. The value of labor power, moreover, is derived not from labor time as such, but from the value of the commodities that the workers buy with their wages. It is thus always from abstract value and surplus value that prices and profits are derived, never from the use-value character of commodities or the technical peculiarities of their production.

However, although Cogoy agrees with Sraffa's finding that the rate of profit together with all prices can be directly derived from relations between physical quantities of commodities, he would like to retain Marx's concept of value, if only to establish a connection between the price relations and the actual social organization of the labor process. His early treatment of the matter carried the title "The Dilemma of neo-Ricardian Theory," and maintained that Sraffa's analysis cannot replace Marx's value theory. While it is necessary to criticize Marx with Sraffa, he held, it is also necessary to criticize Sraffa with Marx, for it remains true that the value relations are the rational foundation for the analysis of price and profit formation, even though the relations between value and price are not those assumed by Marx. In his second and more extensive treatment of the same subject matter, Cogoy still speaks of a "value structure and price structure," but only to reject the former in favor of the latter.[27] If a transformation of values into prices in the Marxian sense is not possible, he asserts, the internal connection between the regulative function of the law of value and the interactions of the different capitals in the formation of the rate of profit is lost and precludes any meaningful analysis of capitalism. Marx's shortcomings with regard to the transformation procedure are now seen as shortcomings of Marx's value theory, due to his failure to pay attention to the complex structure of technological interdependence linking the various industries. If the law of value still has a central place in the comprehension of the system and its developmental tendencies, this is only as a reflection of the social relations of production in a broad, nonquantitative way. Actually, the technical forms that realize the socialization of labor are more important than the vague value relations that seemingly point to the socialization of capital production via the average rate of profit. The abstract value concept must therefore make room for principles based on the technological use-value structure of capitalist production, or for that matter, of any kind of production. But at this point we can take leave of Cogoy, for he has made the irrevocable jump from Marxism to neo-Ricardian theory, with which we will deal at another place.[28]

To sum up: the insistence of neoclassical theory upon the point that there is no transformation of values into prices, and the concurrence with this position on the part of the neo-Ricardians, is also shared by Marx, if only for the reason that there is no way to expose the value relations in quantitative terms, to prove their equivalence with the price relations. If the transformation of values into prices were possible, it would suggest choice between value and price theory. Why, then, deal with value at all, since the real world of capitalism is one of price relations? Indeed, it has been said that

> in so far as the problems which are posed for solutions are concerned with the behavior of the disparate elements of the economic system (prices of individual commodities, profits of particular capitalists, the combinations of productive factors in the individual firm et cetera) there seems to be no doubt that value calculation is of little assistance. Orthodox economists have been working intensely on problems of this sort for the last half century and more. They have developed a kind of price theory which is more useful in this sphere than anything to be found in Marx and his followers.[29]

Nevertheless, the value concept should be retained because "it makes it possible to look beneath the surface phenomena of money and commodities to the underlying relations between people and classes."[30] As we have seen, some of the more recent contributors to the literature on the value-price problem share this opinion, which reduces the value theory to a mere theory of exploitation.

In this whole discussion the relevance of bourgeois price theory is taken for granted. The problem is with value, not with price. After all, prices are observable; they are what they are, whether or not they are traceable to underlying value relations. But they are what they are also aside from bourgeois price theory, which deals with a "pure price system," not with the prices encountered in the real world. This "pure theory" plays the same role with regard to actual prices that Marxian value theory plays with regard to the prices of production. The prices of "pure theory" are also unobservable. "The economist's definition" of price, it is said, "is surely not easy to implement except in the most artificially simplified instances. That is why businessmen do not follow the economist's mode of analysis but adopt simplified rules of thumb."[31] Within its limited field, bourgeois price theory has only explanatory functions; if it had operational meaning, it would no longer refer to the assumed self-adjustability of market relations.

Bourgeois price theory presents a static system and as such has no connection with the dynamic reality. It makes theoretical assumptions and draws conclusions from them that preclude empirical verification. It always remains the theory of an imaginary price system. It insists upon the interdependence of all prices and their derivation from the prices of final goods, as equilibrium prices, although it is now admitted that the aggregate demand may not equate with the aggregate supply. The resulting discrepancy between theoretical price and real price leaves the latter unexplained. Until recently, price theory disregarded the distribution of income, for it assumed that each factor of production, be it labor or capital, finds its proper reward in accordance with its marginal product, so that all incomes of factor owners equate with the respective contributions of these factors to the production process. In this way, the price system determines the distribution of income, whatever it may be, and in any case, the "science of economics" restricts itself to the study of the allocation of commodities through the "revealed preferences" of the consumers under whatever conditions of distribution. This theory, which is now under attack, cannot account for the actual price relations and their changes. It does no more "than to translate the queer concepts of the capitalists, who are in the thralls of competition, into a more theoretical and generalizing language and to attempt a vindication of the correctness of these conceptions."[32]

It could not have entered Marx's mind to have a price theory apart from value theory. The actual price relations and their historical development are only the market expression of value relations, which are the determining element of capital expansion. Prices change with changes in value relations and the latter change with changes in the system as a whole, following on the accumulation of capital. The derivation of prices from values shows itself in changes in the general price level and in the average rate of profit.

Outside of these changes, alterations of relative prices signify no more than temporary reactions to shifts of supply and demand within the existing value relations. They are met by counter-shifts and can be disregarded. Whatever these changes in relative prices may imply for individual capitals, they do not affect the state of the economy as a whole and its developmental tendencies.

Not being a primer for businessmen, Marxian theory has no desire to trouble itself with individual price determination, or with particular businesses and their profitability. In a dynamic system, such as capitalism is, "economizing" on the basis of price is in any case dependent on the behavior of the system as a whole, a fact to which the bourgeois theory of "risk and uncertainty" bears witness in its own fashion. Insofar as empirical proof of the determination of price by value is possible, it is by comparing general price levels of the past with those of the present, or those of more with those of less capitalistically developed nations. As the increasing productivity of labor decreases the value of commodities, lower values find their expression in lower prices.

We may as well point out at once that value may fall without a change in price, or even with increasing price, though this would merely indicate a devaluation of money. Just as for any other commodity, the value of a money commodity, gold or silver, is determined by its cost of production plus the average rate of profit; its price falls with the decline of its value, somewhat modified by changing supply and demand relations. But as commodity money is supplemented by other types of money, an inflation of the money supply may lead to prices that seemingly contradict the reduction of the commodities' value content. It is therefore on the assumption that the law of value extends over the money supply that the decreasing value of commodities finds its expression in lower prices.

Aside from statistically ascertainable changes in the general price level, it is the existence of a general rate of profit that verifies the effect of the value relations upon the price and profit relations. It is of course only in a manner of speaking that the establishment of the average rate of profit constitutes a "value transfer" between different capital entities. Actually, the "transfer" is not observable, but is the outcome of price movements enforced, unbeknownst to economic agents, by value relations. The general rate of profit does not take the place of the law of value; the latter shows itself in the average rate of profit. Price movements are dependent on value relations because the reproduction and accumulation of capital is accomplished not in terms of use values but in terms of exchange values. The physical production process serves the reproduction of the physical requirements of society only insofar as they are compatible with the maintenance and the enlargement of capital. As the use value aspect of commodity production, and of the commodity itself, precludes an exchange of goods measured in terms of quantities of abstract labor time, due to the different rates of exploitation, different conditions of production, and different organic compositions of the various capitals, commodity exchange in a capitalist society is possible only in terms of prices that both derive and deviate from labor-time values.

Prices precede the capitalist system and continue with it, even though they are now associated with the specifically capitalist relations of production. It was their existence that raised the question of their meaning within capitalist commodity production and led to the discovery of the value relations upon which they rest. But the emergence of value theory changed nothing in the fact that price relations determine the exchange process. No question of an actual transformation of values into prices could, or can, arise in a system that functions only on the basis of price relations. But the value relations also exist; that is, it is a self-evident fact that commodities must be produced, and are produced, by human labor, so that the various commodities may be distinguished in terms of the quantities of labor time required for their production. The social character of commodity production demands an allocation of the total social labor in such proportions as assure the existence and the enlarged reproduction of the system, and this must be accomplished by means of a process of exchange in which no one is aware of the actual requirements of the system as a whole in its material or use-value aspects. A substitute for this "awareness" must be reached through price movements, which by themselves have no direct connection with the labor-time quantities incorporated in commodities. Because it is through price, and not value, that social production and exchange find some sort of regulation, price must account for the necessary allocation of labor among the various spheres of production, and the profitability of any kind of production, required for the existence of the system as a whole.

That such a system cannot be conceived as an equilibrium system seems obvious. But this has nothing to do with its existence and its continuation. As the regulator of capital production, Marx's law of value implies no more than the setting of definite social boundaries to the movements of prices and profits through which the system operates. These boundaries, again, are recognizable only in price and profit relations, which turn an apparent "equilibrium"—suggested by the expansion of capital—into the disequilibrium of crisis. This leads us into the next chapter. At this point it suffices to state that it is most importantly in the disturbances and the recurrent crises of capitalist production that the determination of the price system by value relations shows itself empirically, though still not in value terms but in terms of price and profit relations. We can thus leave the "transformation problem" to the mathematical wizards of the "post-Marxian production economics."

Value
and
Capital

Given the value character of capitalist production, the increase of the productivity of labor and the expansion of capital are different expressions for the capitalization of surplus value. This process changes the organic composition of the total social capital. Historically, Marx related,

> it can be assumed that under the crude, pre-capitalist mode of production, agriculture is *more productive* than industry, because nature assists here as a machine and an organism, whereas in industry the powers of nature are still almost entirely replaced by human actions (as in the craft type of industry, etc.). In the period of stormy growth of capitalist production, productivity in industry develops rapidly as compared with agriculture, although its development *presupposes* that a significant change as between constant and variable capital *has* already taken place in agriculture, that is, a large number of people have been driven off the land. Labor productivity advances in both, although at an uneven pace. But when industry reaches a certain level the disproportion must diminish, in other words, productivity in agriculture must increase relatively more rapidly than in industry.[1]

With capitalist production being the dominant mode of production, it determines the increase of productivity in all spheres of production and allocates social labor accordingly.

Capital expansion increases not only the productivity of labor but also the number of wage workers and with it the mass of surplus value. But just as capitalist development presupposes an increase in the productivity of precapitalist labor, so the extension of the capitalist mode of production requires a steadily increasing productivity of its labor force. Only the increase of surplus value ensures its expansion and territorial extension through the transformation of surplus value into additional constant and variable capital. It is through accumulation that capitalism spreads itself in space, by transforming additional labor into wage labor in the simultaneous pursuit of absolute and relative surplus value. Capitalist production thus tends to become universal by creating the world market through the expansion of capital. While commodity exchange gave rise to capitalist production, the production of capital now determines the growth of markets; they are dependent on the accumulation of capital. This implies, of course, that if there should be a limit to the extraction of surplus value from a given number of workers, there would also be a limit to the extension and the enlargement of capital.

Historically, capital expansion starts with a very low organic composition of capital. Profits are low because the use value of labor —in other words, its productivity—is still quite limited. It is for this reason that, at first, the increase of capital relies on absolute surplus value, on extraordinarily long working hours and the most ferocious exploitation of the laboring class, still more accentuated by a cut-throat competition for the still meager mass of the social surplus value. Accumulation is here a precarious process because of the low organic composition of capital. At a certain stage of development, however, the organic composition of capital begins to rise significantly and supplements in increasing measure the absolute with relative surplus value, indicating a rise in the productivity of labor-power. The accumulation of capital can now proceed by shortening the labor time in general and necessary labor time— that which produces the value of variable capital—in particular.

The second phase of capital expansion is predominantly based on relative surplus value, on the reduction of the variable as against the constant capital. While the exchange value of labor power declines, its use value for capital increases. Of course, the decline of the value of labor power does not imply any reduction of the workers' living standards, for progressively less labor time is required to produce the commodity equivalent representing the variable capital. Although, and *within definite limits*, the value of labor power is variable, in his abstract model of capitalist accumulation in *Capital* Marx assumed that it remains unimpaired throughout the analysis, i.e., that it always corresponds to the commodity equivalent necessary to produce and reproduce the social labor power, whatever that may imply in terms of quantities of commodities in use-value terms. More use values, expressing a sufficiently lower exchange value, will, of course, improve the living conditions of the laboring class even while the latter's exchange value declines, without ceasing to express the value of labor power as that which is required for its reproduction in accordance with the prevailing social habits and conditions. The value relations of capitalist production do not imply any definite physical level of existence for the working class, but rather levels that at any particular time allow for the accumulation of capital.

At first glance it may seem that if accumulation and the rising productivity of labor are one and the same process, the resulting immanent decline of the labor-time value of commodities should be fully compensated by a respective quantitative increase of the mass of the produced commodities. However, the question is not one of maintaining but of enlarging the surplus value for purposes of accumulation. A given capital must become a larger one. But the increasing productivity of labor decreases not only the value of labor power but also that of the already accumulated capital. As the existing capital is "measured" not by its own historical costs of production, but by the lower costs that constitute the additional constant capital, the enlargement of capital as exchange value is constantly held back by the declining exchange value of the previously accumulated capital. In order to enlarge the total constant capital in value terms, the newly produced surplus value must not only cover the costs of new investments but also the loss of value of the old capital brought into being under less productive conditions. The absolute growth of capital thus requires a rate of surplus value large enough to cover both the new investments and the devaluation of the existing capital. This situation finds its source in the twofold character of the commodity as an exchange value and a use value.

The total social capital includes both constant and variable capital. If increased productivity of labor means that more commodities are produced in less time, fewer workers are needed to produce the same or a larger mass of commodities. Although the number of workers diminishes in relation to production, the expansion of capital through newly invested surplus value enlarges the number of workers absolutely. But the absolute growth in the number of workers accompanies their relative decline with respect to the growing social capital. And as only the variable capital yields surplus value, the rate of profit on total capital must fall as the organic composition of capital rises, unless the rate of surplus value increases fast enough to maintain the given rate of profit on the accumulating capital. According to Marx, "the rate of profit expresses the rate of surplus value always lower than it actually is. The rate of profit would be equal to the rate of surplus-value . . . only if the entire invested capital were paid out in wages."[2] A constant rise of the organic composition of capital must lower the rate of profit even with a rising rate of surplus-value. The total surplus value, Marx pointed out,

> is determined first by its rate, secondly by the mass of labor simultaneously employed at this rate, or what amounts to the same, by the magnitude of the variable capital. One of these factors, the rate of surplus-value, rises in one direction, the other factor, the number of laborers, falls in the opposite direction (relatively or absolutely). To the extent that the development of the productive power reduces the paid portion of the employed labor, it raises the surplus-value by raising its rate; but to the extent that it reduces the total mass of labor employed by a certain capital, it reduces the factor of numbers with which the rate of surplus-value is multiplied in order to calculate the mass. . . .
> The compensation of the reduction of the number of laborers by means of an intensification of exploitation has certain impassable limits. It may, for this reason, check the fall of the rate of profit, but cannot prevent it entirely.[3]

The tendency of the rate of profit to fall may be *demonstrated* by the *artifice* of letting the organic composition of capital rise on the assumption of a stable rate of exploitation. Under such conditions, the rate of profit falls proportionally to the increasing organic composition of capital, thus revealing the dependency of capital accumulation on a rising rate of surplus value. The fact of accumulation thus attests to a sufficient increase of surplus value despite the tendential fall of the rate of profit, which will not be noticeable in the price relations of the market.

> A fall in the rate of profit and a hastening of accumulation are . . . only different expressions of the same process as both of them indicate the development of the productive power. Accumulation in its turn hastens the fall of the rate of profit, in as much as it implies the concentration

of labor on a larger scale and therewith a higher composition of capital. On the other hand, a fall in the rate of profit hastens the concentration of capital and its centralization through the expropriation of the smaller capitalists . . . This accelerates on the one hand the accumulation, so far as mass is concerned, although the rate of accumulation falls with the rate of profit.[4]

The manifold world of capitalism—the global nature of the exchange relations, the dynamic character of the expansion process, and the countless possible deviations from the basic rules of the socially determined production and exchange process—makes it extremely difficult, if not impossible, to identify particular events in the value relations underlying the system of capitalist production. It is less difficult to observe occurrences proving or disproving the value character of capitalist production, which discloses itself in capitalism's historical development. The proof of the labor theory of value is to be found not in its abstract logical consistency but in the actual course of capitalist development, in whether or not this development verifies a trend deducible from value theory.

Marx's *Capital*, then, is first of all a theory of capitalist development. Marx reserved for later work more detailed elucidations of the capitalist world of appearance as determined by the essential value relations. These relations, however, are as empirical as the actual world of experience. The theory is abstract, not in the sense that it is a mere conceptual working hypothesis, but literally, in that it abstracts from all the less essential and continously changing surface phenomena of the market economy, which exist only by virtue of the social production relations in their capitalistic garb. These relations *are* the actual capitalist world. If market and price relations appear in various deceptive forms during capitalist development, they could not take on these disguises unless the real basis of capitalist production, namely, the capital–labor relation as a value relation, remained intact.

This is what makes it possible to construct a theoretical model of capitalist production that disregards the many modified forms in which the capital-labor relations, as value relations, assert themselves in the commodity-producing society. This construction is empirical insofar as it reveals the basic structure of capitalism, which remains unaffected by whatever happens within the market relations. While an analysis of capitalist production based on nothing but value relations does not tell the whole story of capitalistic development, it does lay bare the dynamics of that development. Whereas it is possible to abstract from the latter, in order to reveal the inescapable trend of development in a society based on surplus-value production, the reverse is not possible; that is, it is not possible to abstract from the value relations in order to grasp the development of market relations. Although these market relations, as price and profit relations, are of an observable nature, they would not exist were it not for the underlying value relations.

Assuming a closed and fully developed capitalist system, restricting his analysis to the production of surplus value and disregarding the problem of its realization, Marx came to the logical conclusion that the value relations of capitalist production explain both the system's rapid rise and its eventual demise. While nothing definite can be said about the historical long-run tendency of the rate of profit to fall, the prevalence of this tendency manifests itself in the actual crisis cycle of capitalist development. Marx's theory of accumulation is thus at the same time a theory of crisis, based on the analysis of the value relations of capital production. As the crisis cycle accompanied the whole of capitalist development, whatever the organic composition of capital at any particular time, it is not the organic composition of capital as such that, with the rate of profit, determines the state of the economy, but a time-conditioned *specific relationship* between a specific rate of exploitation and a specific organic composition of the total capital.

Marx's model of capitalist production pictures an imaginary system, free of all the obstacles that hide the real relations of production and often seem to contradict them. But his analysis is imaginary only insofar as it abstracts from the changing market appearances of the unchanging social production relations, which assure the production of surplus value through the fetishistic value character of social production. As the latter determines the real, observable motions of the capitalist world, Marx's theory of accumulation, as the theory of the tendential fall of the rate of profit, restricts itself to a contradiction inherent in capitalist production, which, although ever present, need not be visible in market events, as it can be counteracted by capitalist reactions for shorter or longer periods of time.

In any case, the very fact of its development testifies to capitalism's ability to increase the rate of exploitation fast enough to offset the declining rate of profit which this development also implies. What empirical evidence exists, quite apart from the specific economic categories considered and the analytical methods employed, verifies what is also obvious to the naked eye, namely, a continuous rise of the composition of capital in both its material and its value aspects. As a result, according to Marx,

> the same development of the social productivity of labor expresses itself in the course of capitalist production on the one hand in a tendency of a progressive fall of the rate of profit, and on the other hand in a tendency to a progressive increase of the absolute mass of the appropriated surplus-value, or profit; so that . . . a relative decrease of the variable capital and profit is accompanied by an absolute increase of both. This twofold effect . . . can express itself only in a growth of the total capital at a ratio more rapid than that expressed by the fall of the rate of profit.[5]

Moreover, the diminishing of the variable capital as compared to the constant

> only shows approximately the change in composition of its material constituents. . . . The reason is simply that, with the increasing productivity of labor, not only does the mass of the means of production consumed by it increase, but their value compared with their mass diminishes. Their value therefore rises absolutely, but not in proportion to their mass. The increase of the difference between constant and variable capital is, therefore, much less than that of the difference between the mass of the means of production into which the constant, and the mass of the labor-power into which the variable capital is converted. The former difference increases with the latter, but in a smaller degree.[6]

When in the course of accumulation the rising organic composition of capital begins to diminish instead of enlarge the extractable surplus value, a period of expansion comes to a halt. The closeness of the "race" of the rate of exploitation with the rate of accumulation, which the former must win to assure the growth of capital, shows itself from time to time in the setbacks of the capitalist crisis. As it is not possible to deduce from price and profit relations the underlying changes in value and surplus-value relations, there is no way to predict at what particular moment an insufficient profitability, due to the rising organic composition of capital, will arrest the accumulation process. The tendency of the rate of profit to fall must turn into an actual fall of market profits in order to disclose its existence.

However, due to the fact that capitalism is beset by many more contradictions than those inherent in value production, a particular economic crisis does not necessarily imply a fall in the rate of profit through changing value relations at the point of production. Discrepancies in supply-and-demand relations may be such as to impair the realization of the produced surplus value on their own accord, and the monetary form of the value relations may lead to financial difficulties disturbing the exchange mechanism. Because the market equilibrium is itself an illusion, the assumption of a frictionless expansion of capital, in the course of which new capital investments provide the necessary demand for an increasing supply, is also illusory, not only because this presupposes a definite level of profitability, which may or may not exist, but also because of the inability of economic agents to assess the system's productive requirements. There may be a lack of necessary investments or failures of invested capitals, which disturb the economy sufficiently to release a crisis situation that would not have arisen if the economic decisions of the capitalists had chanced to be in closer harmony with the requirements of the system as a whole.

The fact that the circulation process of capital is not immune to crisis situations has led to various explanations of crisis as a disturbance in supply and demand relations, caused either by the overproduction of commodities or by the underconsumption of the population—and here in particular, by the limited consuming power of the laboring class. All such explanations are based on the incorrect assumption that production has no other purpose than that of satisfying the consumption needs of the population. Indeed, in modern price theory it is consumption and the changes in consumption patterns that determine the production process. From this point of view, a crisis should be preventable if all that is produced is also consumed, inclusive of the productive consumption of the expanding capital. Moreover, an overproduction of some commodities would imply an underproduction of others, not the general overproduction of all commodities that characterizes the capitalist crisis due to the tendential fall of the rate of profit, and that can only be overcome by the resumption of the accumulation process. Besides, the limited consuming power of the laboring class is a condition of capital production, not a cause of crisis. And, in fact, crises are overcome by a relative reduction of the variable capital, expressing the increasing productivity of labor and playing a larger surplus value into the hands of capital.

Marx's main concern was with the crisis of overproduction, or overaccumulation, of *capital*, which has its roots in the value character of the social production relations and is thus the crisis mechanism specific to capital. It is capitalism's susceptibility to recurrent crises of overaccumulation that points to its historical limits, because it implies an ever-narrowing base of exploitation as the result of expansion. It is the inescapability of this development which Marx's abstract model of capital accumulation reveals, and which cannot be altered short of the abolition of this mode of production. The capitalistic *reactions* to this trend may lead to continuous changes in the market structure, eliminating some crisis elements and introducing new ones, but they cannot do away with the trend itself, short of ending the system. Whatever happens in the process of development must therefore be subjected to value analysis, in order to grasp its meaning, its possibilities, and its limitations. Marx's abstract model of capital expansion delineates a trend of development that must be recognizable throughout the system's various modifications. If it is not recognizable, of course, the model has no validity and the law of value is not the law of capitalist development.

Aside from historical changes in the general price level, for Marx it is the crisis that is the definite proof and the empirical verification of the law of value as the hidden regulator of the capitalist production and exchange process. If the market mechanism could *by itself* regulate the capitalist economy, there would be no general crisis (and indeed, for this reason, until quite recently bourgeois economics had no crisis theory, no way of accounting for the business cycle). The alternation of periods of economic expansion with periods of contraction is an alternation of periods of rising and falling profits, which overlap at the crisis point. That is to say, at the highest point of expansion the rate of profit begins to fall drastically, while at its lowest point it may begin to climb again, provided a rate of surplus value sufficing for a further accumulation of captial has been regained.

During a period of rapid capital expansion generally more attention is paid to the increase of production than to the productivity of labor engaged in this production. Full utilization of productive resources, comprising relatively inefficient as well as more efficient means of producton, and the employment of less productive along with more productive workers, although actually diminishing the average rate of productivity, may at first lead to higher profits through larger sales and higher prices. The higher prices lessen the need to maintain a given wage level; wages may rise together with profits. The expansion of capital, on the basis of a given level of profitability, creates for all individual capitals the competitive need to partake in the general upswing. The extension of the credit system bolsters the expansion of production by reducing or eliminating the need for immediate profits. Once set in motion, capital expansion is as blind a process as capitalist production itself, until it reaches objective limits in the constraint set by the unknown social value relations.

Because the value relations are not recognizable in their price forms, prices can move relatively independently of their value determination. But this only means that the price relations lose contact with the real relations of production and exchange. As relative prices, as well as the general price level, are affected by supply and demand (as determined by the accumulation of capital), prices may deviate from their value base in either a negative or positive direction, depending on whether the system expands or contracts. When the general expansion of production, initiated by the expansion of capital, outruns the growth of profits in terms of prices, and finally, in terms of value, due to the simultaneous rise in the organic composition of capital, the expansion comes to a halt. But this first comes to light in market and price relations, in the form of an actual decline of profitability, which discourages further capital investments.

Since the accumulation of capital depends on the value relations of capitalist production, the interruptions of the accumulation process due to changes in these relations can only be caused by arising disparities between the surplus value required by a given total capital for its further expansion and the total surplus value actually produced. Just like accumulation itself, a lack of profitability testifies to the determination of capital production by value and surplus-value relations. While the drive for accumulation is a drive for exchange value *per se*, in *abstraction* from its use-value embodiment, the productivity of labor is bound to the *concrete* possibilities of increasing the use value of labor power and therefore to the physical-technical apparatus of production. There is no way consciously to coordinate production as such with value production, in such a way that the productivity of labor will always conform to the accumulation requirements of capital. A violation of this necessary relationship has first to project itself into the market sphere through price and profit relations that are disruptive of capital accumulation, and thus demand a reorganization of these relations by means of further price and profit changes.

Although prices and profits can never be more than the value and surplus value produced, this is a matter of what has been in fact produced, not of the rate of accumulation required, given the total capital already amassed. The equivalence of prices and profits with value and surplus value is a condition of capitalist production that does not guarantee an equivalence of the mass of the produced surplus value with the surplus value required for a further productive—that is, profitable—enlargement of capital. Because of the relative decline of the variable capital in the course of the rise in the organic composition of capital, the mass of surplus value may decline even though its rate increases. There is no way to determine the "proper" relationship between the increasing productivity of labor and the relative decline of the number of workers with regard to the total capital, so as to bring the mass of surplus value in conformity with the required rate of accumulation.

A capitalist crisis and the ensuing depression signify the arrest, or the decline, of capital accumulation, which disrupts the circulation process and thus shows itself as an overproduction of commodities. Already produced surplus value, earmarked for the expansion of capital, remains in its money form and thus fails to function as capital. A falling or low rate of profit indicates that new investments would not yield the customary rate of profit and thus would reduce the already low rate of profit even more. For this reason no new investments are made. The curtailment of investment appears as an overproduction of means of production, as well as an overproduction of consumption goods, for workers who would have been employed in the case of an enlarged reproduction of capital are now also idle. The shortage of surplus value, coming to light in an actual fall of the rate of profit, thus appears on the market as a reduction of the effective demand for all sorts of commodities. Unless ways and means are found to increase the surplus value, a prolonged depression sets in. But the law of value, which explains the descent from prosperity to depression, also explains the ascent from depression to prosperity—as involving a change in value relations favorable to a further expansion of capital.

The new ascent is accomplished by a reversal of the process that led to the depression. While the rise of the organic composition of capital leads to a state of overaccumulation and a consequent decline of the rate of profit, the stagnation and decline of economic activity in the course of the depression lowers the organic composition of capital and increases the rate of profit. The depression diminishes the value of constant capital through disinvestment, bankruptcies, and the sale of commodities and securities at ruinous prices. The same, though partly unused, productive apparatus now represents a lower exchange value, so that the relationship between constant and variable capital is altered. Although the variable capital is also reduced through unemployment, it now stands in relation to a constant capital whose use value is largely unimpaired while its exchange value has been considerably lowered. This has a similar effect in exchange-value terms as the increasing productivity of labor has in use-value terms. More commodities, namely means of production, are now expressed by a lower exchange value and this decline of exchange value is compensated by a larger quantity of use values, just as the reduction of the value content of the single commodity is compensated by a greater quantity of use values. The decline of exchange value indicates a lowered state of the organic composition of capital and therefore a higher rate of profit on the given mass of surplus value.

This of course is a process detrimental to many capitalists, as well as to the unemployed and even the employed workers. But for the capitalist system as such, the changes in value relations provide a fresh basis for a renewed upswing of the economy. Moreover, the large amount of unemployment keeps wages at a lower level than previously and increases productivity through job competition and the elimination of less-productive workers. The frantic attempt by capitalists to secure their capital and maintain its profitability in the face of falling prices, through the restructuring of the production process and the application of technical innovations, raises the productivity of labor and—in time—restores for the successful capitalists a rate of profit that provides the starting point for new large-scale investments. But all this is quite obvious. What the depression brings about is a general attempt to lower costs through the increase of labor productivity and a general change of the capital structure involving the assignment of lower value to the same, or even a larger, productive apparatus (that is, to lower the organic composition of capital without lowering its productive capacity).

A depression implies the *concentrated* destruction of capital values; in fact, it expresses all capitalistic contradictions in a more intense fashion. The elimination of capital values also takes place during "normal" periods of capital accumulation, but to a lesser extent, which leaves the expansion process unimpaired. Accumulation is at the same time a process of capital concentration by the smaller capitals. Capital competes by cheapening commodities, and this depends on the productiveness of labor and therefore on the scale of production. Reproduction on a larger scale implies the concentration of capital, even though the number of individual capital entities may grow. It becomes, however, increasingly more difficult to form new capitals, as the initial minimum capital required increases constantly. The concentration of capital is implemented by its centralization, which, through the formation of stock companies, corporations, takeovers, and mergers takes place

> by a mere change in the distribution of already existing capital, a simple change in the quantitative arrangements of the components of the social capital. Capital may in that case accumulate in one hand in large masses by withdrawing it from many individual hands. . . . Centralization supplements the work of accumulation by enabling the industrial capitalists to expand the scale of operations . . . [thus hastening] at the same time the revolutions in the technical composition of capital, which increase its constant part at the expense of its variable part and thereby reduce the relative demand for labor.[7]

The concentration and centralization of capital, abetted by the credit system, is also quite obvious and is hypocritically bewailed in bourgeois economic literature.

The lowering of the organic composition of capital in the depression period is tantamount to a return to a lower level of capital expansion. This is destruction of capital, not its accumulation.

And though it helps prepare the way for a resumption of the accumulation process, the new upswing itself must not only restore but exceed the previously amassed capital in value terms. In spite of the setbacks of the accumulation process, each new phase of expansion must lead to a larger capital value and so to a still higher organic composition of capital. Without this, there would be capital stagnation, not its accumulation. To be sure, the forced lowering of the organic composition of capital in the depression only accentuates a procedure which accompanies the whole accumulation process. Although it is the need to increase surplus labor that occasions material-technical changes in the production process, such changes may diminish the growing discrepancy between the constant and variable capital in value terms and thus, to some extent, hold back the fall of the rate of profit. But the slowing-up of the rise in the organic composition of capital, through the cheapening of its constant part, is itself an expression of the increasing productivity of labor and a reaction to the diminishing profitability of the accumulating capital. It may retard the rise of the organic composition but cannot prevent it altogether, for capital accumulation is nothing else than the enlargement of the value of the constant capital.

Marx's economic categories are not those of bourgeois economic theory. The tendency of the rate of profit to fall, as a consequence of the accumulation of capital, may be denied simply because it is not directly observable. Just as the value relations take on the form of price relations and their "regulatory" power asserts itself through the capitalist crisis, so the abstract tendency of the rate of profit to fall comes to light in its actual but temporary decline in the contracting capitalist economy, as well as in the various attempts on the part of the capitalists to restore the profitability and accumulation of their capitals.

In periods of accumulation, the mass of profit increases absolutely, while its rate diminishes relative to the rising organic composition of capital. But the total mass of profit may be large enough to expand the existing capital. Empirically, then, the fall of the general rate of profit shows itself not in a decline of actual profit rates but in a slowing-down of the rate of accumulation, which, of course, implies the decline of capital production itself. Because "all additions of value must be more than compensated by the reduction in value resulting from the decrease in living labor,"[8] the relative or absolute decline of the latter's role within the total social capital must impair its profitability or its accumulation, or both at the same time. This is a deduction from value theory, which, though logically unassailable, must be substantiated by the actual capitalist development. However, "measurements" both of the rate of profit on a given total capital and of the rate required for its augmentation, as well as of the state of the organic composition of the total social capital, not only involve conceptual difficulties but seem to defy empirical verification in quantitative terms. Although the movements of capital, as expressed in its concentration and centralization, in the crisis cycle, and in the retardation of its rate of expansion, are deducible from value theory, and qualitatively are obvious to everyone, they cannot be described in numerical-statistical terms. This is due not so much to the abstract character of all theory and to methodological ambiguities as to the actual inaccessibility of the data required to evaluate the movements of capital. After all, this is a capitalistic system outside of conscious social control and therefore unpredictable in its quantitative interrelations and their constant changes, except insofar as they are determined by the social relations of production as value relations, which show themselves as general tendencies within capitalist development.

The more consistent capitalist ideologists see the automatic self-regulation of the market economy as its only "rational" regulation, which implies, of course, that its quantitative features are to be found in the existing price and profit relations, whatever they might happen to be. Those who look for data useable for affecting the course of economic events must find analytical procedures that differentiate the price and profit data with respect to their origin and their destination, in order to assess their convergence or divergence from theoretical assumptions. They must be satisfied with data that at best allow for a very partial and approximate apprehension of past economic occurrences. These data are produced by professional economists within the framework of their theoretical preconceptions. No other data are available for any attempt on the part of the Marxist investigator to dress his theoretical findings in empirical-statistical garb. He will not find the economic categories valid for the system as a whole, but merely price and profit aggregates for a selected part of the capitalist economy, which will not divulge the changing value relations beneath the historical price and profit relations and their effect upon the accumulation of capital.

Given the practical difficulties in the way of disentangling the value relations from their price and profit forms, attempts at empirical substantiation of the value-determined developmental tendencies of capitalism, however praiseworthy, are not very promising. The rising organic composition of capital can correspond to an increase as well as a decrease of the mass of profit, depending on the degree of labor exploitation. If the labor-time values of the constant and variable capital, as well as that of the surplus value, could be known, it should be possible, in principle, to establish the movements of the rate of profit in the course of the accumulation process. But this is not possible, precisely because capital accumulation, or what is the same, the increasing productivity of labor, implies continuous but differentiated changes of the value content of these three categories of capital. Although the growing productivity affects these categories simultaneously, it does not do so in equal measure. Their "synchronization," which allows for the expansion of capital, only exists as a tendency, not in the form of definite quantities discernible at any particular moment in time. It is brought about through the averaging price and profit movements, which account not only for the general rate of profit, but for this rate within the changing interrelations of the value content of the three components of capital.

As the value relations of the organic composition of capital are also physical-technical production relations, changes in the latter reflect those in the value relations, and vice versa. The rise of the organic composition of capital will to some extent be visible in the enlargement of the productive apparatus and the mass of raw materials, in the relative reduction of the number of workers thereby employed, and in the physical output of production. This makes it possible to describe *one aspect* of the accumulation process in physical-technical terms and to see the development of capital as that of a continuous growth of production. Economic difficulties may then likewise be adjudged as of a physical-technical nature, due either to the scarcity of factors in the sphere of production or to changes in the effective demand. The price or money expressions of the growth and the movements of social production do not refer here to shifts in value relations, but merely to their material or utility aspects and to their variations in the course of the production process. The *decisive* relationship as regards the accumulation process, namely, the relationship of surplus value to the exchange value of the total social capital, or the value side of the organic composition of capital, is here totally disregarded. Although the expansion of exchange value is the sole concern of capitalist production, the latter is seen only as aiming at an increase of production in the form of capital goods and commodities for purposes of consumption. From such a viewpoint, it suffices to note no more than the growth and decline of the social product as material quantities expressed in price terms.

However, prices relate not to these material quantities, but to their value content, as modified by the general rate of profit. There is no parallel development of material and value production within the rising organic composition of capital. A rise in capital composition, considered only in its material aspect, does not imply anything definite as regards the mass or the rate of profit, which is always bound up with the changes in the value of the total social capital and their effects upon the surplus value brought forth by the laboring class. Prices in capitalist society do not represent the physical nature of production of commodities, but the changing socially determined abstract labor-time values incorporated in them, and the equally socially determined dispersion of the total social surplus value over the various capitals as revealed by the average rate of profit. While noticing the changes in the technical composition of capital, bourgeois economic theory does not concern itself with the changes in the value relations occasioned by them. As the value content of capital production plays no part here, no distinction is made between the expansion of production and the accumulation of capital, and no theoretical account is given for the declining rate of profit, even when this phenomenon finds empirical acknowledgement.

Although with different interpretations, both the bourgeois economist and his Marxian critic have to accept the economic data at hand, however inexact and restricted it may be. As the value-determined organic composition of capital contains the technical composition, the development of the latter will throw some light upon the development of the former. However dimly, it will still reveal one aspect of the expanding capital structure. This must in some measure substantiate the Marxian deductions from value theory or, at any rate, not contradict them. While it is true that the categories of bourgeois economic theory have no connection with the value relations of Marxian theory, they do encompass the changing relationships between the growing physical mass of the accumulating constant capital and the relatively diminishing number of workers employed by it. And as the decreasing value of the variable capital shows itself empirically in a relative decline of the number of *productive* workers, the fact of this decline bears on the rising organic composition of capital, whether it is expressed in value terms or merely in terms of the number of workers vis-à-vis the amassed total capital.

It is of course true that such analogous processes reveal no more than a general trend, which as such will not satisfy the desire of the strict empiricist for data that are at once explanatory and operational. It is often asserted that while Marx's theory transcends bourgeois economic theory in order to solve "economic problems" that cannot be satisfactorily dealt with by bourgeois price theory, it must, for that reason, be as empirical as any other science. It is assumed, in brief, that Marx's *Capital* is a better part, but still a part, of the "positive science" of economics, whereas it is actually its opposition. Marxian theory aims not to resolve "economic problems" of bourgeois society but to show them to be unsolvable. Marx was a socialist, not an economist. In Marxian theory the concrete phenomena of bourgeois society are something other than they appear to be. Empirically discovered facts have first to be freed of their fetishistic connotations before they reveal empirical reality. The abstract generalizations of value theory disclose the laws of development of a system that operates with a false comprehension of the concretely given facts. The inductively won data do not correspond with, but camouflage, the real social relations of production. Bourgeois economy is not an empirical science but an ideological substitute for such a science; a pseudo-science, despite its scientific methodology.

Willingly or unwillingly under the sway of the ruling ideology, the bourgeois economist takes the capitalistically determined economic categories for granted without being able to verify them empirically. Were this not the case, bourgeois theory would be less eclectic than it actually is, and would have a greater ability to predict events on the strength of its empirical findings. Bourgeois economics has evolved no theory, however, that can account for the actual capitalist development—or even for short-run market trends, which would give it some practical applicability. Of course, no statements about the economy can be made without recourse to some observation of the real world. As a result there exists a great amount of descriptive material that may be confronted with the theories these facts are supposed to verify.

With respect to capital formation—the goal of capitalist production and the special interest of Marxism—the data assembled by bourgeois statisticians neither confirm nor disconfirm Marx's theory of accumulation as deduced from value theory. But neither do they confirm or disconfirm the notions of bourgeois theory insofar as these are relevant to the development of capitalist society. The comprehension of the elicited data requires a theoretical conception of the nature and the purposes of society. In the bourgeois view, "the fundamental purpose of the complex economic system of modern society is to increase the economic welfare of the country's inhabitants—that is, to provide more goods to satisfy their natural wants, present and future."[9] If this is taken seriously, then, of course, the formation of capital assures the welfare of society and the social mechanisms of the accumulation process are only means to this end. On the basis of such a theory, there is no way to understand or to explain the actual course of development, and the theory itself must falsify the facts assembled to give it credence.

Although it is freely admitted that all empirical findings with regard to capital formation are merely "conjectural rather than tested, partial rather than complete, suggestive rather than definitive,"[10] they are nonetheless deemed "essential if we wish to speculate, in a systematic fashion, on the bearing of past trends upon the prospects for some projected future."[11] The trend of capitalist development discernible in the expansion of production and the enlargement of the productive apparatus, insofar as they are expressible in statistical terms, can not verify the Marxian predictions with respect to the value components of capital, yet, as suggested above, this trend indicates the changes in the technical composition of capital in the course of accumulation. According to Simon Kuznets's data for the United States, the effect of technological changes in the past

> has been to increase both total output and demand for capital for the
> economy as a whole, and the greater the rate of technical change, the

greater the rise of output and the net demand for capital. While the statement can be nothing more than crude conjecture, it is most reasonable to assume that a projected high rate of potential technological change means a high projected rate of demand for capital—net of any contractions on the part of industries competitively and adversely affected by the new technology.[12]

The developmental trend of the value composition of total capital—that is, the more rapid growth of the constant relative to the variable capital—will find some kind of reflection in its technical composition, in a relatively faster growth of the mass of means of production vis-à-vis the growing labor force. According to Kuznets's estimates, "the stock of capital, both net and gross, grew at high rates. From 1869 to 1955, net capital stock increased to about 16 times its initial level; gross capital stock net retirements to 18 times."[13] This implied

a marked growth in capital per person and per member of the labor force. Net capital stock per head rose, over the period as a whole, to about 4 times its initial level . . . at a rate of about 17% per decade. Since the labor force grew at somewhat higher rates than total population, the rate of growth of capital stock per member of the labor force was somewhat lower than that of capital per person. . . . The important finding is that with the exception of net capital stock the supply of capital goods per worker grew at a slightly increasing rate through most of the period, the decline in the rate of growth emerging only in the most recent interval, 1929 to 1955.[14]

If one would deal only with the visible physical-technical process of capital production—apart from value considerations—something like Kuznets's findings should emerge because of the use-value aspect of the exchange-value relations. These findings thus confirm rather than contradict Marx's deductions from value theory. However, even these findings are quite dubious because of the inadequacy of the data on which they are based. The statistical patterns of past developments possess no predictive powers because

the possibilities of testing the persistence of these patterns under varying conditions are limited; and in the attempts to support empirically found patterns by explanatory hypotheses, it is rarely possible, in the present state of our knowledge, to assign to such explanatory links empirical coefficients that would necessarily produce the specific trend rates or secular proportions found. For lack of adequate testing and of specific explanation, some major features of the orderly patterns may be sufficiently in doubt to overshadow any apparently precise quantitative projections.[15]

While Kuznets's skepticism with regard to the utility of his own statistical compilations derives from their quantitative inadequacies, for others statistical evidence is highly unreliable also because of its qualitative shortcomings. According to Oskar Morgenstern, for instance, the error components in the various time series are of such a magnitude as to make them practically useless. Apart from outright falsifications and misrepresentations to serve specific business interests, or even governmental purposes, the statistical evidence so confidently offered, particularly with respect to the national income and the rates of economic growth, is simply not "computed with the stated or demanded degree of refinement and reliability."[16] Of course, economics being an empirical science, the only solution Morgenstern can offer is to "develop a statistical theory (with experimental application) which would allow us to recognize the direction and extent of such willful distortion of information and to eliminate their influence. Such theory, unfortunately, does not exist."[17] Until it has been developed, it has to be admitted "that the economy moves in a deeper penumbra than thought possible, that economic decisions, by business and government alike, are made largely in the dark."[18]

The quest for a quantitative test of Marx's accumulation theory—by submitting it to the data at hand—is thus doubly confounded by the miserable state of the statistical evidence and by the need to translate it into Marxian categories.[19] Although not an *a priori* statement, Marx's theory cannot find unambiguous verification in purely quantitative terms but must appeal to qualitative changes, which for their part, and however imperfectly, imply the presence of quantitative relationships not accessible to observation. Bourgeois economic theory, too, uses nonnumerical evidence in order to buttress its own quantitative findings, although its static character does not even raise the question of qualitative change. Although the abstract value theory is largely axiomatic and based on hypothetical assumptions, this is not only for reasons of a lack of empirical-statistical material at the time it was developed, but also because the price categories cannot be reduced to value relations even with an abundance of empirical data. The value relations gain their prognosticative force by way of recognizable qualitative changes throughout the capitalist development. There is no doubt, of course, that there are definite quantitative relationships beneath all the qualitative changes, but they are not discernible in a system that finds its "regulation" in the vicissitudes of market events.

As regards its verification in qualitative terms, Marx's theory of accumulation has fared rather well in the empirical world. The general trend of development has not gone counter to Marx's deductions from value theory. The elimination of competition through competition, the increasing concentration, centralization, and monopolization of capital, the increasing productivity of labor, the crisis cycle, the capitalist domination of the world market, the increasing social polarization of labor and capital, and a growing industrial reserve army are all undeniable and generally acknowledged. From the viewpoint of Marx's theory, these occurrences imply, given the expansion of capital, the tendency of the rate of profit to fall, even when the actual profit rates appear to be stable because they are capitalistically "measured" not by the relationship between the surplus value and the value of the total capital, but by capitalistic expenditures in relation to their market returns. When the value of the mass of capital at the disposal of the capitalists grows faster than the rate of profit declines, the mass of surplus value will yield the same rate of profit despite the rising organic composition of capital. But this *same rate* of profit presupposes the *relatively larger* mass of capital; without it, the rate of profit would show a decline. The stable rate of profit under conditions of a rising organic composition of capital merely attests to capitalism's ability to immunize the fall of the rate of profit through the increase of surplus value.

We have already pointed out that the contradictory movement immanent in value production, namely, the increase of surplus value and the decline of the rate of profit, must resolve itself —in time—in a decline of the rate of accumulation and finally in the objective impossibility of extracting from the shrinking variable capital component of capital the quantities of surplus value required for its further profitable expansion. The last statement follows, of course, from a logical projection of the value-determined production process into the indefinite future. Although actually indeterminate in an empirical sense, the validity of this logical projection is attested to by the crisis cycle, which offers us, so to speak, a temporary representation of the long-run trend of capital expansion as determined by its immanent contradictions. However, the temporary loss of profitability and the consequent inability to continue the accumulation process have until now always led to the restoration of a rate of profit sufficient for the further expansion of capital. If this should remain so, then, of course, the tendency of the rate of profit to fall, alone, will tell us nothing about the destiny of the capitalist system.

Apart from acute crisis situations, the customary rate of profit may be maintained even with a declining rate of accumulation, for this decline prevents or delimits the further rise of the organic composition of capital and thus upholds the rate of profit. The latter may then be maintained under less dynamic conditions and its fall would come to the fore not as such but as a slowdown of the accumulation process. This, of course, would imply deteriorating economic conditions and the growth of unemployment as a lesser quantity of surplus value is transformed into additional profit-producing capital. But, again, the slowing-down of the expansion process may itself be regarded as a prolonged crisis situation, to be terminated by a new spurt of accumulation, unless it should be persistent enough to resemble a permanent crisis which could end only in the destruction of the capitalist system. Because past experience shows that crises can be overcome, one can ask why this should not continue into the future and, perhaps, forever. Although it is true that a steady decline of the rate of accumulation, as the visible result of the tendential fall of the rate of profit, must eventually lead to the end of all accumulation and therewith to the end of capitalism, there is no way of determining when the system will reach such an impasse.

Because the rate of profit and with it the rate of accumulation depend on the relationship between the surplus value and the value of the total capital, and because both these items are not knowable with any degree of certainty for any capitalist country, not to speak of capitalism as a world system, only the concretely given conditions of capitalist society allow for some time-conditioned estimates of its possible directional movements. World capitalism is not the closed system of Marxian theory, and the logical conclusions drawn from the development of the latter can serve only as a "guiding thread" of orientation through the otherwise almost impenetrable and contradictory development, in the course of which the same economic laws can imply the rise as well as the decline of the system.

However, Marx's abstract model of accumulation rests on the assumption that the social production relations of capitalism will remain what they were at their inception, despite all the possible modifications of the market structure. Because the "economic laws" of capitalism are not really such, but the fetishistic appearances of social relations, they will have to be ended by social actions. In his revolutionary expectations, therefore, Marx did not rely on the implications of the law of the falling rate of profit for the future of capitalism, but on possible reactions of the laboring class to a system able to maintain itself only through the continuous increase of exploitation, and which at the same time must put its future at risk by undermining the very conditions of exploitation upon which it rests. Marx did not expect, or predict, the end of capitalism because of a diminishing rate of accumulation and the decline of the rate of profit, but because these tendencies, immanent in capital production, were bound to bring forth social conditions that would become increasingly unbearable for always larger layers of the working population, and so to create objective conditions out of which subjective readiness for social change might arise.

Theory
and
Reality

Marx's abstract model of capital accumulation concerns itself solely with the immanent contradictions of this process. It does not pretend to depict the actual course of capitalist development, even though the general direction of this development is determined by the value relations of capital production. It deals with the social relations basic to capital as such, independently of their changing appearances in the expanding capitalist economy. While the model reveals a trend inherent in capital production, only on the basis of knowledge of concrete social conditions and the actual state of the economy is it possible to venture some predictions as to the probable further course of events and to formulate policies to cope with these contingencies.

While Marxian theory can confidently predict the crisis cycle of capitalist development, it is not able to foresee a particular crisis, unless it should already be apparent in market occurrences that indicate its certain approach. This *detailed* insight is gained from past empirical experience. While Marxian theory can confidently insist upon the inevitability of the capital concentration and centralization process, it cannot be aware of its tempo or its specific effects upon the formation of capital at any particular point in time. Though the fall of the rate of profit is an unavoidable outcome of capitalist production, there is no way to predict when this tendency will overwhelm the counter-tendencies through which it shows itself—in particular, the increase of surplus value with respect to a particular organic composition of capital. And finally, although the accumulation process displaces labor relative to the growing mass of capital, it is not possible to say at which stage of development the number of unemployed will grow absolutely, whatever the conditions of capitalist production.

Marx's theory of accumulation, in which the pattern of capitalist development is deduced from value theory, finds its empirical verification in the actual increase of social misery, in the relentless concentration and centralization of capital, in the increasing polarization of society between wage labor and capital, and in the recurrence of always more general crises in the course of the capitalization of the world economy. This capitalist development, while of a cyclical nature, is nevertheless progressive, in that each phase of expansion is followed by another of a higher organic composition of capital. This implies that with the absolute growth of the variable capital and the surplus value created by it, despite their relative decline with respect to the accumulating capital, the growing capital may, for an indeterminate time, for all practical reasons "disprove" Marx's abstract capital analysis and its foreshortened perspectives. The modifications the system undergoes in the very course of its development may set aside the general law of accumulation, at any rate for considerable periods of time, and thus meet the optimistic expectations of the ruling class and raise doubts among the exploited classes about capitalism's vulnerability.

Like everyone else, Marx was a child of his time and must be understood in the context of that phase of capitalist development which he himself experienced. His critique of bourgeois society evolved in a period of rather rapid capitalist development. Though this was still largely restricted to England, it was obvious that a similar hastened development would take place throughout the West and, via the world market, affect the world at large. This historical juncture allowed for, and demanded, a theory of the dynamics of capitalist production, if only to comprehend its actual development and its social implications. Although the gestation of capitalism had been a long drawn-out and rather slow process, by the middle of the nineteenth century it had gained enough momentum to permit recognition of its impact upon the foreseeable future. It had set aside most of the social and economic obstacles to its own evolution and unmistakably exposed its own incongruities. Foremost among these was the rapid accumulation of capital at the expense of the increasing misery of the laboring population.

There exists a large enough literature devoted to the early development of capitalism—the industrial revolution, the conditions of the working classes in the various capitalist nations, the first attempts to form working-class organizations, and the laborers' actual struggles for the improvement of their living and working conditions—to obviate the need to discuss this historical phase of capitalist development here. The social distress and unrest caused by these conditions impressed itself upon all layers of society and led to a rather pessimistic outlook with respect to the future of capitalism. Yet, by and large, to the bourgeois mind this dismal state of affairs had nothing to do with the capitalist mode of production but had its source in the "niggardliness of nature," the "multiplication of man," and the economic law of diminishing returns as formulated by David Ricardo. The trend of development seemed to point toward a stationary state and increasing social misery, which might, perhaps, be somewhat alleviated by a more equal system of distribution.

For Marx, in direct contrast, it was precisely the rapid development of capitalism that caused the increasing social misery:

> The greater the social wealth, the functioning capital, the extent and energy of its growth, and, therefore, also the absolute mass of the proletariat and the productiveness of its labor, the greater the industrial reserve-army. The same causes which develop the expansive power of capital develop also the labor-power at its disposal. The realtive mass of the industrial reserve-army increases therefore with the potential energy of wealth. But the greater this reserve-army in proportion to the active labor-army, the greater is the mass of a consolidated surplus-population, whose misery is in inverse ratio to its torment of labor. The more extensive, finally, the lazarus-layer of the working-class, and the industrial reserve-army, the greater is official pauperism. *This is the absolute general law of capitalist accumulation.*[1]

To this declaration Marx added that like any other law, this one too "is modified in its working by many circumstances," which, however, do not affect its general validity. The modifications are largely due to the cyclical movements of capital, which expand or contract the industrial reserve army and therewith also the "lazarus layer" of society, which comprises those unfortunates who are no longer able to sell their labor power to capital. As the general law of accumulation expresses itself in the diminishing variable capital, general misery is bound to grow with the enlargement of the industrial reserve army. This misery shows itself not so much in the lowering of wages, which cannot for long fall below the reproduction requirements of labor power, as in a growing mass of impoverished people living and dying on the offal of society. This general law of accumulation has been modified in its effects—precisely because of its validity—by the welfare legislation enacted in the developed capitalist nations in order to mitigate its potential threat to the stability of society. The costs of this by-product of accumulation are distributed over the whole of society, although they can actually only be paid out of the surplus value produced by the productive workers. As this surplus value diminishes relative to the profit requirements of the accumulating capital, it is only a question of time until the accumulation of capital reveals itself openly as the accumulation of social misery.

Marx's prediction of increasing misery in the course of accumulation met with the capitalist apologists' particular scorn, for it was obvious that the workers' living standards and working conditions were improving all along. While the actual miseries that accompanied capitalist development could not be denied, they were now relegated to an irrevocable past, to difficulties in the early stages of capitalist production that had completely and forever been overcome before the end of the nineteenth century. And if both labor and capital were prospering, what sense was there in speaking of a tendency of the rate of profit to fall? A relatively long period of successful capital expansion created an ebullient optimism that also affected the working class. It also agitated the organized labor movement, whose spokesmen hastened to deny that Marx had really meant what he had said. However, though doubtless influenced by the actual social misery of the working class at the time *Capital* was written, Marx's theory of increasing misery was not based on this, but was the result of his value analysis of capital production. If capital accumulation proceeds in accordance with the law of value, the increasing misery of the laboring population is one of its inescapable consequences.

Marx's concern was not with the miseries prevailing in past societies but only with that brought forth by the specific conditins of capitalist production. Unemployment and pauperism have been a highly visible feature of capitalism throughout its development, even though they have waxed and waned with the ups and downs of the business cycle. The unemployed sector of the working class grew with the growth of the latter and either depressed or stabilized the going wage rates. Unemployment became the dominant problem of capitalist society during prolonged periods of depression and forced upon the bourgeoisie some modifications of the general law of accumulation. When the periods of expansion and contraction of the economy are taken together, as they must be when dealing with the accumulation process as a whole, there can be no doubt that unemployment has risen steadily, as the absorption of part of the industrial reserve army in periods of expansion has not fully compensated for the expulsion of workers from the production process during periods of depression. Taking good and bad times together, that is, there can be little doubt that the ratio of unemployed to employed workers increased with the accumulation of capital, for the latter implies the relative decline of the variable within the total capital.

Although to varying degrees in different countries, estimates of unemployment are notoriously inadequate, tending to understate its extent. In the United States, for example, "the method for calculating unemployment is rigged, deliberately designed to conceal the true level, understating it by almost half."[2] But even on the basis of such inadequate statistics, at the end of 1975 the *International Labor Organization* estimated

> that unemployment had expanded to the highest level recorded in the last 40 years in the 23 countries covered by its survey. The total jobless in 18 European countries, the United States, Canada, Japan, Australia and New Zealand reached 17.1 million. In the depth of the world depression during the 1930s unemployment in the same 23 countries is said to have topped 25 million, with the jobless rate in many of them reaching 20 to 35 percent of the labor force. If account is taken of the jobless workers' dependents, 40.4 million persons were suffering from the unemployment situation in 1975.[3]

Because the number of employed may grow together with an increase in unemployment, it is now suggested that attention should be paid to the employment rather than to the unemployment figures when judging the performance of the economy, "for the picture one gets from looking at the employment rate varies significantly from that which is obtained by concentrating on the jobless rate alone."[4] But this will not alter the fact that the unemployment rate grows faster than the employment rate. It merely shows that the recorded business expansion was not sufficient in recent years to absorb a decisive number of the unemployed, as had been the case in previous periods of expansion. And thus unemployment, with its accompanying pauperization, remains, despite the growing number of jobs and the various welfare measures and insurance schemes.

According to a congressional study, prepared by M. H. Brenner of John Hopkins University, analyzing the relevant statistics for the United States over a period of 40 years, there exists a direct link between "the actions which influence national economic activity—especially the unemployed rate—and physical health, mental health and criminal aggression."[5] Although this is quite obvious, without any statistical evidence, it has not the same effect as the naked hunger that stalked the United States, and other countries, during the Great Depression. This may explain the general complacency toward the systematic deterioration of social life. But just as the price of labor power varies with changing historical conditions, its value comprising more or fewer commodities, so too misery has a historical character and represents different states of being under different circumstances. Misery is not experienced as a specific state of starvation but as impoverishment relative to customary living standards. People's reactions to a persistent impairment of customary living conditions may be just as radical as those that may result from a state of semistarvation produced by the constant increase of pauperization. What "increasing misery" means will be determined by those subjected to it, not by any "objective measure" of what people may be capable of enduring. In this sense, even in the highly developed capitalist nations the modifications of the general law of capitalist accumulation will not prevent the increase of social misery.

In Marx's view, the growing misery is due not to the increase of exploitation but to the limitations set to it by the value character of capitalist production. The increasing exploitation of a given number of workers—which has no particular relation to their living standards and working conditions—makes possible the growth of capital but at the same time reduces its variable component and thus decreases the potential for its further accumulation. Just as in the world at large the poor suffer from both capitalization and the lack of capitalization, so in each capitalist country the proletariat suffers from both exploitation and the lack of it, but far more intensely under the latter condition. As in Marx's day capitalism was still restricted to a few nations, it was in these areas that the general law of accumulation revealed its concrete meaning in the scourge of unemployment. But with the territorial extension of the capitalist mode of production, and the capitalist domination of the world market, the distribution between employed and unemployed became more dispersed, affecting different nations in unequal measure in accordance with their stage of capitalist development. Thus, insofar as the growth of capitalism can be held responsible for growing misery on the world scale, through capitalism's impact on its underdeveloped regions, this must be added to the miseries associated with the accumulation of capital in the developed capitalist countries.

Just as the historians of capitalism have produced a whole library of documentary proof of the miseries of the "lower classes" during its earlier stages, so there exists today a no less impressive collection of data on increasing impoverishment in the so-called "developing nations," which comprise the large majority of the world's population. There is then no point in adding new descriptions to the mass of material already at hand, especially as the relevant facts are uncontested general knowledge. This almost universal impoverishment which has accompanied the expansion of capitalism into a world system reveals the continuing validity of Marx's general law of capitalist accumulation. The latter is not contradicted, but rather substantiated, by the vast improvement of the conditions of broad strata of the working class in the dominating capitalist nations, which constitute a small minority within the world proletariat and a somewhat larger minority within their own nations.

As a competitive concentration and centralization process, accumulation simultaneously reduces the number of capital entities relative to the total mass of capital and the number of workers employed in industry. While it becomes increasingly more difficult to form new capital units in the capitalistically advanced nations, these difficulties are far greater in less-developed countries, unless capital from the former enters into the social fabric of the latter. But this mainly serves capital expansion in the dominant capitalist nations and holds back capital formation in the underdeveloped countries. The competitive advantages of the long established and highly concentrated capital entities are such, at home and abroad, as practically to preclude the emergence of new capitalist undertakings of a lower organic composition and therewith a larger labor force. While the capitalist mode of production becomes in-

increasingly more general, it does not absorb the same quantity of labor power it used to assimilate at earlier stages of development. What capital expansion takes place does so by creating a surplus population unable to live either outside or inside the capitalist system.

There can be little doubt that Marx believed the concrete manifestations of the general law of accumulation would appear sooner and more convincingly than has actually been the case. The law cannot, however, be disproven for the simple reason that its full impact may await the future. For this reason, of course, it can also not be proven, for capitalism may modify itself to an hitherto inconceivable extent and set the law aside. All that can be asked is whether or not the law can be seen at work in the discernible tendencies of capitalist production. And here there can be no doubt of its existence, even though its consequences have been less direct and more drawn-out than Marx contemplated.

Marx seems to have underestimated the resiliency of capitalism and its ability to adapt to the changing conditions of the accumulation process, because of the difficulty in foreseeing the degree of the development of the productivity—and exploitability—of labor possible at any moment through the application of machinery and the advancement of the applied sciences. He did emphasize that a rapid development of the sciences accompanied and conditioned, even as it was conditioned by, the rise and expansion of capital. While technological changes in the production process are at first quite accidental and sporadic, they are soon systematically searched for in the competitive pursuit of new products and cheaper methods of production. Such changes improve productivity, which implies the reduction of living labor relative to means of production and the mass of output. But this rise in the organic composition of capital can be offset by the increasing mass of commodities in such a way as to maintain or even increase the rate of profit on capital, if only for some time. Thus it is not possible to predict exactly what impact science and technology will have on the value-determined capitalist production process.

The concept of the rising organic composition of capital refers to the totality of the social reproduction process, that is, to both the social relations and the social forces of production. These are not separable in the sense that one is the sole determinant of the other. When we consider historically differentiated societies it is of course possible to recognize specific social forces of production that correspond to definite social relations and to distinguish them from those developed by other social formations. But within a *given* society it is not possible to derive changes in the social relations of production from the development of the social forces of production. In capitalism the productive forces change constantly within the unaltered social relations of production, and it is precisely the constancy of the latter that allows for the accumulation of capital in value and in physical terms. As the capital-labor relationship fosters the development of the forces of production, so it also hinders their unfolding, as soon as this conflicts with the social relations of production.

For Marx, the development of fixed capital indicated "to what degree general social knowledge has become a direct force of production, and to what degree, hence, the conditions of the process of social life itself have come under the general control of the general intellect and been transformed in accordance with it."[6] Yet this side of the development of the productive forces, and its immense acceleration through the capitalist relations of production, always remains subordinated to the value relationships between necessary and surplus labor and to their changes as determined by the accumulation of capital. Technological and scientific development by itself, as the determiner of the conditions of social existence, may have validity for a future society, but it has no independent meaning with regard to the capitalist system. It is for this reason, according to Marx, that the forces of production cannot be reduced to a matter of technological development, for they embody as well the social activities released by their class-determined course. Just as it is not science and technology but capital that represents the productive forces and their historical boundaries in modern society, the proletarian revolution would be the greatest of productive forces by destroying the capitalist relations of production. History is the history of class struggle, not of technology.

For the bourgeoisie itself, until quite recently "technological changes were the *terra incognita* of modern economics."[7] They played no part in static market theory. From this point of view, capital formation results from savings, which by expanding the physical-technical capital per worker increases the output per worker at any given technological level. A mathematically conceived "production function" serves to analyze the structural changes between different "factors of production," in order to determine which proportion between them will yield the greatest output from the given inputs. The more capital-intensive production becomes, the greater the output and thus also the general well-being of society. Because in the bourgeois view it is consumption that regulates the allocation of economic resources, the technologies involved merely reflect the supply and demand relations of the market.

Those economists who paid attention to the dynamics of capitalist production, such as Thorstein Veblen and Joseph Schumpeter, found its driving force in technological changes that were bound to upset the market equilibrium, only to lead to its reestablishment at a more advanced technological level. For them, not capital but technology is the decisive element in the evolution of the capitalist system.

Similarly, the disregard of the physical-technical aspect of capital expansion on the part of neoclassical economists found its end with the arrival of the various capitalist "growth theories." What had hitherto been largely ignored now became the sole determining feature in economic theory, in order to explain capitalist development without sacrificing the equilibrium concepts of market theory. At this point, we merely want to draw attention to this reversal of economic theorizing without entering into the subject matter itself, and to make clear in advance that no connection exists between Marx's theory of accumulation and the current growth theories, which either try to accommodate the physical aspects of capital expansion to the imaginary consumer choices on the market, or try to determine the distribution of the social product from technological relationships within the production process. For Marx, the general law of accumulation prevails whatever the modifications brought into the capitalist reproduction process by the growth of the productive forces, as expressed in the mass and the character of the fixed capital and their effects upon the exploitability of labor power, as it is precisely this growth which reveals the contradictions of the capitalist system and points to its eventual demise.

Technological development, as determined by the accumulation of capital—or, what is the same, the use-value aspect of exchange value or capital—implies the centralization of capital in physical and in value terms. According to Marx, this centralization extends the original expropriation of the precapitalist laboring classes, which created the "free" wage worker, to capital itself, by playing the property of many capitalists into the hands of a few. This increasing monopolization of the social capital, deducible from value theory, refers of course to a process developing over an indeterminate period of time. It is not possible to tell at what particular time the numbers of constantly newly arising capital formations must diminish to leave the exploitation of the world proletariat to a decreasing number of giant corporations, able by their existence to prevent the successful rise of new capitalist enterprises. However, the concentration and centralization of capital is an empirically observable process with regard both to its magnitude and to its effect upon the capitalist economy as a whole. It is for this reason that the fact of the concentration and centralization of capital, first recognized by Marx, is no longer denied and has not only been the subject of a great amount of literature,[8] but has led, albeit without success, to various attempts to arrest its further development by legislative measures.

Whether income derives from profit, interest, or rent, it is in each case related to ownership, or part-ownership, in particular businesses. Such a business may be a giant corporation, a large or small industrial establishment, a commercial farm, an extraction business such as mining or lumbering, a real estate brokerage, and so forth—all of these businesses representing a certain market value in money terms. Most of the larger businesses are the property of many shareholders. The rights to a firm's property and its yields are marketable and the object of much trafficking on the stock markets. A company's real resources and their evaluation on the market are not identical, and shareholders may partake not only of actual profits but also of "profits" made through the sales of their shares. The expectations of large dividends increase the price of shares while, conversely, fear of a firm's declining profitability will lower share prices. The capital of a modern corporation is thus a fluctuating magnitude that may change even from day to day, whereas its actual material base, its real property and equipment, will change only by way of accumulation (or disaccumulation).

In early capitalism enterprises were mainly owned by individuals or small groups who quite generally considered the costs of their capital equipment the basis for its capitalization. Under modern conditions, it is the real as well as the expected profitability that determine the projective evaluation of an enterprise. The expectations may or may not be realistic—this gives the capital market its speculative character. However, speculative gains or losses, while affecting individual fortunes, do not affect the real state of the economy and its actual profitability, even though a "stock market boom"—that is, the speculative expansion of fictitious capital and fictitious profits—may very well bring an already existing crisis situation to a head, as was the case in the United States in 1929.

Although there still exist many small businesses whose capital belongs to and stays in the hands of particular persons or families, and even very large businesses (especially in extraction industries and in real estate) where the whole of the assets are privately controlled, the great mass of capital is concentrated in large corporations and has the form of widespread stock ownership. In the United States, for example, there are about 17 million stockholders. But although many people own some stock, very few own the great bulk of it. Only 2 percent of all shareholders control about 58 percent of all common stock, and 1 percent of preferred stockowners control 46 percent of all preferred stock. Big business is still in the hands of multimillionaires who control the corporations through their concentrated stockholdings. In the 1950s, for instance, the late J. Paul Getty, president of the Getty Oil Company, personally owned 12,570,039 shares or 79 percent of the shares of his company, representing a market value of more than $300 million. Families such as the Mellons, the Fords, and the du Ponts controlled through their concentrated shareholdings the corporations with which they were associated, and in several cases their holdings exceeded the value of the Getty properties. To own just 10 percent of the outstanding stock in ventures such as the Standard Oil Company (Rockefeller) meant to hold 21,658,999 shares, worth more than $1.516 billion. In some cases, even 1 percent represented a staggering sum of money. The Watson family interest in the International Business Machine Corporation (I.B.M.), of which they are the founders, comprised a total of 243,570 shares representing a market value of $108 million, or under 1 percent of the company's total market value of $12.2 billion. Individual shareholders in many corporations controlled more than 10 percent of all their outstanding stocks with market values in the hundreds of

millions of dollars. The concentrated shareholdings may be compared with those of the *average* shareowner in particular companies, which for General Motors were 275 shares and for Wool-
worth 17 shares.[9]

The concentration of property has been accelerating since
these estimates were made and, via the multinational corporations,
has been internationalized to such an extent that the sales volume
of some large corporations exceeds the gross national product of
many nations.[10] This trend is not unique to the United States but
is observable in all capitalist countries. Besides these private corporations there also exist utility corporations dealing with water, gas,
electricity, oil, sewage, communications, and transportation. In
some nations, predominantly in Europe, such corporations are directly owned by municipal, state, or national public authorities. In
other countries, and predominantly in the United States, they are
private corporations whose operations are partially covered by
public law. Public control of these organizations consists mainly in
regulating the rates they charge for their services, and the determination of returns on their investments, which are usually oriented
to what is considered a "fair return" in view of the prevailing profit
rates. Occasionally, some form of regulation also affects their investment policies. The control of these corporations is highly centralized by way of holding companies in association with great
banking houses. To secure the highly concentrated control, stock
issues are generally limited, and long-term bonds are the preferred
form of financing. The practices of control differ in different nations and for different companies, but the actual operations of the
utility enterprises, whether private, public, or of mixed ownership,
do not differ from the business practices of other corporations.

Ownership in the large corporations is not identical with control. It is clear that there is no way for the 2 million stockholders
of a company such as American Telephone and Telegraph to exercise any kind of control over its transactions. The wide diffusion
of stock ownership not only allows but demands minority control,
and the greater the dispersion the less stock is needed to maintain
control of a corporation. A concentrated 10 percent ownership of
all of a company's outstanding stock usually suffices to secure
control over it. In theory, the stockholders ultimately control the
management of corporations through their legal right to dismiss an
unwanted management; in practice, however, concentrated minor-

ity holdings, in combination with management, usurp all decision-making power and can hardly if ever be challenged. Although this is not necessarily the case, managers and directors of corporations are usually also shareholders. But they enjoy their power not so much by virtue of their share ownership as by their possession of the managerial positions. The larger a company with respect to number of share-owners, the greater is the practical separation of ownership from control. But the larger the concentration of stock-ownership within a corporation, the greater is the control over management exercised by the concentrated minority stockholders.

Minority control over capital is further enhanced through its "pyramiding" or "amplification" by way of holding companies and interlocking directorates. The holding company is a device for bringing under single control the properties of one or more corporations, by pyramiding voting control over their securities and thus controlling a large amount of capital with a minimum of investment. The interlocking directorates seat the same persons as members of boards of directors in a number of separately organized corporations, able to impose a uniform policy on all of them.

Aside from the owners of nonvoting stock, it is clear that even those with voting rights are not able, and usually do not even try or care, to influence corporation policies. This is the responsibility of the board of directors, a small number of persons who in turn select the professional management which actually carries on the corporations' business operations. Although the directors are supposedly elected by the stockholders, the latter cannot do so directly but make use of "proxies," who represent and exercise their votes. In a going concern, the proxy is usually a member of the board of directors, and though at times there occur "proxy fights" for the control of corporations, they do not affect corporate management as a self-perpetuating group determining its own successors. Generally, the ordinary shareholders find themselves in the position of passive claim holders.

Although ownership and control do not coincide in the modern corporation, there is normally no divergence of interest between the passive claim holders and the active business leaders. Both are interested in the maximization of profits. As with capital generally, so also must corporate capital's operations be directed toward profit making and the formation of additional capital. A lack of profitability or a capital loss imply the eventual extinction of the organization. Nor can there be a difference of interest between the owners and the managers of a business, for the latter's position and income (even as nonowners, or insufficient owners) depend on the existence and thus on the profitability of the corporation under their management. Actually, the managerial class forms the largest single group in the stockholding population, which fortifies their interest in the profitability of corporate enterprise both from the side of management and from the side of ownership.

Management of corporations, though largely independent of the great number of their stockholders, may be subjected to outside control by investment banks and financial groups through the latter's supply of long-term credits. Financial interests are likely to acquire power in a firm when it is either in the process of rapid expansion or in financial distress. Those who give financial support, particularly for purposes of reorganization, usually exact some determination over a company's policies through the selection of its board of directors and its chief executives. But even independently of a corporation's credit requirements, financial interests may acquire influence in, and even control of, a company through devices such as the purchase of minority interests, the creation of voting trusts, and the pyramiding of holding company structures. However, the controlling powers of banks and financiers over business have been weakened in recent times because of competition by insurance companies and pension funds for new industrial bond issues, and because of the increasing ability of corporations to finance their expansion out of retained earnings. But whether the centralized control of corporations is exercised by "inside" or "outside" management, the operation of the corporation itself demands the same emphasis on profitability as does ownership combined with direct control.

The concentration and centralization of capital implies its contradictory movement toward monopolization. In analogy with Newtonian physics, in which the forces of attraction and repulsion keep the universe in balance, economists saw in the market forces of supply and demand an equilibrium mechanism secured by competition under laissez-faire conditions. At first, this idea was not so much a description of reality as a political demand, expressing the needs of the rising bourgeoisie within the mercantile conditions of the feudal regime. But free competition became an actual social fact. Although the "ideal" of noninterference in the competitive market was not, and could not be, reached, nevertheless up to the beginning of the twentieth century it was private market competition that largely determined the character and the development of capitalist society.

Whatever the individual businessman may think about free competition, in his practical business affairs he must try to escape the pressures of competition by ways and means that, in their effects, reduce the number of his competitors either in absolute terms or relative to the total growth of the economy. By fair means or foul, he will search for extra profits, for a temporary monopolistic market position, for a larger share of the demand, so as to prevent the always threatening destruction of his own business through competition. Each isolated cost reduction leads to a market advantage, soon to be lost again through its more general application. It is in this way that competition breeds monopoly and monopoly succumbs to competition. It is thus not really possible to speak of competition without speaking of monopoly, for both are merely aspects of one and the same market process.

In bourgeois market theory, monopoly was not inherent in competition but was its direct opposite, which hindered the proper functioning of the price mechanism. Until quite recently, market theory was based on an abstract model of perfect competition. But this model lost what limited relevance and justification it had with the progressively increasing monopolization of the business world. "Imperfect" or "monopolistic" competition refers to market situations that are neither perfectly competitive nor completely monopolized. In such a market, no single firm can as yet control prices at will, but the limited number of competitors does change prices from what they might be under more perfect competition. The buying and selling of commodities on a very large scale assures some degree of monopolistic price control. Imperfect competition is thus associated with big business, and because the latter dominates present-day capitalism, the economists' concern is no longer with perfect competition but with what is called "workable competition," a term that accommodates all degrees and combinations of competition and monopoly.

The businessman's attitude to competition and monopoly is quite flexible. If he finds himself in monopolistic market position, he will simply enjoy it; if not, he will denounce monopoly in favor of "fair" competition. While competition is always accompanied by temporary monopolies, because some enterprises succeed sooner than others in reducing their costs, monopolistic situations are also brought about through cut-throat competition. In order to drive competitors out of business, some firms will deliberately inflict upon themselves temporary losses through price discrimination, excessive discounts, rebates, etc., and in this way gain a greater control over prices as well as a larger share of the available market demand. Cut-throat competition is practiced by both small and large businesses, particularly during depressions.

Quite apart from all "unfair" competition, however, it was the mere growth of the market economy by way of competition that led to the concentration and centralization of capital and to large-scale enterprises, and which accentuated the monopolistic aspects of the simultaneously competitive and monopolistic market reality. While in early capitalism there is more competition than monopoly, in late capitalism there is more monopoly than competition. The variety of market situations that can affect prices, through the diminishing or increasing number of competitors on either the demand or the supply side, was given a variety of technical expressions, such as oligopoly, oligopsony, duopoly, and duopsony. Some of the market relations described by these terms rarely, if ever, find a counterpart in reality, but serve the theoretical economists in their speculative constructions. Monopoly (a single seller) and its counterpart monopsony (a single buyer) may at times exist in a special line of business. But this condition can hardly be maintained. Monopoly is always accompanied by competition and is itself a form of competition. It prevails to varying degrees in different kinds of business activities, as some lend themselves to more monopolization than others. Big industry, for instance, is less competitive than agriculture and has therefore more control over prices than the latter. But even the more competitive businesses will try to overcome their disadvantages by achieving a modicum of monopolization, as for instance in farmers' attempts to control prices through cooperative associations. There exists, then, in each nation and in the world at large, a great conglomeration of more or less competitive and more or less monopolistic businesses, their control over prices varying from zero to complete determination.

Even monopoly prices, however, are not arbitrarily set but

retain some definite relation to the total market situation. The higher the monopoly price, the smaller will be the demand for commodities offered at this price, for the market demand is itself limited by the total social income. What has been "overpaid," so to speak, in the monopoly price cannot be expended on commodities subjected to more competitive conditions. The demand in the competitive business sphere will diminish, and, as competition increases, competing enterprises will reduce their prices. For firms with a low profit margin this may well spell ruin. On the basis of a given social income, which determines the existing demand, monopoly prices force other prices below what they would be under more perfect competition. What takes place here is a "transfer" of income from the more competitive to the less competitive businesses. This "transfer" is accomplished through the reduction or elimination of competition in some enterprises and depends on the persistence of competition in others. However, this "transfer" need not affect the absolute size of any business income under conditions of flux, that is, with a growing social income and an expanding market demand. The increasing social productivity and the extension of markets may be such as to allow for monopoly prices as well as for competitive prices still high enough to assure a sufficient profitability. Only under conditions of stagnation and decline would the increasing monopolization be accompanied by a continuous destruction of smaller and more competitive enterprises, a process that would find its "logical" end in the complete monopolization of the economy, which would also be the end of the capitalist market.

The prevailing conditions of imperfect competition still incorporate a great deal of undiluted competition. There are everywhere in the capitalist world countless small businesses, particularly in farming and the retail trade, which do not have the slightest control over prices. Such businesses are still open to anyone with the necessary funds and the illusion of success in a world dominated by big business. Their cost prices are codetermined by prices set by monopolistic competition, while their sales prices are often determined by the fiercest type of price competition. The bankruptcy rate of such businesses is very high and their relative weight in the business world is as minimal as their number is large. Thus there exist at the same time two different markets: the traditional market where supply and demand determine competitive prices, and a market where administered prices determine supply and demand. Administered prices may, but do not necessarily, indicate monopolistic competition. Instead of engaging in costly price competition, some enterprises rather adhere to more or less uniform prices—either by unwritten agreements arrived at by consultation, or by accepting the "price leadership" of one of the larger firms in the business. If the product is homogeneous, as in the production of steel, for example, prices will be raised or lowered in accordance with those set by the dominant company.

It is often said that the absence of price competition in the larger part of the modern market does not signify the end of competition but merely a change of form, in that price competition is replaced by competition via advertising, brand names, credit terms, and variations and improvements of the products themselves. But this rivalry has more restrictive than competitive functions, as it tends to consolidate and expand existing monopolistic positions and to safeguard them against possible intruders. The reluctance to engage in price competition is not a special characteristic of large enterprises; even smaller ones do not favor that type of unrestricted competition which the economists held essential for the proper functioning of the economy. Whatever the economists may think about the necessity of a competitive price mechanism, the practical businessman's concern must always be with his profitability, no matter what the given market conditions. If he could make a larger profit by lowering prices, and thereby force others to follow suit, he probably would do so. But it is precisely because he can better enlarge his profits by way of administered prices that he prefers to cut his production rather than his price. This choice stems not from an evil design to violate "economic laws" and the "public interest," but from the principle of profit maximization as a necessary condition for the existence and the future of any business.

With the growing size of industrial enterprises grow also their fixed charges and their overhead costs. These costs are relatively constant, whereas a firm's sales may fluctuate widely. To maintain profitability, sales must have a definite relation to costs. If costs are lowered, commodity prices too can be lowered, but this by itself is no guarantee of larger sales, or of sales large enough to yield a profit over costs. What can be gained in terms of sales by a reduction of price is often insignificant as regards a firm's profitability. In order not to lower profits, price competition requires a rapidly expanding market demand. Without it, the lower prices and the more "sticky" costs will reduce the profit margin. If demand does not expand sufficiently, prices can only be cut at a loss. Under such conditions, businessmen will prefer to restrict production by informal agreements, which stabilize prices at the most comfortable profit level. The decline of price competition is thus not only a consequence of the rise of big business but also a result of a declining rate of capital expansion, experienced by the businessmen as a decline of the market demand.

The concentration of capital should have made it obvious that the competitive price mechanism of bourgeois equilibrium theory has no bearing on capitalism's development. In bourgeois parlance, however, "the economies of large-scale production," brought about by the increase of productivity through more and improved capital equipment, merely reduce production costs and lower prices. But they also eliminate the high-cost producers and drive them out of the market. By being an instrument of competition, mass production is also an instrument of concentration and monopolization. Yet it took more than a hundred years of this development before bourgeois theory discovered the existence of monopolies within the laissez-faire system and their effects upon profits and prices, and turned from the analysis of competition to that of monopolistic price formation.

In contrast, Marx's value theory of accumulation finds empirical verification in the undebatable and generally acknowledged fact of the increasing concentration and centralization of capital. In Marx's model of capital production competition "regulates" the capitalist economy through the formation of an average rate of profit. It is thus clear that the progressive elimination of competition must interfere with the formation of a general rate of profit and in this manner disrupt its "regulatory" force. While the law of value continues to determine capitalist development, its effect upon the distribution of surplus value diminishes with the increasing monopolization of capital. It places a disproportionate amount of the social surplus value into the hands of monopolies and reduces that which falls to the competitive capital. But like competition, monopolization can only affect the distribution of the socially available surplus value, not its actual mass. The tendency of the rate of profit to fall remains, and shows itself first in the reduction of competitive in favor of monopolistic profits. What the one gains, the other loses. The escape from the averaging process of competition on the part of monopoly capital, through its control of prices, implies lower prices and lower profits for the competitive capitals and therewith the decrease of their number within the total social capital. To the same measure, then, that monopoly capital does away with competition, it also removes the source of its monopolistic profits, which tend to become the profits as determined by the actual degree of exploitation with respect to the total capital. Monopoly profits will become the social average profit, which will rise or fall with the increasing productivity of labor in relation to the changing organic composition of the total capital.

The elimination of competition by way of competition and the consequent increasing monopolization of capital does not affect Marx's theory of accumulation and its effect upon the general rate of profit, except insofar as the progressive loss of the "regulatory" force of competition—with respect to the distribution of surplus value—increases the general disorder of the capitalist system and its susceptibility to crises and depressions. Through the effect of monopolization upon the allocation of the social labor in terms of use value, crisis situations become more devastating and less easy to overcome. The distribution of the social surplus value, via the general rate of profit, is also a mechanism through which the requirements of the capitalist reproduction process are met in use-value as well as in exchange-value terms, while a more or less arbitrary monopolistic rate of profit distorts this close connection in favor of the privileged exchange-value expansion of the monopolistic capital. Capital is bound to lose, in increasing measure, even that degree of coherence which satisfied its own social requirements at earlier stages of its development.[11]

If one strips the constantly increasing centralization of capital of its contradictory (that is, its capitalistic) character, then, according to Marx, the unmistakable trend toward centralization indicates

> that production loses its private character and becomes a social process, not formally—in the sense that all production subject to exchange is social because of the absolute dependence of the producers on one another and the necessity for presenting their labor as abstract social labor (by means of money)—but in actual fact. For the means of production are employed as communal, social means of production and therefore

not determined by the fact that they are the property of an individual but by their relation to production, and the labor likewise is performed on a social scale.[12]

This same process, however, which allows for a socialist perspective with regard to society's further development, only intensifies the contradiction between the social forces and the social relations of capital production, and therewith the aggravation of social conflicts within deteriorating economic conditions.

While there is no denial of the centralization of capital, and while the directly experienced crises cannot be talked away, Marx's prediction of the polarization of capitalist society into two major classes is generally considered as incorrect as his prediction of increasing misery. The industrial working class, though vastly larger than it was a hundred years ago, still comprises the smaller part of the world's population. Even if white-collar workers and the laborers in capitalist agriculture in both the developed and underdeveloped nations are included in the working class, and though

> no exact, or nearly exact, figure for the total could possibly be given, ... it is quite safe to say that it could not be less than 500 million. That is less than the population of China alone, about the same as the population of India, probably something less than one-sixth of the population of the world. The number to be absorbed (in the capitalist system) is therefore vast; but the number that has been absorbed is also very large. The rate of expansion that is needed to absorb the remainder ... is certainly no greater than that which has been achieved hitherto.[13]

As John Hicks says, five-sixths of the world's population stands outside the capitalist system, without thereby being freed from capitalism's impact upon their conditions of existence. This points of course to difficulties in maintaining, or increasing, the rate of capital expansion, due to the levels of concentration and centralization of capital already reached and to their effects upon its variable component. What expansion does take place does not require, as in the past, the same number of additional workers, even if the rate of expansion should be the same. The great mass of the world population, which is no longer able to exist in traditional ways, is also not able to find a way into the labor market. Because capital is nothing but extracted surplus value, it should, by its nature, be inclined to absorb the maximum of available labor-power, for even absolute surplus value is capable of augmenting capital. The fact, then, that the mass of unemployed and underemployed is constantly growing on a worldwide scale, means that while the world is not polarized between capital and wage labor, it is certainly polarized between the beneficiaries of the capitalist system and an ever-growing proletariat of which only a declining number find themselves counted within the working class.

The bourgeois economists adjudge the relative reduction of the number of industrial workers through the expansion of capital to be a refutation of Marxian theory. "In the developed countries," it is said, for instance, "a true proletariat still exists, but it has become a minority, and furthermore, unfortunately, an impotent minority. Under these circumstances Marx's interpretation of history ceases to have much meaning."[14] While some economists, as seen above, confidently await the involvement of all people as workers in the capitalist system, for others the working class has already ceased to exist, in the sense that it has been completely integrated into the capitalist system. The integrated or classless society is being realized "through a process of political dialogue, compromise, and the sheer working out of the social consequences of a long-continued process of economic growth."[15] Such hopeful projections are based on a total misapprehension of the capitalist system and its developmental tendencies. It is precisely because of the diminishing number of productive workers that the apparent integration of the working class turns into the disintegration of the capitalist system and prevents the hoped-for absorption of the world proletariat into the capitalist system through the progressive reduction of its rate of expansion.

Actually, of course, the large majority—up to 80 percent— of the population in the developed capitalist countries are wage workers, for they have to sell their labor power to capitalist enterprises and public institutions for wages and salaries. While it is true that the income differentials within this large mass of dependent wage receivers are such as to prevent their simple description as members of one uniform working class, their combined income remains subjected to the changing value and surplus-value relations of the capitalist system as a whole. While one part of the working class reproduces itself through the value of its labor power, another part receives its income out of the surplus value gained through the application of variable capital. The production process implies the circulation process and the costs of the latter have to be covered by the surplus value gained in production. Although the capital-labor relation prevails in both the circulation and the production process, the wages and salaries paid out in the former must be derived from the profits made in the latter. The cost of circulation reduces the mass of surplus value available for capitalists' consumption and for the accumulation of capital.

The increasing productivity of labor, which implies the relative decline of the variable within the total productive capital, must not only prevent a possible fall of the general rate of profit but must also compensate for the increasing costs of circulation. This increase is itself a consequence of the increasing productivity of labor, for the growing mass of commodities, produced with less and less labor, requires a disproportionate increase of the labor employed in distribution. This disproportionality has its source, on the one hand, in the enlargement and extension of the market and, on the other hand, in the as yet unresolved fact that the increase of productivity in the distribution process proceeds at a slower pace than in the production process. Whereas the production process becomes increasingly more centralized into fewer and bigger enterprises, the distribution process is increasingly "decentralized," as it has to reach the far-spread and widely dispersed consumer market. The slower advance in the productivity of the so-called service sector of the economy depresses the rate of profit. While its disproportional growth may absorb a part of the workers displaced by the increasing productivity in the production process, this itself is an additional contributor to the decline of the rate of accumulation, in which the decreasing profitability of capital comes to the fore.

The pressure exerted upon the rate of profit by the disproportionate growth of unproductive vis-à-vis productive (that is, profit-producing) labor can be relieved only by a further increase of the productivity of labor in general and that of productive labor in particular. Meanwhile, the movements of the rate of profit affect both of these layers of the working population and set them equally in objective opposition to the capitalist need to maintain its profitability. It is then not its *occupational character* that characterizes the proletariat but its *social position* as wage labor. The diminution of the industrial working class implies the growth of the working class irrespective of the type of employment it is engaged in.

There are still social groups that possess some degree of independence within the otherwise mutual dependence of labor and capital, but their progressive disappearance is making for the continuing polarization of capitalist society. Although generally determined by the capitalist relation of production, it was predominantly agriculture, retail trade, and the free professions that allowed for an existence outside the wage system. It was these social layers that comprised the middle class hovering between labor and capital. The progressive decline of this class is an observable fact, as the retailer makes room for the supermarket and family farms turn into industrial enterprises based on wage labor. This process is observable everywhere, but particularly in the United States. It shows itself in the constant decrease of the farm population, the elimination of share-cropping and the high capitalization of agriculture. According to the Agricultural Department of the United States Census Bureau, fewer than one American out of 25 lived on a farm in 1975, while as recently as 1935 it was one out of four. Farm population declined 14 percent between 1970 and 1976. Nearly 37 percent of this loss occurred over just one year, from 1975 to 1976. During the last six years the number of black persons living on farms dropped from 900,000 to 500,000. The reduction of farm labor was accompanied by a 20 percent increase of production and the utilization of a larger acreage. The number of farms dropped from 6.8 million to 2.8 million between 1935 and 1976.[16]

Marx's expectation that at a certain stage of capitalist development productivity in agriculture must increase more rapidly than in industry has been verified in the growing mechanization of agriculture, which has indeed raised its productivity beyond that prevailing in industry. With mechanization abetted by, and even forced upon, the larger farm entities by the highly centralized food industry, agriculture turned from a labor-intensive into a capital-intensive branch of production, creating on its part a surplus population which joins that in the urban centers. While raising the rate of profit, this also implies a still higher organic composition of the total social capital. But there is no way to deal with this contradictory development except through the further increase of productivity. While a decline of productivity reduces the rate of accumulation, the decline of the latter intensifies the decrease of productivity. Since 1965 productivity in the United States has been declining, which is only another way of saying that the rate of accumulation has decreased; this, again, implies an insufficient profitability, hindering the expansion of capital to the extent necessary for the maintenance of what is called full employment and the full utilization of productive resources. As a cyclical phenomenon this only repeats with some variations what happened in every previous situation in which decreasing profitability showed itself in a decling rate of accumulation.

Whatever the shortcomings of the measurement of productivity, economic statistics provide some terms for its appraisal. According to the Council of Economic Advisers to the U.S. Government, the decrease of productivity finds its main cause in, among other things, "the inadequacy of investments."

> Between 1948 and 1973, business spending on new plant and equipment added 3% a year to the capital investments supporting each manhour of work. Since then this capital-labor ratio has increased only 1.75% annually.[17]

Of course, the reasons for this decline are not looked for in capital production itself, but in excessive wages or in governmental tax policies which "slow the introduction of cost-cutting labor-saving machinery," induce inflation and thus make "businessmen even more hesitant to spend on new machinery."

This situation raises the question of the profitability of capital. Only a decline of profits, relative to the existing capital, could explain the capitalist reluctance, or inability, to expand production through additional, more productive investments. As in all previous depression states of the economy, the rate of profit, now a practical concern, becomes a theoretical one. However this rate may be calculated from the available statistical data, if the methods applied to this end are used consistently, or brought under uniform denominators, even this inadequate data will display a definite trend over time, showing whether the rate of profit rose, fell, or remained the same. According to a study undertaken by William D. Nordhaus,[18] the rate of return of nonfinancial corporate capital in the United States has been consistently falling since 1966, despite an erosion of the effective corporate tax rate and liberalized depreciation allowances. This poor performance of corporate profits is also observable in most of Western Europe. In the United States, all corporate profits as a share of Gross National Product dropped considerably, though in cyclical fashion, throughout the period from 1948 to 1973. The 1971-73 ratio was 57 percent of the 1948-50 average. "The postwar decline occurred in two distinct movements, 1948-54 and 1966-70, separated by a period during which the share fluctuated within a narrow band, mostly because of cyclical movements."[19] The decline since 1966 was drastic enough to induce Nordhaus to raise the questions: "What lies behind the crumbling profit margins? Is the decline a statistical artifact? Was labor able to increase its share by aggressive bargaining? Or does the declining share of profit portend the euthanasia of the capitalist class, and indeed of capitalism itself?"[20]

We are here only concerned with the recognition of the actual fall of the rate of profit that resulted from Nordhaus's investigation, not with his own explanation for this occurrence.[21] Other explanations, such as the decline of productivity during the same period, are given by other economists. Of course, this only leads back to the question of why there was such a decline, since it could have been prevented by a faster rate of accumulation; and this only returns us to the original question of why the rate of profit fell. Nordhaus's findings were soon challenged, though with respect not to the facts themselves but only to their interpretation. In 1977 Martin Feldstein presented a paper at the Brookings Panel on Economic Activity, which, while acknowledging the recent radical fall of the rate of profit—that reached a thirty-year low in 1974 of only 6.4 percent—submitted that this was due to special circumstances, which do not allow for the proposition that there has been a gradual downward trend in the rate of return.[22] As in the past, so also now, a lower return period may well be terminated by a new rise of profits, excluding the probability of its permanent fall. And of course, a permanent fall of the rate of profit would imply a permanent depression and thus an early end of capitalism.

It was the actual fall of profit rates that disturbed bourgeois economists sufficiently to take a new look at this long forgotten problem. The problem also attracted attention during previous periods of crisis and depression, only to be dropped again as soon as a new upswing ensued. But as profits allegedly accrue to capital in its capacity as a "factor of production," the reason for their decline has been searched for everywhere except in the capitalist relations of production, and therefore in the value composition of capital. What is of interest here is only that the realities of the capitalist development impress themselves even upon the economists and in this manner substantiate, if only indirectly, Marx's theory of accumulation. All the issues raised by Marx finally find their reflection in bourgeois theory, which attempts to cope with them and perhaps turn them to capitalist advantage. And as the actual development of capitalism does not strictly follow the abstract pattern of Marx's theory, simply because of the capitalist reactions to the value-determined course of events, it is quite possible to reject this theory even while considering the concrete conditions by which it is verified.

All critical appraisals of Marx's theory have centered on the fall of the rate of profit, denying the logical consistency of the argument and its empirical verification. Out of the welter of such critical assessments we may select at random a recent book by F. M. Gottheil, which investigates Marx's economic predictions in general and that of the falling rate of profit in particular. Gottheil states correctly that for Marx, "the rate of profit will decline whatever the rate of surplus-value."[4] However, Marx also saw, he continues, that if he "permitted surplus-value to vary *without restraint*, then little could be said concerning the fall of the rate of profit."[5] But if the relation between surplus value and the rate of profit is wholly dependent upon the rate of productivity, Gottheil proclaims, then "the rate of profit increases as the number of laborers declines. So, too, does total output."[6]

Thus far, Gottheil only restates Marx's own propositions. But while Marx's model of capital expansion serves to clarify the theory of the falling rate of profit, by assuming an upper limit of expansion at the point where it is no longer possible to overcome the fall of the profit rate through an increase of suplus value, Gottheil maintains "that an infinite increase in surplus value will raise the rate of profit infinitely, whatever the organic composition of capital."[7] "Incorporating productivity considerations into Marx's demonstration of the upper limit, he says "substantially alters the conclusions."[8] In other words, Gottheil finds Marx's theory logically flawed, because "specific parameter values must be assumed in the profit-rate equations before such a decline will occur. Whatever else Marx does, he does not prove that the specific values required for the falling-rate-of-profit prediction can be derived from his model."[9]

However, it is not Marx's theory but the actual periodic decline of profit rates that must prove the reality of the fall of the rate of profit, which Marx's theory tried to explain by applying the labor theory of value to the analysis of the expansion of capital. What were the restraints that prevented an "infinite increase" of surplus value from coping with the increasing organic composition of capital and its effect upon the rate of profit? For Marx, the restraints are built into the system by the double nature of capital production as the production of both exchange value and use value. The "infinite" expansion of exchange value—and it is only this that can find consideration in capitalism—is limited by the use-value aspect, that is, by the degree of exploitability of labor power, not to speak of ecological constraints independent of every social formation.

Although Gottheil imagines that he can prove Marx wrong on his own grounds—that is, on the basis of the theory of value—his argument depends on reference to the production process as such and not to its value determination. And of course, if we see capitalist production merely as a material production process, excluding from its technological side, so to speak, the assumption of a rise of productivity steadily enlarging the total capital, this leaves no room for a falling rate of profit. Though Gottheil points out that "the value of labor power is determined by the real subsistence of the family unit, or the real costs of reproducing the laboring class,"[10] he overlooks that these costs imply a (changing) relationship between necessary and surplus labor in the value-determined production process. The cheaper reproduction of the laboring class implies the reduction of the necessary part of total production in order to ensure the accelerating formation of capital. But the necessary part cannot be reduced to zero, so that its decline must slow the growth of the productivity of labor as capital accumulates. What Gottheil does not comprehend is that the increasing productivity of labor is only the other side of the decreasing value of labor-power, or the reduction of the ratio of variable to constant capital. It is not the increasing productivity of labor in use-value terms, but the increasing appropriation of surplus labor in exchange-value terms, that makes possible the continuous expansion of capital. No matter how great the increase of the productivity of labor, it always means a relative reduction of the number of workers employed by a given capital, and accordingly a shift in value relations that must affect the rate of profit on total capital. It is then only a question of time until the disparity between the increasing productivity of labor and the decreasing application of labor power (where the one compensates for, but also conflicts with, the other) comes to light in a lower rate of accumulation and a slower rise of the organic composition of capital.

In order to avoid misunderstandings, it should be recalled that the increase of the productivity of labor in exchange-value terms remains always bound to its increase in use-value terms. A commodity like any other, labor power is at the same time the source of surplus value, as its use involves both necessary and surplus labor, measured by paid and unpaid labor time. The productivity of labor and the quantity of its products cannot be divorced from the working time applied in the production process. Just as the necessary labor time cannot be reduced to the point at which all labor becomes surplus labor, this working time delimits the rising productivity, as it cannot be extended at will beyond the humanly bearable. With these absolute limits in mind, and on the assumption of a closed system and a constant working population, it follows logically that the increase of productivity, like the increase of surplus value, is finite and must reach an upper limit as the organic composition of capital rises.

Now, capitalism is not a closed system with a constant working population; nonetheless, the mechanism modeled by Marx on the assumption of these conditions must also characterize, although with far-reaching modifications, the actual expanding capitalism and its variable working population, for it is the mechanism that makes capitalism possible in the first place. It is, so to speak, its "inner logic," which determines the course of its development in a definite direction and makes this trend predictable. Because in an expanding capitalism, the growing productivity of labor is accompanied by an absolute growth in the number of workers, their decline relative to the growing capital may not be perceptible, except in the formation of the industrial reserve army, and the rate of profit may remain the same, or even increase, as the composition of capital rises. The fall of the rate of profit remains then a mere tendency within the accumulation process. But this tendency is real nevertheless, just as the law of value is operating even though it is not perceivable in the price relations of the market. In fact, the theory of the falling rate of profit is just another name for Marx's labor theory of value.

As the labor theory of value finds validation in the capitalist crisis, it does so through the reduction of the profitability of capital. The loss of profitability and the periodicity of crisis cannot be explained except in terms of a discrepancy between the profits actually produced and those required for further profitable capitalist expansion. Whatever theory has been advanced to explain this, all theories agree that the crisis implies a loss of profitability, disinvestment instead of investment, the widespread destruction of capital, and large-scale unemployment. All theories also agree that the end of the crisis and the depression it brings in its wake presuppose the restoration of the profitability of capital, although the means suggested to this end differ in accordance with the particular crisis theory. From a Marxian point of view, the generality of the crisis —that is, the fact that it embraces all aspects of the economy— has its central source in the decline of the rate of profit, or, what is the same, in the "regulating" power of the law of value, which controls the otherwise unregulated and blindly proceeding production process.

For Gottheil, that the rate of profit must fall as a consequence of capital production is a mere assertion on the part of Marx.

> Without making explicit the relationship between the rate of surplus value and the capital composition," he says, "no law concerning the movement in the rate of profit can be formulated. . . . If certain parameter values are assumed, then the rate of profit will fall. If, however, different sets of parameter values are selected, the rate of profit will increase. Since Marx provides no insight into the estimation of future parameter values, the prediction concerning the falling rate of profit is logically untenable.[11]

What Gottheil demands of Marx is not a prediction, based on observable social production relations and their consequences for capitalist development, but exact quantitative knowledge of future relationships between the rate of surplus value and the composition of capital. As these relationships cannot be known in the present, they are even more out of reach for the future. It is in the nature of the fetishistic unfolding of capital that nothing of the changing relations between the rate of surplus value, the composition of capital, and the rate of profit is visible as such. All these changes manifest themselves implicitly in the expansion or contraction of the economy determined by price changes. But as these price relations, whatever they may be, are derived from the value relations of capitalist prodution, the movements of capital, in their dependence on the rate of profit, can be traced to the social relations of production as value relations. Marx did not attempt to solve insoluble problems; he merely tried to explain the actual capitalist development within the realm of the possible. And here, the parameter values of the different economic categories, while varying in their application, vary within the invariable setting of the capialist relations of production, which determine the changing weights of the different parameter values in the system as a whole and in the course of its development.

It is not the possible fall of the rate of profit to which the critics of Marx object, but the elevation of this phenomenon into an "economic law" that determines the trend of capitalist development. And indeed, if the fall of the rate of profit merely accounts for the business cycle, and has no further implications, there is no reason to assume a secular one-directional movement of the profit rate pointing to the eventual collapse of the capitalist system. According to Marx, of course, "economic laws" *per se* do not exist at all, even though the production and reproduction process is at all times and under all conditions not only a social relationship but also the metabolism between man and nature. This latter aspect is a natural necessity and not an "economic law." To speak of "economic laws" is to refer to changing man-made arrangements —social production relations—which rule, while they last, a specific mode of production but do not apply under different circumstances. The "law of the falling rate of profit" is nothing but a law of capitalist expansion, and is such only so long as value production determines the social production process. Here the subjugation of the working class under the exploitative capital-labor relations is so thoroughly mystified as to appear as an unalterable "economic law," controlling society as if it were a natural law, whereas in fact it is nothing more than an alterable system of production relations with a limited historical perspective.

To demonstrate the historical limitations of the capitalist mode of production, these limitations must already be present in the system, as an objective trend of its development and in the existence of subjective forces arising in opposition to it. Acknowledging the impossibility of seeing the future in precise detail, and recognizing the limitations of economic analysis for the comprehension of economic events, Marx was satisfied with the discovery of the general law of accumulation, based on the social production relations.

The validity of Marx's theory shows itself in the real world, beset as it is with recurring crises of always wider dimensions and greater destructive power. The contradictions inherent in the capitalist system, already present long before Marx was born, formed the starting point for his economic analysis. These contradictions are still with us, but are now not only suffered but also understood. Marx's theory of capital accumulation stands or falls not because of limitations set to economic analysis by the analyzed system itself, but with the actual development of capitalism as a viable social system of production.

It is interesting but understandable that most of the critics of Marx dwell in the sphere of "pure theory," in order to challenge the logical consistency of one or another aspect of Marx's theories. When they present empirical evidence, they do so quite selectively, pointing to the successful phases of capital expansion, and disregarding past periods of crisis and depression as mere aberrations that leave the essential stability of the system unaffected. This nonchalance broke down during the Great Depression of 1929, only to be regained with the new upswing of capitalist production after World War II. From a Marxian point of view, however, it is the phase of contraction, not that of expansion, which is of foremost importance. For it is during periods of severe depression that the irrationality of the system reveals itself to the fullest and the illusion of its immortality suffers the greatest damage. Here the concrete conditions contradict their own ideological support and bring forth a greater awareness of the true nature of capital. Due to the narrowing base of exploitation, which characterizes the accumulation of capital, the expansion of capital implies its susceptibility to crises and depressions of increasing severity. As all economic activity is geared to the accumulation of capital, it must contract with every decline in the rate of accumulation, and thus with every fall in the rate of profit as experienced in changing market relations.

The difficulties in the way of blind adjustment of the rate of exploitation to the accumulation requirements of capital show themselves in the frequency and the severity of capitalist depressions. However, frequently occurring crisis situations point to a relative ease in the resumption of the accumulation process, such as accompanied the early stages of capitalist development. At later stages, depressions became less frequent, but of a more devastating nature, embracing a larger mass of capital and a greater number of the population. The global extension of capital led to crises of a worldwide nature, affecting in growing measure even the capitalistically undeveloped regions, which saw, added to their own plight, that caused by their contacts with the capitalist world. It is in the increasing depth and duration of the capitalist crisis that the secular fall of the rate of profit shows itself, and any objective description of capitalism's history up to the present provides empirical proof of Marx's theory.

The inability or unwillingness of present-day bourgeois theory—and not only bourgeois theory—to comprehend the capitalist system and its development rests upon a profound conviction, which also characterized classical political economy, that there is no other possible mode of production than the capitalist one. The system itself is supposed to provide society with rationality through its members' pursuits of their special interests. While the early confidence in the blessings of the "invisible hand" has largely vanished, this has not affected the belief in the necessity and rationality of the prevailing relations of production, even if they require, and in increasing measure, the use of many visible hands. The "rationality principle" implies, of course, that production is carried on to satisfy the consumption needs of society. Even some Marxists have great difficulties in seeing the capitalist system as an irrational one and thus restrict their criticism to the unequal distribution that goes with the capital-labor relation. Presumably, this inequality causes the disproportionalities in the production process, devoted, as it should be, to the production of consumption goods, so that the underconsumption of the workers causes the overproduction of commodities and therefore the crisis cycle of the capitalist system. For Marx, however, capitalism is an irrational system precisely because it does "accumulate for the sake of accumulation" and for that reason finds its barrier in itself. "Production for the sake of production" is obviously not only irrational but is seemingly also precluded by the capitalist need to realize surplus-value in the sphere of circulation.

Perhaps the best way to comprehend the capitalist system is to start by imagining a social system in which the alleged, but inapplicable, capitalist principle of production for the sake of consumption has been realized. In that case, production and its expansion would be determined by the existing and changing consumption needs of the population. It would be these needs in their use-value form that would have to be provided for by production and the production of means of production in their use-value forms. The rationality of this system would be of a purely technical-organizational character, without any consideration of the values of commodities, which, by their nature, are independent of their use-value forms and therefore divorced from the actual requirements of social production and consumption, except insofar as these requirements serve the amassing of capital in its abstract value form. In a system free of value relations, production and consumption would be complementary processes and the possible difficulties encountered in coordinating the one with the other would also be of a technical-organizational nature.

Not so in capitalism. The quest for maximum profits which motivates each capitalist enterprise, and indeed is necessary for the maintenance of its existence, implies that the surplus value on the total social scale must exceed those consumption requirements that have to be met out of the produced surplus value. Part of the latter must be reinvested to expand the economy through which the accumulation of capital in its value form is realized. The size of this part is determined by the magnitude of the already accumulated capital, irrespective of its relations to the consumable part of the surplus value. And just as only the growth of the total social capital allows for the expansion of the single capital entities, so the profitability of the latter is a precondition for the expansion of the total capital. The accumulation of capital implies, then, the expansion of production in relative independence from, and even at the expense of, consumption, and involves a relatively faster growth of means of production than of production in general.

Indicating a successful accumulation of capital, the increasing means of production in turn increase the production of consumption goods through the absolute growth of the variable capital and a greater affluence with respect to capitalists' consumption. Still the question remains: how can the value of this disproportionately expanding constant capital, which retains its capital value in its constantly reproduced and enlarged fixed part (the means of production), be realized through the exchange process in the sphere of circulation? Of course, this question can only arise on the assumption that the capitalist system tends toward a state of equilibrium. If we drop this unwarranted assumption, the problem resolves itself in the accumulation of capital. Throughout its existence capitalism finds itself in a state of disequilibrium, made possible by the capital-labor relation and the production of surplus value. Being determined by the accumulation of capital, the changing allocation of labor changes the market relations in favor of capital goods, although the enlarged means of production, implying a rising productivity, also bring forth an enlarged production of consumer goods. The capital-output ratio may, or may not, increase output in terms of products so as to justify the additional capital. But it cannot do so in value terms unless productivity exceeds the rise of the organic composition of capital. Otherwise the value of the enlarged output will lag behind the value of the accumulated capital, even though both may have become larger.

Seen from the point of view of the total social capital, one part of the produced surplus value, namely that reinvested in additional means of production, cannot be realized within the exchange relations of a given market, for it cannot find an equivalent counterpart within the circulation process. The individual producers of capital goods do of course find a market for their products—at any rate, so long as capital as a whole expands. But they find this market—so to speak—outside of the circulation process of commodity exchange as they drive their production beyond the confines of the given market. What happens here is somewhat similar to the image developed by Keynesian macroeconomics, that is, the expansion of production beyond the effective market demand; with the difference, however, that it is restricted to productive capital expanding in anticipation of future profits and growing markets. It is an addition to the existing capital which, though measured in price and therefore value terms, disrupts the given supply and demand relations insofar as they find their determination in the consumption requirements of capitalist society. The capital-output ratio may remain the same or be altered, yet the out itself changes qualitatively by incorporating a relatively larger mass of capital goods.

This process is made possible (and opaque) by the money form of value and by the fact that the circulating money represents at all times only a part of the total mass of circulating commodities. As any commodity can take the form of money, and the latter any commodity form, capital can be expressed in money terms and money can be considered latent capital. The existing capital represents, *but is not*, a given quantity of money. But through its monetary denomination it can *assume the function of money*. Likewise, money from whatever source can be turned into capital. Although the quantity of money does rise with the general expansion of production, it does not necessarily rise in equal measure. In fact, it is a principle of capital production to minimize the use of commodity money in order to reduce the costs of circulation. There is then no obstacle in the way of a continuous expansion of capital from the monetary side, although a contraction of the economy will appear as a shortage of money because of the contraction of the circulation process.

The mass of capital goods in excess of those required for the simple reproduction of capital and the mass of consumption goods, as determined by the antagonistic distribution relations, represent a part of the total surplus value in the form of additional capital. It appears then that the accumulation of capital takes care of the disequilibrium conditions within which capitalism must move. So long as capital expands with the increasing productivity of labor, there is no realization problem, in spite of the changing allocation of labor associated with it and despite the relatively decreasing variable capital. The relative decrease of consumption only leaves a larger part of the surplus value for purposes of expansion, and the production of means of production proceeds at a faster pace than general production. It is in this manner that capital "deepens" and spreads itself as the industrialization process on a world scale, and in the process realizes the whole of the surplus value. As the expanding capital is expressible in money, the possession of this capital in its physical form fulfills the requirements of capitalist production—that is, the transformation of a given amount of money into a larger one.

It remains true of course that each capitalist enterprise must justify its expansion by the returns on its capital, and to that end must be able to sell its enlarged output on the market. But this market does increase, and only increases, because of the general expansion of capital through additional investments out of the existing surplus value. The reproduction of capital on an enlarged scale—the goal of capitalist production—finds its consummation in the progressive capitalization of the world economy. There is then no *material obstacle* in the way of a continuous expansion of capital, as the world is far from being capitalized, and because all that is required to this end are additional means of production and the application of labor power.

The difficulties of capitalism have thus to be searched for elsewhere, as they are neither to be traced to the physical production process nor to be found in the process of circulation. What remains then as a cause of crisis and stagnation is the accumulation process itself, or rather, the recurrent inability to produce enough surplus value to secure the profitability of the expanding capital. The growing capital increases the output of products. Among the latter are also capital goods, which constitute the physical expansion of capital. In monetary terms, to repeat, the expansion of capital within the total expansion of production raises no problems, as the surplus value involved in this process finds its realization in an enlarged productive apparatus. However, capital in the form of means of production yields no surplus value; it merely transfers its own value, in shorter or longer intervals, to the produced commodities that enter the market. With the relative decrease of variable capital the source of surplus value diminishes with respect to the accumulated capital, even though the capital-output ratio must remain the same.

For the rate of profit not to decline, output must grow faster than the constant capital, which is only another way of saying that the rate of exploitation must exceed the rate of accumulation. As far as can be established on the basis of the unreliable statistics we have, this was the case during the last century, although accumulation was interrupted by a series of depressions. On the basis of the then existing capital structure, the rate of exploitation apparently sufficed to ensure the expansion process. This may explain the rather rapid accumulation of capital during this period. Since the first decade of the present century, however, the capital-output ratio has stabilized, which is to say that the rate of accumulation

has slowed down, relative to the existing capital. But as the accumulation of capital is also a concentration process and thus
plays larger profits into fewer hands, the accumulating capitals
were not for some time aware of the decline in profits. And because the centralization process can raise the rate of profit even in
the absence of capital concentration, simply by the reorganization
and different utilization of the existing capital, a relative stagnation of capital does not at once express itself in lower profits. On
the other hand, the hastened concentration and centralization of
capital can also be seen as measures forced upon capital to maintain its profitability. Insofar as these measures compensate for a
lack of sufficient new investments, they hold down the rising organic composition of capital, thus bolstering the rate of profit at
the expense of accumulation. But while the profit rate may be
maintained, general economic activity stagnates, for it cannot advance without the production of additional capital. Sooner or later,
the stagnation leads to a crisis, which can be overcome through the
resumption of the accumulation process.

As long as the share of surplus value within the value of the
total output allows for both capitalistic consumption and new investments adequate to the already existing capital, the rate of
profit will not fall, even with a rising organic composition of capital, or in bourgeois terms, with the increase of the ratio of capital
to net output. But this is just the point: while the rate of profit
must fall with the rising organic composition of capital, a more
rapid increase of the rate of exploitation, visible in larger output,
prevents this tendency from showing itself in the actual profit
rates. To progress, capitalism must constantly raise the productivity of labor, that is, reinvest in more efficient means of production
through the accumulation of capital. A slowing-down of the rate
of accumulation, or even capital stagnation, while on the one hand
reducing or preventing the rise of the organic composition of capital and thereby stabilizing the rate of profit, on the other hand
will lead to a sudden fall of profits through the reduction of total
production, on account of the lack of new investments. A part of
the surplus value remains in its monetary form, in which it does
not yield surplus value, and to that extent reduces the total mass
of profit over time.

As capitalist production is the *production of capital* via the
production of commodities, a lack of new investments can only

have one cause, namely, the fear that such investments may prove to be unprofitable and therefore senseless. This fear is not a psychological phenomenon but derives directly from the fact that the rate of profit on the functioning capital already shows a strong tendency to decline. The reason for this decline is not discernible, for it has to do with capital as a whole, with the total social mass of surplus value in relation to the total social capital. But while not discernible, it nonetheless affects all individual capitals, although to varying degrees, and determines their individual decisions with regard to investment policies. The fall of the rate of profit precedes the decline, or the arrest, of accumulation, which is thus merely the outward expression of the fall of the rate of profit inherent in the expansion of capital. The falling rate of profit is thus the signal for the disruption of the spiraling disequilibrium of capital production, as a necessary condition for its continuing development.

Without the resumption of the accumulation process, the *raison d'être* for capital production would be gone. It is thus in the capitalist reactions to decreasing profitability that Marx's theory of accumulation finds its obvious verification. These reactions, whatever their consequences, have only one purpose, namely, the increase of surplus value through a further increase of the productivity of labor, for the restoration of the profitability of the expanding capital. This is, and always was, the *only solution* suggested by the capitalists and by the "science of economics" to overcome a period of economic decline, even though this means accumulation for the sake of accumulation, regardless of social consequences.

REVOLUTION
AND
REFORM

Introduction

On the basis of its assumptions, Marx's model of capitalist production could only end in the collapse of the capitalist system. However, this collapse was not conceived of as the automatic outcome of economic processes, independent of human actions, but as the result of the proletarian class struggle:

> Along with the constantly diminishing number of magnates of capital grows the mass of misery, oppression, slavery, degradation, exploitation; but with this too grows the revolt of the working class, a class always increasing in numbers, and disciplined, united, organized by the very mechanism of the process of capitalist production itself. The monopoly of capital becomes a fetter upon the mode of production, which has sprung up and flourished along with it, and under it. Centralization of the means of production and socialization of labor at last reach a point where they are incompatible with their capitalist integument. This integument is burst asunder. The knell of capitalist private property sounds. The expropriators are expropriated.[1]

The history of the labor movement, which from a bourgeois point of view has no connection with the foregoing economic analysis, is from a Marxian point of view of the utmost importance and the very reason for concern with the problems of political economy. This holds with respect to wide-ranging issues of historical materialism, as well as to the narrower question of capitalism's destiny. For Marx, social history is the history of class struggles, determined by the class-related contradictions characterizing any particular social formation. The *general* development of the social forces of production brings forth *particular* social relations of production, and the combination of these determines the ruling ideology as the consciousness of a given mode of production. Material social forces determine ideational development, a fact that is rather obvious and even trivial *after* it has been recognized and formulated.

Class relations and exploitation are as old as known history. But they have different forms depending on the mode in which surplus labor is extracted by a ruling class. This in turn depends on the state of the productive powers available at any particular time. Because a given mode of production is most advantageous for an established ruling class, it will be defended by this class against any alteration that might diminish its power and its control over the social product. By the same token, however, it will hinder the further development of the social powers of production and set itself in opposition to emerging social needs that require changes in the mode of production, and to innovations arising within the process of production itself. The continuous *reproduction* process always changes any particular process of production, but to varying degrees. The changes may be so slow as to be almost imperceptible, which accounts for the static conditions that prevailed in some social formations for long periods of time. But even these societies had a history simply through the alterations, however limited, in the production processes.

Radical or revolutionary changes in modes of production presuppose the rise of new classes within the existing social relations, for history, however determined by objective necessities, has to be actualized through people's subjective determination to alter the existing social relationships. This determination will express itself in a new ideology, but both are the results of the changes that have taken place within the existing social relations of production.

Marx summed up this materialist conception of history, which served as a "leading thread" in his economic studies, as follows:

> In the social production which men carry on they enter into definite relations that are indispensable and independent of their will; these relations correspond to a definite stage of development of their material powers of production. The sum total of these relations of production constitutes the economic structure of society—the real foundation, on which rise legal and political superstructures and to which correspond definite forms of social consciousness. The mode of production in material life determines the general character of the social, political and spiritual processes of life. It is not the consciousness of men that determines their existence, but, on the contrary, their social existence

determines their consciousness. At a certain stage of their development, the material forces of production in society come in conflict with
the existing relations of production, or—what is but a legal expression
of the same thing—with the property relations within which they had
been at work before. From forms of development of the forces of production these relations turn into their fetters. Then comes a period of
social revolution.[2]

If this situation may be *described* as one wherein the "economic structure of society" determines its "legal and political
superstructure" and its "definite forms of social consciousness," in
order to bring out the point made by historical materialism, this
does not imply an actual separation of "structure" and "superstructure" with the latter explained by the former, but merely
states the fact that the material production process is *consciously*
undertaken and thus conceptualizes the identity of a given state of
the social powers of production with its corresponding social production relations. It is in terms of this two-sided totality, at once
material and ideational, that historically evolving social formations
are differentiated.

Although it is possible mentally to break up the totality of
the social production and reproduction process into its various
manifestations in the political, legal, and ideational spheres of social practice, these aspects cannot be concretely isolated and
weighted with respect to their importance within the social system
as a whole. In other words, it is not possible to say that the political, legal, and ideational activities may, *on their own accord*, affect the economic processes and codetermine their development,
for the superstructure *is the expression* of the socioeconomic
structure. This may be grasped by analogy with the value-price relations in capitalism, where the value relations must express themselves in the different form of price. It is not that the superstructure merely reflects the economic base, but that this base is what
it is by virtue of its specific superstructure.

Just as capitalist price relations are both distinguishable and
undistinguishable from value relations, so the superstructure in
any social formation is also separable and inseparable from the
socioeconomic structure. If we speak of the one, we speak of the
other, and in either case we speak of no more than the material
production processes that allow society to exist. This implies, of
course, that a fundamental change of society affects its "structure"

and "superstructure" simultaneously, that is, that no socially significant political, legal, or ideational change can take place apart from changes in the relations of production and the state of the productive forces of society, and that basic changes only occur in the latter accompanied by corresponding alterations of the "superstructure." It is therefore not possible to change a social system from the side of its "superstructure" alone—as for instance, by way of politically induced reforms—for such changes must always stop short at that point where they would jeopardize the existing social production relations. A change of the latter is only possible by way of revolution, which overthrows the "base" together with the "superstructure."

However, due to the development of the social forces of production, a social formation represents not only itself but also another society in embryonic form. The gestation period of the new society varies in accordance with the degree of change, spontaneous or consciously induced, in the social reproduction process. In societies without such changes, the productive forces and social relations will remain stagnant. Such societies have no history, although they may display class relations of one sort or another. Historical materialism concerns itself solely with developing societies. But changes in these societies are bound sooner or later to break down the stagnation of more static societies and alter their course.

Although incorporating technical innovations, the social forces of production are not reducible to technology. The transformation of the relatively static feudal-mercantilist economy into the dynamic capitalist system, for instance, was due not to technological changes but to the extension of a given technology over a wider field of application, by way of changes in the relations of production that opened the way for the vast development of the productive forces experienced in the Industrial Revolution.

The precapitalist era was based on agriculture, considered the only source of a surplus product making possible the nonproductive life of the land-owning ruling class. At least part of the total social product was a "gift of nature," exceeding the results of the applied agricultural labor. This state of affairs found expression in the economic theories of the Physiocrats, who spoke of the "sterility" of all production outside of agriculture. In this theory, in contrast to mercantilist notions, a surplus arose in the sphere of production, not in that of circulation, or the exchange of commodities. Indeed, there was only a minimal exchange between agricultural products and those manufactured in the urban centers. The surplus was extracted from peasant labor, operating under conditions of self-sufficiency, which included the labor-producing agricultural implements; it was thus a clear case of expropriation, not of exchange relations. Whatever manufactures and handicrafts there were implied a technology exclusively and directly devoted to satisfying the needs and habits of the ruling class. There was also exploitation in the cities, in the sense that the city laborers produced not for themselves but for the ruling class, even though part of their products also served their own needs. But both their products and their surplus product were made possible by the agricultural surplus. Whatever technical development there was, was determined not by the accumulation of capital but by the needs and habits of the ruling class. If there was accumulation, it took not the abstract form of exchange value but that of use value.

With the means of production in the hands of the agricultural producers, the latter's exploitation implied compulsory labor, which was also extended over the infrastructure as forced or corvée labor. Under these conditions, any improvement of the productivity of agricultural labor would merely increase the surplus product falling to the landowning class and its state apparatus. There was, then, no incentive for technical innovation on the part of the peasantry, but rather the desire to work as little as possible in order to reduce the degree of their exploitation. The resulting stagnation of agricultural production set a limit to technological development in general, as it was almost totally dependent on the agricultural surplus. To increase this surplus was the sole concern of both the ruling classes and the urban population, as a precondition for the satisfaction of wants and the betterment of their living standards. This was eventually accomplished through the incorporation of agriculture into the exchange relations within and between the urban centers, brought about through a further division of labor within the existing class relations. In order to make the agricultural surplus grow, it was necessary to deprive the peasant population of control over their means of production and so force them out of their self-sufficiency and into the competitive market economy.

This was a twofold accomplishment, effected from the side

of agriculture and from that of the merchant class as mediators of the exchange process. It involved the extension of market relations and commodity production over all of social production and the gradual transformation of labor into wage labor. While the commercialization of agriculture in England and France occasioned the "enclosure" movement, which drove a great deal of the peasantry from the land or transformed them into agricultural wage laborers, it also extended cottage industry, or the "putting out" system, from a supplementary to a main form of production. Provided by merchants with means of production and raw materials, peasants turned into wage laborers and merchants into capitalist entrepreneurs. Social relations became in increasing measure capital-labor relations and it was this fact that, by its generalization, expressed the growing social powers of production and the emergence of a new class accumulating surplus labor as surplus value and capital.

To cut a long and rather well-known story short, it may be said that with the increasing capitalization of agriculture, the way was open to bringing the whole of social production under the dominance of capital. Occupying a position between the landed aristocracy and the rural and urban proletariat, the middle class widened its field of operation with the extension of wage labor and the competitive pursuit of exchange value as an abstract and apparently limitless form of wealth, bound not to any specific form of property but to all forms in which surplus value materialized itself. New methods of production evolved to increase the profits on invested capital and technical innovations were searched for and introduced, not for the limited purpose of increasing the well-being and the luxuries of the ruling class, but in order to extract more surplus value out of all types of labor. While not in theory, at any rate in practice the capitalists were fully aware of the fact that a man's labor "may mean either the personal act of working, or the effect which is produced by that act. In the first sense, it must be allowed that a man's labor is properly his own . . . but it does not follow . . . that the effect of his laboring . . . must likewise be properly his own."[3]

With surplus value the goal of production and wage labor the only means of existence for a growing number of people, production accelerated in accordance with increasing exploitation. Of course, this social transformation was accompanied by all sorts of serious dislocations of the economy and its political system, affecting not only the working population but all of society. Industrial capital and its demand for profits grew at a relatively faster pace than capital based on agriculture, and set itself in opposition to the latter. Surplus value in the form of rent, thanks to the monopoly position of landed property, escaped the averaging process of profit rates and lowered the profits of industrial capital. The antagonism between the landed interests and those of the advancing bourgeoisie characterized the early stages of capitalist development and found expression in the aspirations of the bourgeoisie for political power and control of the state. This antagonism resolved itself in the bourgeois revolutions, which in one way or another turned feudal relations into the capitalist relations of production and production itself into the production of capital.

To be sure, this historical process did not manifest its nature as clearly as did its final outcome. Ideologies encompass the past as well as the future and refer not to special but to putative general interests. They can thus be isolated from the specific purposes and concerns they serve under particular conditions and class relations. It is by virtue of this that they are indispensable for the maintenance as well as for the overthrow of given social relations, precisely because they cut across otherwise unbridgeable class differences. While history is being made, the apparently indivisible unity of the mode of production and its political and ideational superstructure is rent apart and seems to reveal competing ideologies with independent powers. But in retrospect, once society has changed, everything comes together again to constitute a particular historical period, characterized by the productive forces released by it, the social production relations associated with them, and the apparently extraeconomic "superstructural" expressions of the material production process.

History is clearly the history of social changes of modes of production and class relations, which have led to capitalist society, the subject matter of Marx's concerns and those of the class at whose expense it exists. There is therefore no longer any history for the bourgeoisie: the development of any new mode of production would imply its own demise as a ruling class. From the point of view of historical materialism, however, capitalism must be analyzed with respect to its specific class relations and their effect upon the development of capital production. Obviously, the emergence of these class relations allowed for an enormous increase of the social powers of production in the form of the accumulation of capital. If the latter is the life's blood of capitalist society, it is here also that this system's historical limitations will be found. If there are none, then of course the bourgeoisie is right and history has come to an end.

Marx's theory of proletarian revolution is thus an integral part of his theory of capitalist accumulation. As capital expands, so does the working class. But while accumulation assures the rule and comfort of the capitalist class, this is due only to the constant increase in the exploitation of labor power, which may or may not be compensated for by improvements of the workers' living standards. This depends on changing value relations, on whether or not the lower exchange value of labor power will be the value equivalent of a greater quantity of use values. According to Marx, to recall, the changing value structure of capital in the course of its accumulation diminishes the rate of profit, even with a rising rate of surplus value, because the mass of surplus value is reduced due to the decline of the variable relative to the constant capital, or, what is the same, to the decrease in the number of workers with respect to the total capital amassed. Of course, just as the lower exchange value of labor power may not contradict a rise of wages in use-value terms, so a rise in the organic composition of capital may be compensated for by an increase of productivity, overcoming the decline of surplus value in each commodity by a disproportionally greater quantity of commodities, so as to restore, or even surpass, the customary rate of profit on capital. This depends in turn on the possibility of a sufficiently high rate of accumulation of capital. This makes the rate of profit in Marx's system indefinite and, aside from the specific assumptions made by Marx in expounding his theory, unpredictable, in a strictly empirical sense. What will interest us here is not so much the economic development of capital as the expectations based on it with regard to the evolution of a revolutionary consciousness on the part of the working class. Like all true revolutionaries, and notwithstanding his scientific bent and materialistic outlook, Marx was a romantic in his thoughts, feeling, and attitudes. Although convinced that "no social order ever disappears before all the productive forces, for which there is room in it, have been developed; and new higher relations of production never appear before the material conditions of their existence have been matured in the womb of the old society,"[4] he saw in the maturing proletariat the most important productive force straining against the capitalist relations of production. History, in Marx's view, does nothing, but must be made by people, by way of class struggle. As an ardent student of the French Revolution, and an observer of, as well as participant in, the revolutionary upheavals of 1848—during which the working class, even within the context of bourgeois aspirations, displayed itself as an independent anti-capitalist force—Marx saw capitalism's future preordained with the proletarian revolution. It was of course not possible, and from Marx's point of view also superfluous, to determine in advance when the capitalist relations of production would cease to further the development of the social forces of production and thus release the objective need for social change. All that was necessary for revolution was the presence of a force within the shell of capitalism representing new social relations in conflict with the capitalistically limited forces of production. In a developed capitalism, any prolonged and deep-going crisis could lead to a revolutionary situation and to the overthrow of capitalism. By breaking the crisis cycle of capital production, the way would then be open for a further unhampered social development. In the early Marxist movement this was seen as a realistic possibility, due to the fact of a growing socialist movement and the spreading recognition that there was an alternative to capitalism.

Objective conditions, changing in the course of capitalist development, would bring forth a subjective readiness on the part of the working class to change the social relations of production. The theory and practice of a growing labor movement was seen as a unitary phenomenon, due to the self-expansion and at the same time the self-limitation of capitalist development. Marx's *Capital*, employing the methods of scientific analysis, was able to proffer a theory that synthesized the class struggle and the general contradictions of capitalism. The actual class struggle would—in time—turn class consciousness into revolutionary consciousness, and the fight over wages and working conditions would become a struggle for the abolition of the wage system, that is, for the ending of capitalism. Class consciousness was seen by the Marxists as one of the results of capital accumulation, emerging out of the master-slave relation in the direct production process, the disproportional increase of exploitation within the capital-labor exchange relations, the observably increasing misery of growing layers of the unemployed and the unemployable, the general wretchedness experienced during periods of depression, and the insecurity prevailing under all capitalist circumstances. On the positive side, there was the capitalistically enforced concentration of great numbers of workers in all industries, inducing the recognition that the laborer was a member of a social class and thus was able to proceed from individual to collective attempts to improve his working conditions. The results of the workers' struggles were seen not only in the improvement of their living standards but also in the recognition of their growing strength in the contest between capital and labor, and in the attendant development of their self-confidence both as individuals and as members of a class. It was thought that out of this class itself and its constant confrontation with the bourgeoisie would arise not only a willingness to assert the workers' temporary interests but also a growing conviction that social production could be carried on outside the capital-labor relation.

These expectations were to be disappointed. Although a growing number of workers became adherents of revolutionary ideas and organized themselves in socialist organizations, a greater number remained immune to socialist ideologies, even though they were prepared to fight for higher wages and better working conditions. The economic struggles found organization in the trade unions; but these organizations did not, as Marx had expected they would, become "schools for socialism," but remained what they were at their outset, a mere phenomenon of the commodity character of labor power. Their concern was with the price of labor power within the capitalist market relations. What socialist ideas had been associated with trade unionism were gradually jettisoned as an unnecessary ballast, and even an embarrassment, hindering the ascent and endangering the legal status of those organizations.

Marx's maxim that the consciousness of a time is that of its social and material production relations holds also for the working class. While the class struggle, as seen with socialist eyes, was supposed to change the consciousness of the laborers, and to some extent actually did so, this change was not in the direction of socialism as a practical goal. Although the class struggle implied awareness of the opposed interests of labor and capital, it did not challenge the capital-labor relation itself, but merely the degree of exploitation as measured by the wage-profit ratio. In order to be effective, the class struggle has to be organized, and the gains made in this struggle must be sustained by making the organizations permanent. The greater the number of organized workers and the need for coordinated actions, the less was their own initiative in determining these activities. The decision-making powers became those of a centralized leadership in a hierarchical bureaucratic organizational structure that came to look upon itself as an instrument to secure its own special interests as a precondition for its activities in behalf of the working class.

Of course, it was the workers themselves who built these organizations and delegated to them control over their own activities. The fact that they did not leave these organizations could only mean that their own demands coincided with those brought forward in their name by the leaders occupying the commanding posts in their organizations. Now, it is true that these leaders, in any case those in the socialist parties, professed to consider the fight for capitalistic reforms as a mere means to reach the revolutionary goals and not as an end in itself; but actually, the struggle for reforms was the only one possible, bringing with it types of organization that were only able to function within the given relations of production and were thus bound, by their very growth and successes, to turn into defenders of the capitalist system, as a precondition of their own existence. They could have no conceivable function in a socialist society, and for that reason did not think in terms of revolutionary change, except rhetorically where this seemed opportune.

The supposed "dialectic" between reform and revolution—the everyday struggle for immediate demands changing into a struggle against the system itself—did not actually lead to a noticeable increase in revolutionary class consciousness, but merely issued into organizational forms of class struggle incapable of making the leap from reform to revolution. To the controlling ideology of bourgeois society was now added the controlling influence of nonrevolutionary organizations over the organized as well as unorganized parts of the working class in a two-sided effort to hold the class struggle within the confines of capitalist society. Marx's expectations as to the revolutionary effect of capital accumulation upon the consciousness of the working class turned out to be erroneous, at least in the ascending stage of capitalist development.

Capitalism
and
Socialism

Whereas Marx's analysis of the social contradictions inherent in capitalism refers to the general trend of capitalistic development, the actual class struggle is a day-to-day affair and necessarily adjusts itself to changing social conditions. These adjustments are bound to find a reflection in Marxian theory. The history of capitalism is thus also the history of Marxism. Although interrupted by periods of crisis and depression, capitalism was able to maintain itself until now by the continuous expansion of capital and its extension into space through an accelerating increase of the productivity of labor. It proved possible not only to regain a temporarily lost profitability but to increase it sufficiently to continue the accumulation process as well as to improve the living standards of the great bulk of the laboring population. The economic class struggle within rising capitalism, far from endangering the latter, provided an additional capitalist incentive for hastening the expansion of capital through the application of technological innovations and the increase of labor efficiency by organizational means. While the organized labor movement grew and the conditions of the working class improved, this fact itself strengthened the capitalist adversary and weakened the oppositional inclinations of the proletariat. But without revolutionary working class actions, Marxism remains just the theoretical comprehension of capitalism. It is thus not the theory of an actual social practice, able to change the world, but functions as an ideology in anticipation of such a practice. Its interpretation of reality, however correct, does not affect this reality to any important extent. It merely describes the conditions in which the proletariat finds itself, leaving their change to the indeterminate future. The very conditions in which the proletariat finds itself in an *ascending* capitalism subject it to the rule of capital and to an impotent, merely ideological opposition at best.

The successful expansion of capital and the amelioration of the conditions of the workers led to a spreading doubt regarding the validity of Marx's abstract theory of capital development. Apart from recurring crisis situations, empirical reality seemed in fact to contradict Marx's expectations. Even where his theory was upheld, it was no longer associated with a practice ideologically aimed at the overthrow of capitalism. Marxism turned into an evolutionary theory, expressing the wish to transcend the capitalist system by way of constant reforms favoring the working class. Marxian revisionism, in both covert and overt form, led to a kind of synthesis of Marxism and bourgeois ideology, as the theoretical corollary to the increasing practical integration of the labor movement into capitalist society.

As an organized mass movement within ascending capitalism, socialism could be "successful" only as a reformist movement. By adapting itself politically to the framework of bourgeois democracy and economically to that of the labor market, the socialist movement challenged neither the basic social production relations nor the political structures evolved by these relations. As regards its significance, furthermore, Marxism has been more of a regional than an international movement, as may be surmised from its precarious hold in the Anglo-Saxon countries. It was above all a movement of a continental Europe, even though it developed its theory by reflection on capitalistically more advanced England. While in the latter country capitalism was already the dominant mode of production, the bourgeoisie of continental Europe was still struggling to free itself from the remaining shackles of the feudal regime and to create national entities within which capitalist production could progress. The economic and political turmoil accompanying the formation of the various European national states involved the proletariat along with the bourgeoisie and created a political consciousness oriented toward social change.

While opposing the entrenched reactionary forces of the past, the rising bourgeoisie also confronted the working class insofar as this class tried to reduce the degree of its exploitation. Despite this early confrontation, the working class was forced to support the aspirations of the bourgeoisie, if only to create the conditions for its own emancipation. From the very beginning of the working-class movement in continental Europe, therefore, there existed simultaneously the need to fight against capitalist exploitation and the need to support the development of capitalism as well as the political institutions it created for itself. The common interest of both the emerging classes—the bourgeoisie and the proletariat—in overcoming the vested interests of the past was already a form of integration that found its reflection in the strategy and tactics of the labor movement, that is, in its striving for political power within bourgeois democracy and the alleviation of economic conditions of the working class within the confines of political eocnomy. As a political movement, however, Marxism could not dispense with its socialist goal, even though practically it could gain no more for the working class than any of the apolitical movements that arose in the established capitalist nations, such as England and the United States, which restricted themselves to the fight for higher wages and better working conditions without challenging the existing social relations of production.

It was thus historical peculiarities that determined the character of the socialist movements in continental Europe—that is, the partial identity of proletarian and bourgeois political aspirations within the rising capitalism. Marxian theory implied preparation for a socialist revolution within a general revolutionary process that could as yet only issue into the triumph of the bourgeoisie, the destruction of the semifeudal state, and the dominance of capital production. After these accomplishments, the road would be open for a struggle restricted to the labor-capital antagonism, which would first pose the question of a proletarian revolution. The way to foster this general development was by partaking in the as yet incomplete bourgeois transformation and by pushing forward the capitalist forces of production, through economic demands that could be met only by an accelerated increase of the productivity of labor and the rapid accumulation of capital.

In the Anglo-Saxon countries, however, the special issues that agitated the European labor movement no longer existed, or did not arise at all, as the capitalist mode of production and bourgeois rule constituted the uncontested social reality. Here the conditions that were goals for the European labor movement were already an established fact and reduced the struggle between labor and capital to the economic sphere. Class consciousness found its expression in pure trade unionism; the ongoing monopolization of capital was echoed by the attempted "monopolization" of labor, as one of the developed forms of general competition in expanding capitalism. This situation foreshadowed the continental labor movement's further development and with it that of its Marxist, or socialist, wing. The more capitalism came into its own, the more the idea of revolutionary change fell by the wayside. The growing trade unions severed their early close relationship with the socialist parties, and the latter themselves concentrated their efforts on purely parliamentary activities to press for social legislation favorable to the working class, through the extension, not the abolition, of bourgeois democracy. For the time being, and the foreseeable future, as Eduard Bernstein, one of the leading "revisionists" of the German Social Democracy and the Second International, put it, "the movement was everything and the goal nothing."

However, organized ideologies do not abdicate easily, and this the less so as their proponents defend not only their convictions but also their positions within the organizations that are supposed to realize the ideological goals. The rather quick rise of the socialist movement allowed for an organizational structure increasingly attractive to intellectuals and capable of supporting a bureaucracy whose existence was bound up with the steady growth and permanence of the organization. The hierarchical structure of capitalist society repeated itself in that of the socialist organizations and trade unions as the differentiation between the commanding leadership and the obeying rank and file. And just as the workers accommodated themselves to the general conditions of capitalism, so they accepted the similar structure of the socialist movement as an unavoidable requirement for effective organizational activity. Although in an entirely different sense from the way the phrase is usually understood, this found a rather apt expression in the interpretation of Social Democracy as "a state within the state."

As in the capitalist world at large, in the Social Democratic movement too there was a right wing, a center, and a left wing, although the struggle between these tendencies remained purely ideological. The actual practice of the movement was reformist, untouched by left-wing rhetoric and indirectly aided by it, as it provided a socialist label for opportunistic activities aimed no longer at the overthrow of capitalism but at organizational growth within the system. Supposedly, bourgeois democracy and capitalism itself would through their own dynamics prepare the social conditions for a qualitative change corresponding to a state of socialism. This comfortable idea was held by all the tendencies within the socialist movement, whether they still believed in revolutionary action to accomplish the transformation of capitalism into socialism, or assumed the possibility of a peaceful nationalization of the means of production through the winning, with a socialist majority, of control of the state.

In any case, the social transformation was cast into the faraway future and played no part in the everyday activity of the labor movement. Capitalism would have to run its course, not only in the already highly developed capitalist nations but even in those just in the process of evolving the capitalist relations of production. It remained true, of course, that devastating crises interrupted the steady capitalization of the world economy, but like the social miseries accompanying the early stages of capitalist production, its susceptibility to crises and depressions was now also adjudged a mark of its infancy, which would be lost as it matured. With the concentration and centralization of capital by way of competition, competition itself would be progressively eliminated and with it the anarchy of the capitalist market. Centralized control of the economy on a national and eventually an international scale would allow for conscious social regulation of both production and distribution and create the objective conditions for a planned economy no longer subject to regulation by the law of value.

This idea was forcefully expressed by Rudolf Hilferding, whose economic writings were widely regarded as a continuation of Marx's *Capital*.[1] Leaning heavily on the work of Michael I. Tugan-Baranowsky, who deduced from the "equilibrium conditions" of Marx's reproduction schemata (in the second volume of *Capital*) the theoretical feasibility of a limitless expansion of capital,[2] Hilferding saw this possibility still very much impaired by difficulties in the capitalist circulation process which hindered the full realization of surplus value. He perceived the capital concentration process in the course of accumulation as a merging of banking capital with industrial capital to create a form of capital best described as "financial capital." It implied the progressive cartelization of capital, tending toward a single General Cartel that would gain complete control over the state and the economy. As the progressive elimination of competition meant an increasing disturbance of the objective price relations, this would mean, of course, that the price mechanism of classical theory would cease to be operative and that the law of value would therefore be unable to serve as the regulator of the capitalist economy.

We are here not interested in Hilferding's rather confused theory of crisis as a problem of the realization of surplus value, due to disproportionalities between the different spheres of production and between production and consumption, because in his view these difficulties do not arrest the trend towards the complete cartelization of the capitalist economy.[3] With the coming to pass of the General Cartel, prices would be consciously determined so as to assure the system's viability. They would no longer express value relations but the consciously organized distribution of the social product in terms of products. Under such conditions, money as the universal and most general form of value could be eliminated. The continuing social antagonisms would no longer arise from the system of production, which would be completely socialized, but exclusively from that of distribution, which would retain its class character. In this fashion capitalism would be overcome through its own development; the anarchy of production and that type of capitalism analyzed by Marx in *Capital* would be ended. The expropriation of capital or, what is the same, the socialization of production, will thus be capitalism's own accomplishment.

Of course, like Marx's "logical" end result of the capitalist accumulation process, the concept of the General Cartel merely serves to illustrate the trend of concrete capitalistic development. But while in Marx's model capitalism finds an inevitable end in decreasing profitability, Hilferding's General Cartel points to an "economically conceivable" capitalist system able to maintain itself indefinitely through the control of the whole of social production. If capitalism tends toward collapse, this is not for economic reasons but must be seen as a political process, as dependent on the conscious resolve to extend the capitalistically achieved socialization of production into the sphere of distribution. Such a transformation is possible only through a sudden political change that transfers control of production from the hands of the cartelized private capital into those of the state. This transformation thus requires the socialist capture of political power within otherwise unchanged production relations.

Such a development seems conceivable given the constant

growth of socialist organization, striving for political power within bourgeois democracy and able to win the allegiance of always larger masses of the electorate, and finally leading to a socialist parliamentary majority and to the control of government. The socialist state would then institute socialism by decree, through the nationalization, or—what is thought to be the same—the socialization of the decisive branches of industry. This would suffice to extend the socialist type of production and distribution gradually to the whole society. Due to capitalism's specific form as financial capital, Hilferding suggested that it would be enough to nationalize the larger banks to initiate the socialist transformation. With this, the economic dictatorship of capital would be turned into what Hilferding—in deference to Marx and Engels—called the "dictatorship of the proletariat."

All this would of course depend on the persistence of the political institutions of bourgeois democracy and the labor movement's fidelity to its socialist ideology. Would the bourgeoisie honor the parliamentary game if it found itself on the losing side? Would the character of the socialist movement remain the same despite its increasing influence and organizational power within the capitalist regime? Even apart from such unasked questions, it is unclear why, if there is no "economically conceivable" end to capitalism, there should arise a political opportunity for its abolition. An economically secure capitalism would guarantee its political security. Moreover, if capitalism socializes the production process on its own, this "socialization" includes the maintenance of the social production relations as class relations, to be carried over into the nationalized form of social production. Indeed, in Hilferding's exposition, the change from private to governmental control does not affect the relation between wage labor and capital, except insofar as economic control is transferred from the bourgeoisie to the state apparatus. Thus socialism, in his view, means the completion of the centralization process inherent in competitive capital expansion, the transformation of private into "social" capital and its control by the state, and therewith the possibility for centrally planned production, which would be distinguished from organized capitalism mainly by allowing for a more equitable distribution.

The theoretical progress made in the socialist movement since its beginnings within the incomplete bourgeois revolution thus consisted in the assertion that, just as the socialist movement fostered capitalist development, fully developed capitalism and bourgeois democracy were now opening the way to socialism. If the workers, for historical reasons, and however reluctantly, aided the rise of democratic capitalism, this very same capitalism was now preparing with equal reluctance, but unavoidably, the conditions for a socialist transformation. The development of wage labor and capital was thus a reciprocative evolution, in which both workers and capitalists functioned as precursors of socialism through the accumulation of capital. All that was necessary in order to play an active part in this historical process was to increase the general awareness of its happening, so as to hasten its completion.

For Hilferding capitalism had already reached its highest stage of development. Notwithstanding the imperialist war and the revolutions in its wake, the prevailing "late capitalism" was for him an organized capitalism, no longer determined by "economic laws" but by political considerations. The capitalist principle of competition was making room for the socialist planning principle through state interventions in the economy. The class struggles over wages and working conditions changed into political struggles, and the wage itself into a "political wage," by way of the parliamentary accomplishments of the socialist parties in the field of social legislation, such as arbitration laws, collective bargaining, unemployment insurance, and so forth, which augmented the "economic wage" and freed it from its value determination. According to Hilferding, the state was not simply, as Marx had called it, the "executive committee of the ruling class," but reflected, through the medium of political parties, the changing power relations between different classes—all of them sharing in state power. The workers' class struggle turns into a fight for the determination of social policy and finally for the control of "bourgeois democracy," or "formal democracy," because democracy belongs to none but the working class, which first had made it a reality through its struggle against the bourgeoisie. Through democracy the workers will gain the government, the army, the police, and the judiciary, and thus realize their longing for a socialist society.[4]

In view of the actual course of events, Hilferding's rationalization of the procapitalistic policies of the socialist parties seems to be of no interest at all. The "democratic road to socialism" led directly to the fascist dictatorships and to Hilferding's own miserable end. However, his concept of socialism as a planned economy under governmental control, one that assumes the functions previously exercised by the centralized but private capital, characterizes almost all of the existing images of a socialist society.

As Marx stopped his analysis short of the expected overthrow of the capitalist system and, aside from occasional very general remarks about the basic character of the new society, left the construction of socialism to the future, so Hilferding stopped short at capitalism's "last stage," without entering into a more detailed investigation of the problems of the transformation of "organized capitalism" into the socialist organization of society. His party colleague Karl Kautsky, however, as the most eminent of Marxists after Marx and Engels, felt obliged to offer some speculations about the possible postrevolutionary situation.[5] He too saw the "expropriation of the expropriators" in the completion of society's democratization, to be accomplished by the working class. The immediate measures to be taken were for him those democratic goals the bourgeoisie itself had failed to bring about—that is, the unrestricted vote, a free press, separation of church and state, disarmament, the replacement of the army by a militia, and progressive taxation. Because class relations had existed for thousands of years and were still deeply ingrained in human consciousness, Kautsky felt that they would not be overcome all at once. Only equality in education would gradually do away with class prejudices. Most of all, however, unemployment would have to be abolished through a system of unemployment insurance that would raise the market value of labor power. Wages would rise and profits diminish or disappear altogether. There would be no need to chase the capitalists away from their leading position in industry, because under the changed conditions the bourgeoisie would most likely prefer to sell their property rights, recognizing that political power in the hands of the working class is incompatible with a capitalist mode of production.

A jest on the part of Marx—to the effect that perhaps the cheapest way to socialism would be the buying-out of the capitalists—Kautsky elevated into a political program. But who would buy the capitalist property? Part of it, Kautsky related, could be bought by the workers themselves, other parts by cooperatives, and the rest by governmental agencies on the local and national

level. The big monopolies, however, could be expropriated outright as detrimental to all social classes, including the smaller capitalists. And because the monopolies constitute such a large part of
the economy, their expropriation would enhance the otherwise
more gradual transformation of private into public property. It
would also allow for a conscious regulation of production and thus
end its determination by value relations. Although labor-time calculation would continue to *aid* the formation of prices, it would no
longer *rule* production and distribution. Money too would lose its
commodity and capital character by being reduced to a mere
means of circulation. The continued utilization of prices and money
would imply, of course, the continuation of the wage system, even
though wages would no longer reflect supply and demand in the
labor market. There would also be wage differentials, in order to
facilitate the allocation of the social labor, which would not, however, prevent a general rise of all wages. Of course, capital would
have to be accumulated and compensation would have to be paid
for the loss of the property rights of the capitalists. Taxes would
have to be raised, for the various and enlarged state functions. For
all these reasons, productivity would have to be increased beyond
the level achieved in the old capitalism, so as to make a higher living standard possible.

   Although preferring compensation for the loss of the capitalists' property, Kautsky is not sure that this will actually be done,
but leaves this issue for the future to decide. He realizes that with
compensation, surplus value, once directly extracted by the capitalists, would still fall to them in terms of claims on the government. However, this extra expense would disappear with the accumulation of additional capital, thus ending the continued exploitation. Besides, Kautsky remarks slyly, if capitalist property
were to exist only in the form of claims on the new public owners,
this unearned income could easily be taxed away. Compensation
would after all amount to confiscation, albeit in a less brutal form.

   The watchword of socialism is, then: more work and higher
productivity. In this respect, according to Kautsky, socialists could
learn a lot from the production methods of the large U.S. corporations. What is more, these methods, as yet limited to the gigantic
trusts, could be even more effective when extended to the whole
of society. The socialist organization of production is thus well
prepared by capitalism and need not be newly invented. The only

requirement is to change the accidental and anarchic character of capitalist production into a consciously regulated production concerned with social needs.

Kautsky's exceedingly tame vision of the state of the future and its relation to the socialist economy was still considered by the right-wing socialists as unwarranted and even dangerous, a threat to the steady progress of the Social Democratic movement. They envisioned this progress in terms of a pure trade unionism of the British and American type, and a pure parliamentarism, which would enable the party to enter into coalitions with bourgeois parties and, sooner or later, perhaps, into government positions. To that end, the Marxist ideology would have to be sacrificed in favor of such evolutionary principles as those propounded by Eduard Bernstein. But Kautsky was the leading Marxist authority and quite unwilling to denounce the Marxist heritage. He was also impressed by the 1905 revolutionary upheavals in Russia and by the great mass strikes that occurred around the same time in a number of European countries. A socialist revolution appeared to him, while not an immediate, nevertheless a future possibility. In this spirit, he wrote his most radical work, *The Road to Power*, against the pure reformism that actuated the socialist parties.[6]

Socialism and its presupposition, political power in the hands of the proletarian state, Kautsky wrote in this work, could not be reached by an imperceptible, gradual, and peaceful transformation of capitalism through social reforms, but only in the manner foreseen by Marx. State power must be conquered. On this point there existed an affinity between the ideas of Marx and Engels and those of Blanqui, with the sole difference that while the latter relied on the *coup d'état*, executed by a minority, Marx and Engels looked to revolutionary actions by the broad masses of the working class —the only revolutionary force in modern capitalism—to lead to a proletarian state, that is, to the dictatorship of the proletariat.

Kautsky's insistence upon the revolutionary content of the labor movement led to a division of the socialist party, in a general way, into an "orthodox" and a "revisionist" wing, whereby the first seemingly dominated ideologically while the other determined the actual practice. Of course, this division was not peculiar to German Social Democracy but, via the Second International, played a part in all socialist organizations. In addition, there were other movements opposing Marxist theory and practice, such as the anarcho-communists, the syndicalists, and the apolitical labor movements in the Anglo-Saxon countries. But it was the Marxist movement which the bourgeoisie recognized as the most important threat to its rule, for it had developed an effective counter-ideology able to subvert the capitalist system. In any case, the success of the apparently "Marxist" revolution in Russia in 1917, its repercussions in the Central European nations, and finally, the subsequent division of the world into capitalist and "socialist" countries, led to a situation wherein any kind of social upheaval in any part of the world received and still receives the label "Marxism."

At this point, however, we are still dealing with the prerevolutionary socialist movement, which found in Hilferding and Kautsky its most exemplary spokesmen. It was their interpretation of Marxism, in the light of changed social conditions, that dominated the socialist ideology. For both, socialism implied the capture of political power through the conquest of the state, either by an evolutionary or a revolutionary process. For both of them, too, capitalism had already prepared the ground for a socialist system of production. All that remained was to remove the value determination of capitalist production, its subjugation to the commodity fetishism of the competitive market, and to organize production and distribution in accordance with the ascertainable needs of society.

It is of course true that Marx and Engels acknowledged the obvious, namely, that the overthrow of capitalism demands the overthrow of its state. For them, the political aspect of the proletarian revolution exhausts itself in overwhelming the capitalist state apparatus with all the means required to this end. The victorious working class would neither institute a new state nor seize control of the existing state, but exercise its dictatorship so as to be able to realize its *real goal*, the appropriation of the means of production and their irrevocable transformation into social means of production in the most literal sense, that is, as under the control of the association of free and equal producers. Although assuming functions previously associated with those of the state, this dictatorship is not to become a new state, but a means to the elimination of all suppressive measures through the ending of class relations. There is no room for a "socialist state" in socialism, even though there is the need for a central direction of the socialized economy, which, however, is itself a part of the organization of the associated producers and not an independent entity set against them.

Of course, for reasons not as yet discernible, this might be altogether utopian, as thus would be a socialist society in the Marxian sense. It has to be tried in a revolutionary situation if a serious effort is to be made to reach the classless society. It may be forced upon the workers by objective conditions, quite aside from whether or not they understand all its implications. But it may also fail, if the proletariat abdicates its own dictatorship to a separately organized new state machine that usurps control over society. It is also not possible to foresee under what particular concrete social conditions the revolutionary process might unfold, and whether or not the mere extension and intensification of dictatorial rule will degenerate into a new state assuming independent powers. Whatever the case may be, it is not through the state that socialism can be realized, as this would exclude the self-determination of the working class, which is the essence of socialism. State rule perpetuates the divorce of the workers from the means of production, on which their dependence and exploitation rests, and thus also perpetuates social class relations.

However, it was precisely the attempt to overcome the apparently utopian elements of Marxian doctrine which induced the theoreticians of the Second International to insist upon the state as the instrument for the realization of socialism. Although they were divided on the question of how to achieve control of the state, they were united in their conviction that the organization of the new society is the state's responsibility. It was their sense of reality that made them question Marx's abstract concepts of the revolution and the construction of socialism, bringing these ideas down to earth and in closer relation to the concretely given possibilities.

Indeed, the construction of a socialist system is no doubt a most formidable undertaking. Even to think about it is already of a bewildering complexity defying easy or convincing solutions. It certainly seems to be out of reach for the relatively uneducated working class. It would require the greatest expertise in the understanding and management of social phenomena and the most careful approach to all reorganizational problems, if it is not to end in dismal failure. It demands an over-all view of social needs, as well as special qualifications for those attending to them, and thus institutions designed to assure the social reproduction process. Such institutions must have enough authority to withstand all irrational objections and thus must have the support of government which, by sanctioning these decisions, makes them its own. Most of all, the even flow of production must not be interfered with and all unnecessary experimentation must be avoided, so that it would be best to continue with proven methods of production and the production relations on which they were based.

In Marxian theory, a period of social revolution ensues when the existing social relations of production become a hindrance to the utilization and further development of the social forces of production. It is by a change of the social relations of production that the hampered social powers of production find their release. Their further expansion might, *but need not*, require a quantitative increase in the social powers of production. By ending the drive to "accumulate for the sake of accumulation" and with it the various restrictions due to this type of abstract wealth production, the available productive power of social labor is set free in a qualitatively different system of production geared to the rationally considered needs of society.

In capitalism the productive forces of social labor, which appear as the productive power of capital, limit their own expansion through the decrease of surplus value in the course of capital accumulation. The applications of science and technology merely hasten this process and become themselves barriers to the formation of capital. But without this formation, production must decline even with respect to the capitalistically determined social needs, first with respect to the enlarged reproduction of capital, and then also with regard to simple reproduction, which would mean the end of the capitalist system. Concretely, this process takes the form not only of recurrent periods of depressions and a long-term trend of economic decline, but also of capitalism's inability to avail itself even of the productive forces developed during its relentless drive for surplus value. Part of the existing productive forces are such only potentially, as they fail to increase the profitability of capital in sufficient measure, or at all, and for that reason are not employed. In economic terms, constant and variable capital remain idle because, if not used capitalistically, they cannot be used at all. Their full utilization would require a change in the relations of production which would disencumber social production of its dependence on the creation of surplus value.

Because the capitalistic increase of the social powers of production has the form of the accumulation of capital, science and technology serve this particular brand of social development and not the latter as such. And because science and technology are limitless in every direction, they can change their direction through a change of the social structure, away from its need to accumulate capital, to the real production and consumption requirements of a society not only "socialized" in the limited sense that its development is determined by the interdependence of the separated commodity producers, but in a truly social sense, implying the prevention of special private or class interests from interfering in the consciously recognized needs of society as a whole. Science and technology would move in different directions than those required by capitalist society.

Moreover, although an expression of the rapid accumulation of capital, its increasing monopolization implies the monopolization of science and technology and their subordination to the specific interests of the centralized capitals. This hinders the increase of productivity in the remaining competitive sectors of the economy and prevents the growth of the social forces of production in capitalistically underdeveloped nations, except insofar as this may suit the special interests of the centralized capitals in the dominating capitalist countries. Finally, the monopolization of the world market plays the bulk of the produced surplus value worldwide into the hands of a diminishing number of internationally operating capitals, at the price of the increasing pauperization of the world's population. At the same time, the national form of capital production prevents its internationalization for an all-round expansion of the social forces of production, which would require consideration of the real needs of the world population within the framework of a socialized world economy. Unable to proceed in this direction, the increasing productive power of capital turns into a destructive power, which today threatens not only the setbacks of new and worldwide wars, but the destruction of the world itself. Under these conditions the capitalist system has ceased to be a vehicle for the growth of the social forces of production. It merely provides the stage for the change of social relations that is the precondition for the resumption of the civilizing process of social labor.

For the theoreticians of the Second International as well, socialism meant a change of the social relations of production, but they saw this change not in the abolition of wage labor but in the sudden or gradual transformation of private into social capital under the auspices of the state. It is true that they also spoke of the end of wage labor, but this implied no more than the negative act of the state's expropriation of capital, which would, presumably, automatically change the social status of the laboring class. It did not enter their minds that the workers themselves would have to take possession of the means of production and that they themselves would have to determine the conditions of production, the allocation of social labor, the priorities of production, and the distirbution of the social product, through the creation of organizational forms that could assure that decision-making powers would remain in the hands of the actual producers. In the statist conceptions of socialism it is not the working class itself that rearranges society. This is done for it, through substitution for it of a special social group, organized as the state, which imagines that by this token it removes the stigma of exploitation from wage labor.

On the whole, it is of course true that the socialist workers themselves shared this concept with their leaders and assumed that the act of socialization would be a function of government. This turned out to be an illusion, but an illusion that had been systematically indoctrinated into the working class. The indoctrination was successful because the procedure it predicted appeared logical in view of the centralizing tendencies of capitalist production and the democratic form of bourgeois politics. The great difference between capitalism and socialism was thus perceived as the mere elimination of the private-property character of capital, or as the complete monopolization of capital under centralized government control, which would serve no longer the specific interests of the capitalist class but the whole of society. But to that end, the state would have to regulate production and thus the labor process, which, under these conditions, seemed feasible only through the maintenance of wage labor.

However, wage labor is only the other side of the capital-labor relation that characterizes capitalist society and determines its productive powers. The complete monopolization of capital does do away, at least ideally, with competitive market relations and does allow for a measure of conscious control of the economy, and thus impairs or ends the value-determination of social production. This may or may not increase the powers of social labor, but it leaves the capitalist relations of production intact. The socialization of production remains incomplete, as it does not affect the social relations of production. The removal of the fetishism of commodity production through its conscious control also removes the fetishistic character of wage labor but not wage labor itself. It continues to express the lack of social power on the part of the working class and its centralization into the hand of the controlling state. The capital-labor relation has been modified but not abolished; there has been a social revolution but not a working-class revolution.

Reform
and
Revolution

The bourgeois political revolution was the culmination of a drawn-out process of social changes in the sphere of production. Where the ascending capitalist class gained complete control of the state, this assured a rapid unfolding of the capital-labor relation. Feudalistic resistance to this transformation varied in different countries. Though capitalism was on the rise generally, its gestation involved both force and compromise, characterized by an overlapping of the new and the old both politically and economically. The ruling classes divided into a reactionary and a progressive wing, the latter striving for political control through a democratic capitalist state. The division between an entrenched autocracy and the liberal bourgeoisie reflected the uneven pace of capitalist development and extended the internal distinctions between reaction and progress to the nations themselves and to their political institutions.

The socialist movement arose in an incompletely bourgeois society in a world of nations still more or less in the thrall of the reactionary forces of the past. This situation led to an expedient but unnatural alliance between bourgeoisie and proletariat. Historically, the opposition of labor and capital had first to appear as an identity of interests, so as to release the forces of production that would turn the proletariat into an independent social class. To partake in the bourgeois revolutions with their own demands did not contradict the postulated "historical goal" of the working class, but was an unavoidable precondition of its future struggle against the bourgeoisie.

Although it has often been asserted that it was fear of the proletariat that induced the bourgeoisie to limit its own struggle against the feudal autocracy, it was rather the recognition of its own as yet restricted power vis-à-vis the reactionary foe that made it draw back from radical measures in favor of its own political aspirations. While the bourgeoisie found support in the laboring population, it was certain that it would find the assistance of the reactionary forces should this prove necessary to destroy the revolutionary initiative of the working class. In any case, time was on the side of the bourgeoisie, as the feudal layers of society adapted to the capitalization process and integrated themselves into the capitalist mode of production. The integration of the apparently irreconcilable interests of the conservative elements, largely based on agriculture, and the progressive democratic forces, representing industrial capital, finally realized the goals of the failed bourgeois revolutions of 1848, which had gripped almost all the nations of Western Europe. Eighteen forty-eight had raised hopes for an early proletarian revolution, particularly because of the devastating economic crisis conditions that had caused the political ferment in the first place. But the years of depression passed and with them also the social upheavals against everything thought to stand in the way of social change. Capital accumulated no less within countries ruled by politically reactionary regimes than in those where the state favored the liberal bourgeoisie.

The modern nation-state is a creation of capitalism, which demands the transformation of weak into viable states, so as to create the conditions of production that allow for successful competition on the world market. Nationalism was then the predominant concern of the revolutionary bourgeoisie. Capitalist expansion and national unification were seen as complementary processes, although nationalism in its ideological form was held to be a value in its own right. In this form, it took on revolutionary connotations wherever particular nations, such as Ireland and Poland, had come under foreign rule. Because capitalism implied the formation of nations, those who favored the first necessarily favored the second, even if only as another presupposition of a future proletarian revolution which, for its part, was supposed to end the national separations of the world economy. It was in this sense that Marx and Engels advocated the formation of nations powerful enough to assure a rapid capitalistic development.

Of course, it did not really matter whether or not Marx and Engels favored the formation of capitalistically viable nation-states, for their influence upon actual events was less than minimal. All they could do was express their own sentiments and preferences with regard to the various national struggles that accompanied the capitalization of the European continent. In these struggles the workers could as yet provide only cannon fodder for class interests that were not their own, or were so only indirectly, in that a rapid capitalist development promised to improve their conditions within their wage-labor dependency. Only in a historical sense was their participation in the national-revolutionary upheavals of the time, and in the ensuing national wars, justifiable, for at the time, they could serve only the specific class interests of the rising and competing bourgeoisie. However, even though history was made by the bourgeoisie, the fact that the latter's existence implied the existence and development of the proletariat made it obligatory to view this process also from the position of the working class and to formulate policies that would presumably advance its interests within the capitalistic development.

As the formation of viable national states involved the absorption of less viable national entities, a distinction was made between nations possessing the potential for a vast capitalistic development and others not so endowed. Friedrich Engels, for instance, differentiated between nations destined to affect the course of history and others unable to play an independent role in historical development.[1] In his opinion, nationalism as such was not a revolutionary force, except indirectly in situations where it served a rapid capitalist development. There was no room for small or backward nations within the unfolding capitalist world. National aspirations could thus be either revolutionary or reactionary, depending upon their positive or negative impact on the growing social powers of production. Only insofar as national movements supported the general capitalist development could these movements be seen as progressive and so of interest to the working class, for nationalism was only the capitalistically contradictory form of a development preparing the way for the internationalization of capital production and therefore also for proletarian internationalism.

Of course, this general conception had to be spelled out empirically, by taking sides, at least verbally, in the actual national movements and national wars of the nineteenth century. According to the degree of their capitalist development, or the clear need and desire for such nation's competitive position within the world economy, their defense implied the defense of the nation, if only to safeguard what had already been gained. The more advanced the working class thought itself to be, the more outspoken its identification with the prevailing nationalism. Where the workers did not challenge capitalist social relations at all, as in England and the United States, their acceptance of bourgeois nationalism with its imperialist implications was complete. Where there was at least ideological opposition to the capitalist system, as in the Marxist movement, nationalist sentiments were extolled in a more hypocritical fashion, namely as a means to transform the nation into a socialist nation powerful enough to withstand a possible onslaught of external counterrevolutionary forces. A distinction was now made between nations clearly on the road to socialism, as attested by the increasing power of the socialist organizations and their growing influence upon society at large, and nations still completely under the sway of their traditional ruling classes and trailing behind the general social development along the socialist path.

A particular nation could thus become a kind of "vanguard nation," destined by its example to lead other nations. This role, played by France in the bourgeois revolution, was now claimed, with respect to the socialist revolution, for Germany, thanks to her quick capitalist development, her geopolitical location, and her labor movement, the pride of the Second International. A defeat of this nation in a capitalist war would set back not only the development of Germany and its labor movement, but along with it the development of socialism as such. It was thus in the name of socialism that Friedrich Engels, for instance, advocated the defense of the German nation against less advanced countries such as Russia, and even against more advanced capitalist nations, such as France, were they to ally themselves with the potential Russian adversary. And it was August Bebel, the popular leader of German Social Democracy, who announced his readiness to fight for the German fatherland should this be necessary to secure its uninterrupted socialist development.

In a world of competing capitalist nations the gains of some nations are the losses of others, even if all of them increase their capital with the enlargement of the world market. The capital concentration process proceeds internationally as well as nationally. As competition leads to monopolization, the theoretically "free world market" becomes a partially controlled market, and the instrumentalities to this end—protectionism, colonialism, militarism, and imperialism—are employed to assure national privileges within the expanding capitalist world economy. Monopolization and imperialism thus provide a degree of conscious interference in the market mechanism, though only for purposes of national aggrandizement. However, as conscious control of the economy is also a goal of socialism, the economic regulation due to the monopolization of capital and its imperialist activities was held by some socialists and social reformers, such as the Fabians of England, to be a progressive step toward the development of a more rational society.

Because a relatively undisturbed growth of labor organizations in ascending capitalism presupposes a rate of capital accumulation allowing at the same time for sufficient profits and for the gradual improvement of the conditions of the laboring classes, the nationally organized labor movement, bent on social reforms or merely on higher wages, cannot help favoring the expansion of the national capital. Whether the fact is acknowledged or not, international capital competition affects the working class as well as capital. Even the socialist wing of the labor movement will not be immune to this external pressure, in order not to lose contact with reality and to maintain its influence upon the working class, regardless of all the ideological lip service paid to proletarian internationalism as the final but distant goal of the socialist movement.

The national division of capitalist production also nationalizes the proletarian class struggle. This is not a mere question of ideology—that is, of the uncritical acceptance of bourgeois nationalism by the working class—but is also a practical need, for it is within the framework of the national economy that the class struggle is fought. With the unity of mankind a distant and perhaps utopian goal, the historically evolving nation-state and its success with respect to the competitive pursuit of capital determine the destiny of its labor movement together with that of the working class as regards the conditions of its existence. Like all ideologies, in order to be effective nationalism too must have some definite contact with real needs and possibilities, not only for the class interests directly associated with it but also for those subjected to their rule.

Once established and systematically perpetuated, the ideology of nationalism, like money, takes on an independent existence and asserts its power without disclosing the specific material class interests that led to its formation in the first place. As it is not the social production process but its fetishistic form of appearance that structures the conscious apprehension of capitalist society, so it is the nationalist ideology, divorced from its underlying class-determined social relations, that appears as a part of the false consciousness dominating the whole of society. Nationalism appears now as a value in itself and as the only form in which some sort of "sociality" can be realized in an otherwise asocial and atomized society. It is an abstract form of sociality in lieu of a real sociality, but it attests to the subjective need of the isolated individual to assert his humanity as a social being. As such, it is the ideological reflex of capitalist society as a system of *social* production for *private* gain, based on the exploitation of one class by another. It supplements or replaces religion as the cohesive force of social existence, since no other form of cohesion is possible at this stage of the development of the social forces of production. It is thus a historical phenomenon, which seems to be as "natural" as capitalist production itself and lends to the latter an aura of sociality it does not really possess.

The ambiguities of ideologies, including nationalism, are both their weakness and their strength. To retain its effectiveness over time, ideology must be relentlessly cultivated. The internalization of ideological nationalism cannot be left to the contradictory socialization process itself, but must be systematically propagated to combat any arising doubt as to its validity for society as a whole. But as the means of indoctrination, together with those of production and of direct physical control, are in the hands of the bourgeoisie, the ideas of the ruling class are the socially ruling ideas and in that form answer the subjective need for the individual's integration into a larger and protective community.

Capital operates internationally but concentrates its profits nationally. Its internationalization appears thus as an imperialistic nationalism aiming at the monopolization of the sources of surplus value. This is at once a political and an economic process, even though the connection between the two is not always clearly discernible because of the relatively independent existence of nationalist ideology, which hides the specifically capitalistic interests at its base. This camouflage works the better because the whole of known history has been the history of plunder and war of various people engaged in building up, or in destroying, one or another ethnic group, one or another empire. "National" security, or "national" security by way of expansion, appears to be the stuff of history, a never-ending "Darwinian" struggle for existence regardless of the historical specificity of class relations within the "national" entities.

Just as monopolization and competition, or free trade and protectionism, are aspects of one and the same historical development, nationalism and imperialism are also indivisible, although the latter may take on a variety of forms, from direct domination to indirect economic and financial control. Politically, the accumulation of capital appears as the competitive expansion of nations and so as an imperialistic struggle for larger shares of the exploitable resources of the world, whether real or imaginary. This process, implicit in capitalist production, divides the world into more or less successful capitalist nations. The specifically capitalist imperialist imperative, or even the mere opportunity for imperialist expansion, was taken up by some nations sooner than by others, such as England and France in the eighteenth century, and was delayed by nations such as Germany and the United States until the nineteenth century. Some smaller nations were not at all able to enter into imperialist competition and had to fit themselves into a world structure dominated by the great capitalist powers. The changing fortunes of the imperialist nations in their struggle for larger shares of the world's profits appear economically in the concentration of the world's growing capital in a diminishing number of nations. This would also result eventually from the expansion of capital without imperialistic interventions on the part of the competing national capitals: it is not competition which determines the course of capitalist development, but capitalist production which determines the course of competition and capitalism's bloody history.

The object of national rivalries is the amassing of capital, on which all political and military power rests. The ideology of nationalism is based not on the existence of the nation but on the existence of capital and on its self-expansion. In this sense, nationalism mediates the internationalization of capital production without leading to a unified world economy, just as the concentration and monopolization of the national capitals does not eliminate their private property character. Nationally as well as internationally capitalist production creates the world economy via the creation of the world market. At the base of this general competitive process lies an actual, if still abstract, need for a worldwide organization of production and distribution beneficial to all of humanity. This is not only because the earth is far better adapted to such an organization, but also because the social productive forces can be further developed and society freed from want and misery only by a fully international cooperation without regard to particularistic interests. However, the compelling interdependency implied in a progressive social development asserts itself capitalistically in an unending struggle for imperialist control. Imperialism, not nationalism, was the great issue around the turn of the century. German "nationalist" interests were now imperialist interests, competing with the imperialisms of other nations. French "national" interests were those of the French empire, as Britain's were those of the British empire. Control of the world and the division and redivision of this control between the great imperialist powers, and even between lesser nations, determined "national" policies and culminated in the first worldwide war.

As crisis reveals the fundamental contradictions of capital production, capitalist war reveals the imperialistic nature of nationalism. Imperialism presents itself, however, as a national need to prevent, or to overcome, a crisis situation in a defensive struggle against the imperialistic designs of other nations. Where such nations do not exist imperialism takes on the guise of a measure to maintain the well-being of the nation and, at the same time, to carry its "civilizing" mission into new territories. It is not too difficult to get the consent of a working class more or less habituated to capitalist conditions, and thus under the sway of nationalism, for any imperialist adventure. The workers' state of absolute dependency allows them to feel that, for better or worse, their lot is indissolubly connected with that of the nation. Unable as yet and therefore unwilling to fight for any kind of self-determination, they manage to convince themselves that the concerns of their masters are also their own. And this the more so, because it is only in this fashion that they are able to see themselves as full-fledged members of society, gaining as citizens of the state the "dignity" and "appreciation" denied to them as members of the working class.

There is no point in being annoyed by this state of affairs and in dismissing the working class as a stupid class, unable to distinguish its own interests from those of the bourgeoisie. After all, it merely shares the national ideology with the rest of society, which is equally unaware that nationalism, like religion at an earlier time, and like the faith in the beneficence of market relations, is only an ideological expression for the self-expansion of capital, that is, for the helpless subjection of society to "economic laws" that have their source in the exploitative social relations of capitalist production. It is true that the ruling class, at least, benefits from society's antisocial production process, but it does so just as blindly as the working class accepts its suffering. It is this blindness which accounts for the apparently independent force of ideological nationalism, which is thus able to transcend the social class relations.

The materialist conception of history attempts to explain both the persistence of a given societal form and the reasons for its possible change. Its supporters ought not to be surprised by the resiliency of a given society, as indicated by its continual reproduction and the consequent recreation of its ruling ideology. Changes within the status quo may be for long times almost imperceptible, or unrecognizable as regards their future implications. The presence of class contradictions explains both social stability and instability, depending upon conditions outside the control of either the rulers or the ruled. In distinction to preceding societal forms, however, the capital-labor relation of social production continually accelerates changes in the productive forces, while maintaining the basic social relations of production, and thus allows for the expectation of an early confrontation of the contending social classes. At any rate, this was the conclusion the Marxist movement drew from the increasing polarization of capitalist society and from the internal contradictions of its production process. Class interests would come to supersede bourgeois ideology and thus counterpose the class consciousness of the bourgeoisie with that of the proletariat.

As stated before, these expectations were not unrealistic and were held by the bourgeoisie as well, which reacted to the rise of socialist movements and the increasing militancy of wage struggles with repressive measures that betrayed its fears of the possibility of a new social revolution. Class consciousness seemed indeed to destroy the national consensus and the hold of bourgeois ideology over the working population. Until about 1880 the theory of the impoverishment of the working class in the course of capital accumulation, and the consequent sharpening of the class struggle, found verification in actual social conditions, and accounted for the radicalization of the laboring masses. This same period, however, which resembled a prolonged social crisis situation, also laid the foundation for a new and accelerating phase of capital expansion which lasted, with occasional interruptions, almost to the eve of the first world war. It provided the objective conditions for the legalization of organized labor and its integration into the capitalist system in economic as well as in political terms.

Of course, the acceptance of organized labor and socialist organizations was not a gift freely offered the working class by a more generous bourgeoisie, but was the result of class struggles— albeit of a limited nature—which wrested concessions from the bourgeoisie and its state, improving the material conditions of the workers and elevating their social status within bourgeois democracy. These concessions could not have been made without a rapid increase in the productivity of labor and a consequent quickening of the accumulation process. But they appeared nonetheless as results of the self-exertion of the laboring population, a class rising within the confines of capitalism, which encouraged the growing illusion that the increasing power of organized labor would eventually turn the working class into the socially dominant class, displacing the bourgeoisie. In reality, the improving conditions of the working class implied no more than its increasing exploitation, i.e., the decrease of the value of labor power with respect to the total value of the social product. However, both the capitalists and the workers think in everyday life not about social value relations but in terms of quantities of products at their disposal for purposes of capital expansion or general consumption. That the improvement in the conditions of the working class resulted from the accelerated growth of their productivity did not diminish the importance of the betterment of their living standards and its reflection in their ideological commitments.

Disappointed by the slow development of proletarian class consciousness in the leading capitalist nations and upset by the latter's ability to weather their crisis situations, and thus to reach always greater heights of self-expansion, the socialists had to admit that Marx's predictions of the impoverishment of the working class and the development of revolutionary class consciousness, as an outgrowth of its class struggle, seemed unsubstantiated by actual events. Friedrich Engels, for instance, tried to explain this dismal condition with the assertion (later to be parroted by Lenin) of a deliberately fostered "corruption" of the working class on the part of the bourgeoisie, which allowed a growing section of the industrial proletariat to partake to some extent of the spoils of imperialism. In this view, a rising "labor aristocracy" within the international working class weakened the class solidarity necessary for a consistent struggle against the bourgeoisie and carried the bourgeois ideology, and here particularly its nationalist aspect, into the ranks of the proletariat. The decline of revolutionary class consciousness showed itself in the steady growth of an opportunistic reformism based on the acceptance of the capitalist relations of production and bourgeois democracy.

In any case, there was no direct connection between the economic class struggle and the revolutionizing of the workers' consciousness. The expectation that the recurrent confrontations of labor and capital over profits and wages would lead to the recognition that the wage system must itself be abolished to end the workers' Sisyphean activities on its behalf was disappointed, due to the simple fact this was not possible at this particular stage of capitalistic development. As long as profits and wages could rise simultaneously—however disproportionately—and the class division of the social product be affected by social legislation, even though this involved economic and political struggles, the character of these struggles was set by the limited demands made by the part of the laboring population still under the sway of bourgeois ideology. Although growing in numbers and in social influence, trade unions and socialist parties remained in a minority position within the population at large and even within the working class as a whole.

Not only were expectations of a possible revolutionary change now relegated to a more remote future, but even the growth of the socialist movement was seen as a long term, prosaic educational effort to win the laboring population to an acceptance of socialist ideology. Notwithstanding the struggles for wages and social reforms, which were themselves conceived of as learning processes, the class struggle was mainly seen as ideological in nature: in the end people would favor socialism because of its more accurate comprehension of the developing reality. One simply had to wait for the time when objective conditions themselves verified the socialist critique of the capitalist system, thus ending the subjective submission of the proletariat to the ruling ideology.

As an organized ideology, socialism opposed the dominant bourgeois ideology; the class struggle became by and large a struggle of ideas and thus the preserve of the proponents of ideologies. Ideologies competed for the allegiance of the masses, who were seen as recipients, not as producers, of the contesting ideologies. Ideologists found themselves in search of a following, in order to effectuate their goals. The working class—apparently unable to evolve a socialist ideology on its own—was seen as dependent upon the existence of an ideological leadership able to combat the sophistries of the ruling class. Due to the social class structure and the associated division of labor, ideological leadership was destined to be in the hands of educated middle-class elements committed to serve the needs of the workers and the goals of socialism.

However limited they were, the parliamentary successes of the socialist parties, which brought an increasing number of representatives of the working class into capitalism's political institutions, not only induced a growing number of educated professionals to enter the socialist organizations but also provided the latter with a degree of respectability unknown at an earlier stage of the developing socialist movement. Leaving economic struggles to the trade unions, the spreading of the socialist ideology was now measured by the number of its representatives in parliament and by their ability to present "the case for socialism" to the nation and to initiate and support social legislation for the improvement of the conditions of the laboring class. Political actions were now conceived of as parliamentary activities, made *for* the workers by their representatives, with the "rank and file" left no other role than that of passive support. In a rather short time, the workers' submission to their intellectual superiors in the parliaments and the party hierarchy was complete enough to turn this incipient class consciousness into a political consciousness derived from that of their elected leadership.

What was at first a tendency within the socialist movement, namely the substitution for proletarian self-determination of a nonproletarian leadership acting on behalf of the working class, later became the conviction and the practice of all branches of socialism, both reformist and revolutionary. Not only its right-wing revisionists but the so-called centrist Karl Kautsky and the leftist Lenin were convinced that the working class by itself was not able to evolve a revolutionary consciousness, and that this had to be brought to it, from outside, by members of the educated bour-

geoisie, who alone had the capacity and opportunity to understand the intricacies of the capitalist system and thus to develop a
meaningful counter-ideology to the ruling capitalist ideology and
so lead the struggle of the working class. Of course, this elitist idea
was itself a product of the rapid rise of the labor movement, which
attracted a growing number of middle-class elements into its ranks.
Ideologically, at any rate, socialism ceased to be the exclusive concern of an awakening proletariat, but became a social movement
with some appeal for members of the middle class.

This class found itself in a process of transformation, caught
between the millstones of capital concentration and social polarization. The old middle class lost its property-owning character and
became in increasing measure a salaried class in the service of the
big bourgeoisie and its state apparatus. It became a managerial
class filling the gap that divided the bourgeoisie from the proletariat and, in the various professions, a class serving the personal and
cultural needs of the divided society. The mediating functions of
the new middle class in support of the existing social production
relations was reflected in the socialist movement by the determination of its theory and practice by its intellectual leadership.
Although some workers were able to advance into leading positions within their organizations, the tone of their politics, as suggested by an alleged predominance of theory over practice, was set
by the intellectually emancipated leadership stemming from the
middle class. This was a question not so much of the relationship
between theory and practice as of the relationship between the
leaders and the led. Policies were made by an elected leadership
and found their parliamentary and extraparliamentary support in
the disciplined adherence of the mass of workers to their organizations' programs and their time-conditioned variations. The
division between mental and manual labor, so necessary for the
capitalist system, was thus also a characteristic of the labor movement.

The rapid influx of middle-class elements into the leading positions of the socialist movement disturbed even its intellectual
founders. Notwithstanding his own reformist inclinations, Friedrich
Engels, for instance, was greatly worried about the increasing subjugation of the self-activity of the working class to the political
initiative of the well-meaning petite bourgeoisie. His own reformism, as he saw it, was after all a mere strategem, not a matter of

principle, whereas the reformism of the petite bourgeoisie tended to eliminate the class struggle altogether in obeisance to the rules of bourgeois democracy. "Since the foundation of the International," he wrote to August Bebel, "our war cry has been: the emancipation of the working class can only be the work of the workers themselves. We simply cannot collaborate with people who declare openly that the workers are not sufficiently educated to be able to liberate themselves, and for that reason have to be freed from above by a philanthropic bourgeoisie."[2] He suggested throwing these elements out of the socialist organizations so as to safeguard its proletarian character.

The workers themselves, however, were unperturbed if not flattered by the attention given to them by some of the "better kind" of people. In addition, they felt the need for allies in their rather unequal class struggle.

But in any case the revolutionary character of socialism was not lost because of the class-collaborationist ideas evolved by its nonproletarian leadership, but because the "strategy" of reformism, as the only possible practical activity, became the "principle" of the organizations in their attempts to consolidate and to enlarge their influence within capitalist society. With respect to German Social Democracy, for instance, it had by 1913 a membership of close to a million and was able to muster 4.5 million votes in national elections. It sent 110 members to the Reichstag. The trade unions had a membership of about 2.5 million and their financial assets amounted to 88 million Marks. The Social Democratic Party itself invested 20 million Marks in private industry and in state loans. It employed more than 4,000 professional officials and 11,000 salaried employees, and controlled 94 newspapers and various other publications. To maintain the party and to assure its undisturbed further growth was the first consideration of those who controlled it, an attitude even more pronounced in the purely proletarian trade unions.

There is no point in describing this process in other nations, even though their labor movements varied in one or another respect from that in Germany. Social Democracy and trade unionism advanced—although more often than not at a slower pace than in Germany—in all the developed capitalist nations, thus raising the specter of a socialist movement that might eventually, by reformist or revolutionary means, or both, transform capitalism into a classless, nonexploitative society. Meanwhile, however, this movement was allowed, and indeed compelled by circumstances, to integrate itself as thoroughly as it could into the capitalist fabric as one special interest group among those which together constitute the capitalist market economy. The specter of socialism, though used by the bourgeoisie to delimit the political and economic aspirations of the working class, remained a mere apparition, unable to destroy the self-confidence of the ruling classes with regard to either their material or their ideological control of society. Dressed in whatever garb, the organized labor movement remained a small minority within the working classes, thus indicating that a decisive weakening of bourgeois ideology presupposes the actual decay of capitalism. Only when the discrepancy between ideology and reality finds an obvious display in persistently deteriorating economic and social conditions, will the otherwise rather comfortable ideological consensus give way to new ideas corresponding to new necessities.

There is also quite a difference between an ideology based on tradition and on actual circumstances, and one based on nonexisting conditions, with relevance to a future which may or may not be a reasonable expectation. In this respect, socialist ideology is at a disadvantage vis-à-vis the ruling capitalist ideology. A powerful exertion of the latter, for purposes of waging war, or even for internal reasons, will create serious doubts regarding the validity or the effectiveness of the socialist ideology even in some of its more consistent supporters. The emerging feeling of uncertainty mixed with the fear of the unknown, which accounts for the mass hysteria accompanying the outbreak of war, will affect the socialists too and induce them to question their own ideological commitments anew. Their critical attitude towards the ruling ideology, to reiterate, does not free them from acting as if they were under its sway, while their socialist convictions cannot be actualized within the given conditions of their existence. They can be carried away by the apparent euphoria of the agitated masses and drown their own ambiguities in the murky sea of nationalism in a spontaneous reassertion of loyalties latent but not yet lost.

Furthermore, there is the objective fact of the national form of capitalism, and therefore of its labor movement, which cannot be overcome by a mere ideological commitment to internationalism, such as can be gained by a loose consultative body as was the

Second International. The various national organizations comprising this institution differed among themselves with regard to their effective powers in their respective countries and thus also with regard to their opportunities to influence national policies. What would happen if the socialist movement of a particular country should succeed in preventing its bourgeoisie from waging war while that of another country did not? Even though "the main enemy resides in one's own country," a foreign enemy may nonetheless attack a nation made defenseless by its socialist opposition. It was the recognition that the road to socialism finds a barrier in unequal capitalist development, which also shows itself in the unequal class consciousness of the laboring population, that induced Marx and Engels to favor one or another country in imperialistic conflicts, siding with those bearing the greatest promise for a socialist future. They could not envision a capitalist development without national wars and they did not hesitate to state their preferences as to their outcome. Pacifism is not a Marxist tradition. It was then not too difficult to rationalize the socialist acceptance of war and even to invoke the names of Marx and Engels in its support.

Notwithstanding the apparently general recognition that in the age of imperialism all wars are wars of conquest, it was still possible for socialists to assert that, from their point of view, they may also be defensive in nature insofar as they prevent the destruction of more progressive nations by socially less-advanced countries, which would be a setback for socialism in general. In fact, this became the flaccid justification for participation in the imperialist war for the majority of socialists in all the warring nations, each national organization defending its own more advanced conditions, against the backwardness of the enemy country. Supposedly, it was the barbarism of the Russian autocratic adversary that demanded the defense of a cultured nation such as Germany, as it was the barbaric aggressive militarism of the still semifeudal Germany that justified the defense of more democratic nations such as England and France. But such rationalizations merely covered up an actual inability as well as unwillingness to oppose the capitalist war in the only effective way possible, namely by revolutionary actions. The international labor movement was no longer, or not as yet, a revolutionary movement, but one fully satisfied with social reforms and for that reason tolerated by a bourgeoisie still able to grant these concessions without any loss to itself. The antiwar resolutions passed at the International's congresses meant no more than a whistle in the dark and were composed in such an opaque fashion as to be practically noncommittal.

In 1909, in the first bloom of his socialist conversion, Upton Sinclair wrote a manifesto calling upon socialists and the workers of Europe and the United States to realize the peril of the approaching world war and to pledge themselves to prevent this calamity by the threat of a general strike in all countries. He sent the manifesto to Karl Kautsky for publication in the socialist press. Here is Kautsky's reply:

> Your manifesto against war I have read with great interest and warm sympathy. Nevertheless I am not able to publish it and you will not find anybody in Germany, nor in Austria or Russia, who would dare to publish your appeal. He would be arrested at once and get some years imprisonment for high treason. . . . By publishing the manifesto we would mislead our own comrades, promise to them more than we can fulfill. Nobody, and not the most revolutionary amongst the socialists in Germany, thinks to oppose war by insurrection and general strike. We are too weak to do that. . . . I hope, *after* a war, after the debacle of a government, we may get strength enough to conquer the political power. . . . That's not my personal opinion only, in that point the whole party, without any exception, is unanimous. . . . You may be sure there will never come the day when German socialists will ask their followers to take up arms for the Fatherland. What Bebel announced will never happen, because today there is no foe who threatens the independence of the Fatherland. If there will be war today, it won't be a war for the defense of the Fatherland, it will be for imperialistic purposes, and such a war will find the whole socialist party of Germany in energetic opposition. That we may promise. But we cannot go so far and promise that this opposition shall take the form of insurrection or general strike, if necessary, nor can we promise that our opposition will in every case be strong enough to prevent war. It would be worse than useless to promise more than we can fulfill.[3]

While Kautsky's pessimism with respect to the possibility of preventing the approaching war proved to be correct, his optimistic assessment of the antiwar position of the German labor movement turned out to be totally erroneous. Moreover, this was not a German peculiarity but had its equivalent, with some slight modifications, in all the warring nations. There were of course exceptions to the rule, but the actual outbreak of war found the large majorities within organized labor, and within the working class as a whole, not only ready to support the imperialist war but ready to do so enthusiastically, which impelled Kautsky to resign himself to the fact that "the International was an instrument of peace but unworkable in times of war." As easy as it had been to discuss the prevention of war, so difficult it proved to act when it arrived. The *fait accompli* of the ruling classes was enough to create conditions that destroyed overnight an international movement that had tried for decades to overcome bourgeois nationalism through the development of proletarian class consciousness and internationalism.

Paraphrasing an old slogan referring to the French nation, Marx once declared that "the proletariat is revolutionary or it is nothing." In 1914 it was obviously nothing, as it prepared to lay down its life for the imperialist notions of the bourgeoisie. The socialist ideology proved to be only skin-deep, powerless to withstand the concerted onslaught of the accustomed bourgeois ideology, which identifies the national with the general interests. As for the working class as a whole, it put itself at the disposal of the ruling classes for purposes of war, as it accepted its class position in times of peace. The capitalist reality weighed heavier than the socialist ideology, which as yet represented not an actual but only a potential social force. However difficult it is to understand the unifying power of bourgeois ideology and its hold upon the broad masses, this difficulty itself in no way alters the force of the traditional ideology. What was more astonishing was the rapidity with which the socialist movement itself succumbed to the requirements of the imperialist war, and thereby ceased to be a socialist movement. It was as if there had been no socialist movement at all but merely a make-believe movement with no intention to act upon its beliefs.

The collapse of the socialist movement and the Second International has been propagandistically described as a "betrayal" of principles and of the working class. This is of course a recourse to idealism and a denial of the materialist conception of history. Actually, as we observed above, the changes the movement had gone through, within the general capitalist development, had long since relegated all programmatic principles to the purely ideological sphere, where they lost any connection with the opportunistic behavior of the movement. The pragmatic opportunism of the reformist movement no longer possessed principles it could "betray," but adjusted its activities in conformity with what was possible within the frame of capitalism. No doubt, the antiwar sentiments displayed at international congresses, and in each nation separately, were true convictions and the longing for perpetual peace a genuine desire, already because of widespread fear that war would lead to the destruction of the socialist movement, as the bourgeois state might suppress its internal opposition in order to wage war more effectively. Not to oppose the war seemed to be one way to assure personal and organizational security, but this alone does not explain the eagerness with which the socialist parties and trade unions offered their services to the war effort and its hoped-for victorious end. Behind this lay the fact that these organizations had become quite formidable bureaucratic institutions, with their own vested interests in the capitalist system and the national state. This accomplishment in turn had changed both the lifestyle and the general outlook of those who filled the bureaucratic positions within the labor organizations. If they had once been proletarians conscious of their class interests, they were so no longer but felt themselves to be members of the middle class and changed their mores and habits accordingly. Set apart from the working class proper, and addicted to a comfortable routinism, they were neither willing nor able to lead their following into any serious antiwar activity. Even their harmless exhortations in favor of peace found an abrupt end with the declaration of war.

To be sure, there were minorities within the leadership, the rank and file, and the working class that remained immune to the war hysteria gripping the broad masses, but they found no way to turn their steadfastness into significant actions. With the war a reality, even the more consistent international socialists, such as Keir Hardie of the British Independent Labour Party, found themselves forced to admit "that once the lads had gone forth to fight their country's battles they must not be disheartened by dissension at home."[4] With socialists and nonsocialists together in the opposing trenches, it seemed only reasonable to rally to "the lads' " support and to provide them with the essentials for waging war. The war against the foreign foe, in short, required the end of the class struggle at home.

The triumph of the bourgeoisie was absolute as it was general. Of course, that minority that upheld socialist principles began at once, if only clandestinely, to organize opposition to the war and to reconstitute the international socialist movement. But it took years before their efforts found an effective response, first in the working class than then in the population at large.

The
Limits
of Reform

However reformable capitalism may prove to be, it cannot alter its basic wage and profit relations without eliminating itself. The age of reform is an age of spontaneous capital expansion, based on a disproportional but simultaneous increase of both wages and profits. It is an age wherein the concessions made to the working class are more tolerable to the bourgeoisie than the upheavals of the class struggle that would otherwise accompany capitalist development. As a class, the bourgeoisie does not favor minimum wages and intolerable working conditions, even though each capitalist, for whom labor is a cost of production, tries to reduce this expense to the utmost. There can be no doubt that the bourgeoisie prefers a satisfied to a dissatisfied working class and social stability to instability. In fact, it looks upon the general improvement of living standards as its own accomplishment and as the justification for its class rule. To be sure, the relative well-being of the laboring population must not be carried too far, for its absolute dependency on uninterrupted wage labor must be maintained. But within this limit, the bourgeoisie has no subjective inclinations to reduce the workers to the lowest state of existence, even where this might be objectively possible by means of appropriate measures of repression. As the inclinations and actions of the workers are determined by their dependency on wage labor, those of the bourgeoisie are rooted in the necessity to make profit and to accumulate capital, quite apart from their diverse ideological and psychological propensities.

The limited reforms possible within the capitalist system become the customary conditions of existence for those affected by them and cannot easily be undone. With a low rate of accumulation they turn into obstacles to profit production, overcoming which effect requires exceptional increases in the exploitation of labor. On the other hand, times of depression also induce various reform measures, if only to withstand the threat of serious social upheavals. Once installed, these also tend to perpetuate themselves and must be compensated for by a correspondingly greater increase in the productivity of labor. Of course attempts will be made, some of them successfully, to whittle down what has been gained by way of social legislation and better living standards, in order to restore the necessary profitability of capital. Some of these gains will remain, however, through periods of depression as well as prosperity, with the result of a general improvement of the workers' conditions through time.

The hand-to-mouth existence of the workers made it never easy to strike for higher wages and better working conditions. Only the most brutal provocations of their employers would move them to action, as a lesser evil than a state of unmitigated misery. Aware of the workers' dependence on the daily wage, the bourgeoisie answered their rebellions with lockouts, as a most efficient means to enforce the employers' will. Lost profits can be regained, lost wages not. However, the formation of trade unions and the amassing of strike funds changed this situation to some extent in favor of the workers, even though it did not always overcome their conditioned reluctance to resort to the strike weapon. For the capitalists, too, the readiness to defy their workers' demands waned with the increasing profit loss on an enlarged but unutilized capital. With a sufficient increase in productivity, concessions made to the workers could prove more profitable than their denial. The gradual elimination of cut-throat competition by way of monopolization and the generally increasing organization of capitalist production also entailed regulation of the labor market. Collective bargaining over wages and working conditions eliminated to some extent the element of spontaneity and uncertainty in the contests between labor and capital. The sporadic self-assertion of the workers made room for a more orderly confrontation and a greater "rationality" in capital-labor relations. The workers' trade-union representatives turned into managers of the labor market, in the same sense as that in which their political representatives attended to their farther-reaching social interests in the parliament of bourgeois democracy.

Slowly, but relentlessly, control over working-class organizations escaped the hands of the rank and file and was centralized in those of professional labor leaders, whose power rested on a hierarchically and bureaucratically organized structure, the operation of which, short of the destruction of the organization itself, could no longer be determined by its membership. The workers' acquiescence in this state of affairs required of course that the activities of "their" organizations provide some tangible benefits, which were then associated with the increasing power of the organizations and their particular structural development. The centralized leadership now determined the character of the class struggle as a fight over wages and for limited political goals that had some chance of being realized within the confines of capitalism.

The different developmental stages of capital production in different countries, as well as the divergent rates of expansion of particular industries in each nation, were reflected in the heterogeneity of wage rates and working conditions, which stratified the working class by fostering specific group interests to the neglect of proletarian class interests. The latter were supposedly to be taken care of by way of socialist politics, and where such politics were not as yet a practical possibility—either because the bourgeoisie had already preempted the whole sphere of politics through its complete control of the state machinery, as in the Anglo-Saxon countries, or because autocratic regimes precluded any participation in the political field, as in the Eastern capitalistically undeveloped nations—there was only the economic struggle. This, while uniting some layers of the working class, divided the class itself, which tended to frustrate the development of proletarian class consciousness.

The breaking up of the potential unity of the working class by way of wage differentials, nationally as well as internationally, was not the result of a conscious application of the ages-old principle of divide and rule to secure the reign of the bourgeois minority, but the outcome of the supply and demand relations of the labor market, as determined by the course of social production as the accumulation of capital. Occupations privileged by this trend tried to maintain their prerogatives through their monopolization, by restricting the labor supply in particular trades not only to the detriment of their capitalistic adversaries but also to that of the great mass of unskilled labor operating under more competitive conditions. Trade unions, once considered instruments for a developing class consciousness, turned out to be organizations concerned with no more than their special interests defined by the capitalist division of labor and its effects upon the labor market. In time, of course, trade organizations were superseded by industrial unions, incorporating a number of trades and uniting skilled with unskilled labor, but only to reproduce the strictly economic aspirations of the union membership on an enlarged organizational base.

In addition to wage differentials, which are a general feature of the system, wage discrimination was (and is) widely cultivated by individual firms and industries in the attempt to break the homogeneity of their labor force and to impair their ability for concerted action. Discrimination may be based on sex, race, or nationality, in accordance with the peculiarities of a given labor market. Persistent prejudices associated with the ruling ideology are utilized to weaken workers' solidarity and with it their bargaining power. In principle, it is of course immaterial to the capitalists to what particular race or nationality its labor force belongs, so long as their skill and propensity to work does not fall below the average, but in practice a mixed labor force with unequal, or even with equal, wage scales engenders or accentuates already existing racial or national antagonisms and impairs the growth of class consciousness. For instance, by reserving the better paid or less obnoxious jobs for a favored race or nationality, one group of workers is pitted against another to the detriment of both. Like job competition in general, discrimination lowers the general wage rate and increases the profitability of capital. Its use is as old as capitalism itself; the history of labor is also the history of competition and discrimination within the working class, dividing the Irish from the British workers, the Algerian, from the French, the black from the white, new immigrants from early settlers, and so on, almost universally.

While this is a consequence of the prevalence of bourgeois nationalism and racism in response to the imperialistic imperative, it affects the working class not only ideologically but also through their competition on the labor market. It strengthens the divisive as against the unifying elements of the class struggle and offsets the revolutionary implications of proletarian class consciousness. At any rate, it carries the social stratification of capitalism into the working class. Its economic struggles and organizations are designed to serve particular groups of workers, without regard to general class interests, and the confrontations between labor and capital remain necessarily within the frame of market and price relations.

Far-reaching wage differentials allow for different living standards, and it is by the latter, not by the labor done, that workers prefer to assess their status within capitalist society. If they can afford to live like the petite bourgeoisie, or come close to doing so, they tend to feel more akin to this class than to the working class proper. Whereas the working class as a whole can only escape its class position through the elimination of all classes, individual workers will try to break away from their own class to enter another, or to adopt the lifestyle of the middle class. An expanding capitalism offers some upward social mobility, just as it submerges individuals of the dominating or the middle class into the proletariat. But such individual movements do not affect the social class structure; they merely allow for the illusion of an equality of opportunity, which can serve as an argument against criticism of the unchangeable class structure of capitalist production.

In prosperous times, and because of the increase in families with more than one wage earner, better paid workers can save some of their income and thus draw interest as well as receive wages from their work. This gives rise to the delusion of a gradual breakdown of the class-determined distribution of the national income, as workers partake in it not only as wage earners but also as recipients of interest out of surplus value, or even as stockholders in the form of dividends. Whatever this may mean in terms of class consciousness for those thus favored, it is quite meaningless from a social point of view, as it does not affect the basic relationship between value and surplus value, wages and profits. It merely means that some workers realize an increase of their income out of the profit and interest produced by the working class as a whole. While this may influence the distribution of income among the workers, accentuating the already existing wage differentials, it does not affect in any way the social division of wages and profits represented by the rate of exploitation and the accumulation of capital. The rate of profit remains the same, whatever part of the mass of profit may reach some workers through their savings. The number of shares held by workers is not known, but judging by the number of shareholders in any particular country and by prevailing average wage rates, it could only be a negligible one. Interest on savings, as part of profit, is of course compensated for by the fact that while some workers save, others borrow. Interest thus increases but also reduces wages. With the great increase of consumer credit, it is most likely that, on balance, the interest received by some workers is more than equaled by the interest paid by others.

As their class is not homogeneous as regards income, but only with respect to its position in the social production relations, wage workers are apt to pay more attention to their immediate economic needs and opportunities than to the production relations themselves, which, in any case, appear to be unshakeable in a capitalism on the ascendant. Their economic interests involve, of course, not only the privileges enjoyed by special layers of the working class but also the general need of the great mass of workers to maintain, or to raise, their living standards. Higher wages and better working conditions presuppose increased exploitation, or the reduction of the value of labor power, thus assuring the continuous reproduction of the class struggle within the accumulation process. It is the objective possibility of the latter which nullifies the workers' economic struggle as a medium for the development of revolutionary class consciousness. There is no evidence that the last hundred years of labor strife have led to the revolutionizing of the working class in the sense of a growing willingness to do away with the capitalist sytem. The strike patterns in all capitalist nations vary with the business cycle, which is to say that the number of strikes, and the number of workers involved in them, decline in periods of depression and increase with every upward trend of economic activity. It is the accumulation of capital, not the lack of it, that determines the workers' militancy with regard to their wage struggles and their organizations.

Obviously, a serious downward trend of the economy, which reduces the total number of workers, also reduces the working time lost through strikes and lockouts, not only because of the smaller number of workers employed but also because of their greater reluctance to go on strike despite deteriorating working conditions. Likewise, trade or industrial unions decline not only because of the rising unemployment but also because they are less able, or not able at all, to provide the workers with sufficient benefits to warrant their existence. In times of depression no less than those of prosperity, the continuing confrontations of labor and capital have led not to a political radicalization of the working class, but to an intensified insistence upon better accommodations within the capitalist system. The unemployed have demanded their "right to work," not the abolition of wage labor, while those still employed have been willing to accept some sacrifices to halt the capitalist decline. The rhetoric of the existing, or newly founded, labor organizations no doubt has become more threatening, but their concrete demands, whether realizable or not, have been for a better functioning capitalism, not its abolition.

Every strike, moreover, is either a localized affair with a limited number of workers engaged in it, or an industry-wide struggle involving large numbers of workers spread over various localities. In either case, it concerns only the time-conditioned special interests of small sections of the working class and seldom affects society as a whole to any important extent. Every strike must end in the defeat of one or the other side, or in a compromise suitable to the opponents. In every case it must leave the capitalist enterprises profitable enough to produce and to expand. Strikes leading to bankruptcies of capitalist firms would also defeat the goals of the workers, which presuppose the continued existence of their employers. The strike weapon as such is a reformist weapon; it could only become a revolutionary instrument through its generalization and extension over the whole society. It was for this reason that revolutionary syndicalism advocated the General Strike as the lever to overthrow capitalist society, and it is for the same reason that the reformist labor movement opposes the General Strike, save as an extraordinary and controlled political weapon to safeguard its own existence.[1] Perhaps the only fully successful nationwide general strike was that called by the German government itself in order to defeat the reactionary Kapp Putsch of 1920.

Unless a mass strike turns into civil war and a contest for political power, sooner or later it is bound to come to an end whether or not the workers win their demands. It was of course expected that the critical situations brought about by such strikes, and the reactions to them on the part of capital and its state, would lead to a growing recognition of the unbridgeable antagonism of labor and capital and thus make the workers increasingly more susceptible to the idea of socialism. This was not an unreasonable assumption but it failed to be substantiated by the actual course of events. No doubt the turmoil of a strike itself brings with it a sharpened awareness of the full meaning of class society and its exploitative nature, but this, by itself, does not change reality. The exceptional situation degenerates again into the routinism of everyday life and its immediate necessities. What class consciousness was awakened turns once more into apathy and submission to things as they are.

The class struggle involves the bourgeoisie no less than the workers, and it will not do to consider exclusively the latter with regard to the evolution of their consciousness. The ruling bourgeois ideology will be reformulated and greatly modified in order to counteract noticeable changes in working-class attitudes and aspirations. The early open contempt of the bourgeoisie for the laboring population makes way for an apparent concern for their well-being and an appreciation for their contributions to the "quality of social life." Minor concessions are made before they are forced upon the bourgeoisie by independent working-class actions. Collaboration is made to appear beneficial to all social classes, and the road to harmonious social relations. The class struggle itself is turned to capitalist account, through the reforms thrust upon the ruling class and the resulting expectations of a possible internal transformation of capitalist society.

The most important of all the reforms of capitalism was of course the rise of the labor movement itself. The continuous extension of the franchise until it covered the whole adult population, and the legalization and protection of trade unionism, integrated the labor movement into the market structure and the political institutions of bourgeois society. The movement was now part and parcel of the system, as long as the latter lasted, at any rate, and it seemed to last just because it was able to mitigate its class contradictions by way of reforms. On the other hand, these reforms presupposed stable economic conditions and an orderly development, to be achieved through increasing organization, of which the reforms themselves were an integral part. This possibility had of course been denied by Marxian theory; the justification of a consistent reformist policy thus required abandonment of this theory. The revisionists in the labor movement were able to convince themselves that, contrary to Marx, the capitalist economy had no inherent tendency toward collapse, while those who upheld the Marxian theory insisted upon the system's objective limitations. But as regards the immediately given situation, the latter too had no choice but to struggle for economic and political reforms. They differed from the revisionists in their assumption that, due to the objective limits of capitalism, the fight for reforms will have different meanings at different times. On this view, it was possible to wage the class struggle in both the parliaments and in the streets, not only through political parties and trade unions, but with the unorganized workers as well. The legal foothold gained within bourgeois democracy was to be secured by the direct actions of the masses in their wage struggles, and the parliamentary activities were supposed to support these efforts. While this would have no revolutionary implications in periods of prosperity, it would be otherwise in crisis situations, particularly in a capitalism on the decline. As capitalism finds a barrier in itself, the fight for reforms would turn into revolutionary struggles as soon as the bourgeoisie was no longer able to make concessions to the working class.

Just as the capitalists are (with some exceptions) not economists but business people, the workers also are not concerned with economic theory. Quite aside from the question as to whether or not capitalism is destined to collapse, they must attend to their immediate needs by way of wage struggles, either to defend or to improve their living standards. If they are convinced of the decline and fall of capitalism, it is because they already adhere to the socialist ideology, even though they might not be able to prove their point "scientifically." It is hard, indeed, to imagine that an asocial system such as capitalism could last for very long, unless, of course, one were totally indifferent to the chaotic conditions of capital production and to its total corruption. However, such indifference is only another name for bourgeois individualism, which is not only an ideology but also a condition of the market relations as social relations. But even under its spell the workers' indifference does not spare them the class struggle, although it is at times only one-sidedly waged through the violent repression of all independent working class actions.

Thus far, reformism has nowhere led to an evolutionary transformation of capitalism into a more palatable social system, nor to revolutions and socialism. It may, on the other hand, require political revolutions in order to achieve some social reforms. Recent history provides numerous examples of political revolutions which exhausted themselves in the overthrow of a nation's despised governmental structure, without affecting its social production relations. Such revolutionary upheavals, insofar as they are not mere palace revolutions, which exchange one dictatorial regime with another, aim at institutional changes and, by implication, economic reforms. Political revolutions are here a precondition for any kind of reformist activity and not an outcome of the latter. They are not socialist revolutions, in the Marxian sense, even if they are predominantly initiated and carried through by the working classes, but reformist activities by more direct political means.

The possibility of revolutionary change cannot be questioned, for there have been political revolutions that altered social production relations and displaced the rule of one class by that of another. Bourgeois revolutions secured the triumph of the middle class and the capitalist mode of production. A proletarian revolution—that is, a revolution to end all class relations in the social production process—has not as yet taken place, although attempts in this direction have been made within and outside the framework of bourgeois politics. Whereas social reform is a substitute for social revolution and the latter may dissipate into mere capitalist reforms, or nothing at all, a proletarian revolution can only win or lose. It cannot be based on any kind of class compromise, as it is its function to eliminate all social class relations. It will thus find all classes outside the proletarian class arrayed against itself and no allies in its attempts to realize its socialist goals. It is this special character of proletarian revolution that accounts for the exceptional difficulties in its way.

Lenin's Revolution

Those in the socialist movement who were thinking in terms of a proletarian revolution were obliged to take all these facts into consideration. In their view, the revolution would not result from a gradual growth of proletarian class consciousness, finding its expression in the increasing might of working class organization and the eventual "legal" usurpation of the bourgeois state machinery, but would be the result of the self-destruction of the capitalist system, leaving the working class no other choice than the revolutionary solution of its own problems through a change of the social structure. And because this choice was restricted to the working class, in opposition to all other class interests, it had to lead to the dictatorship of the proletariat as the precondition for its realization.

In other words, the change in working-class ideology, being by and large a reflection of bourgeois ideology, would be the result of capitalism's decay and collapse. The dissipation of bourgeois self-confidence and class consciousness through the uncontrollable decomposition of its economic base, and therewith its political power, would also break its ideological hold over the working population. However, this was not a question of merely waiting for the expected economic and political catastrophe of bourgeois society; it involved preparation for such an eventuality through the organization of that part of the proletariat already possessed of revolutionary consciousness. The larger this organization, the less difficult it would be to instill its own ideas into the minds of the rebellious masses to aid their reactions to the disintegrating capitalism. Waiting did not imply passivity, but the legal or illegal forging of ideological and practical instruments of revolution.

The objective conditions for a proletarian revolution were to be found in devastating economic crisis conditions from which the bourgeoisie would be unable to extricate itself in time to allay their social consequences. As the social upheavals would be of a violent nature, it would be necessary to arm the proletariat for the destruction of the bourgeois state machinery. The problem was how to get the arms required to this end. But as a severe international crisis would most likely lead to imperialistic wars, or the latter issue into economic crisis conditions, which could not be dealt with in the usual "normal" ways, it was conceivable that an aroused and armed working class might turn its weapons against the bourgeoisie. Even short of war, it was not entirely precluded that a part of the armed forces of the bourgeoisie would side with the rebellious workers if they displayed enough energy to initiate civil war. And because imperialism was itself a sign of the deepening contradictions of capital production, its wars could be regarded as gigantic crisis conditions and as so many attempts at their solution by political means. In any case, what revolutions have taken place— the Paris Commune and the revolutions of the twentieth century in Russia and Central Europe—grew not out of purely economic crises but out of war and defeat and the general miseries associated with them.

We may recall here Karl Kautsky's answer to Upton Sinclair, referred to earlier, which expressed the rather vague hope that "after the war, after the debacle of a government, we may get strength enough to conquer the political power." At that time, as the official defender of Marxian orthodoxy, Kautsky still spoke of the conquest of power by revolutionary means and of the dictatorship of the proletariat. While a proletarian revolution, as a consequence of the sharpening of the existing class contradictions, was for Kautsky not a determinable occurrence, a revolution growing out of war and defeat seemed to him a certainty, even though its success remained questionable.[1] Kautsky's most faithful disciple, Lenin[2] —at the same time, and with the experience of the Russian Revolution of 1905 behind him—likewise associated war with revolution. In a letter to Maxim Gorky in 1913, he pointed out that "a war between Austria and Russia would be a very useful thing for the revolutions throughout Eastern Europe, but it is not very probable that Franz-Josef and Nicky will give us this pleasure."[3] Soon thereafter identifying the "age of imperialism" as "capitalism's last stage of development" and as "the eve of the pro-

letarian revolution," Lenin saw the first world war as the beginning
of an international revolution and consistently called not for the
restoration of the capitalist peace but for turning the imperialist
war into civil war.

If somewhat belatedly, Franz-Josef, Nicky, and all the other
potentates of Europe finally provided the revolutionaries and all
their other subjects with the pleasures of war. The pleasure did not
last long, due to the war's destructiveness with respect to human
lives and capitalist property. But once it started the bourgeoisie
could not conceive of an end to it except in terms of positive results,
that is, victory, expropriation, and annexation. Like business in
general, the war had to be profitable and to that end concentrate
more capital into fewer hands on an international scale. However,
the expectation that the war would turn into revolution, at least in
the defeated nations, also had to wait some time for its realization.
As envisioned by Lenin and other revolutionaries, this happened
first in Russia, because it was the "weakest link in the chain of imperialist powers." And it happened not because it provided the
Russian revolutionaries with objective conditions to be utilized to
win the workers to their side, but because of the population's own
war-weariness and the breakdown of both the war machinery and
the economy on which it depended.

Unlike its aftermath in October 1917, Russia's February Revolution of the same year was a truly spontaneous event, even
though it was preceded by a series of increasingly more ominous
social and political conflicts involving all social classes and the
autocratic government.[4] The military defeats and a relentless deterioration of economic conditions led to lock-outs, strikes, hunger
riots, and mutinies in the army, culminating in enormous mass
demonstrations, confrontations with the authorities, and finally in
the fraternization of decisive groups of the military with the rebellious masses. There were of course also politically organized forces
at work, attempting to inject their definitely demarcated goals
into the disaffected masses and to give them a socialist direction,
but at that time they were too small and ineffective to make much
of a difference. On the contrary, instead of leading the upheaval,
they were led by it, and adapted themselves to its elemental force.

The Russian revolution could not be a socialist revolution,
something that, in a sentence, implies the abolition of wage labor
and the socialization of all the means of production. Such a revo-

lution presupposes a developed capitalism and the existence of a proletariat able to determine the social production process. Such conditions did not exist in Russia except in the first stages of their development. But they appeared to exist in Western Europe, which, consequently, was that part of the world in which a socialist revolution could conceivably take place. A Russian revolution could lead only to the overthrow of tsardom and the institution of bourgeois rule. On the other hand, a socialist revolution in Western Europe would most likely preclude the continued existence of a bourgeois Russia, just as it had not been possible to preserve Russian serfdom within a bourgeois Europe. The relationship between the expected socialist revolution in the West and a possible revolution in Russia had already agitated Marx and Engels, both coming to the time-conditioned and speculative conclusion that a revolution in Russia, if it spilled over into Western Europe, might lead to conditions that could prevent the rise of a full-fledged Russian capitalism. In that case, the still existing communal form of agricultural production, the *mir*, might prove an asset for the socialization of the Russian economy. However, the assertion of this faint possibility was more a concession to the Russian Populists (Narodniks), who were at that time the only revolutionary force in Russia, than a real conviction and it was therefore allowed to be forgotten.

With the rise of a Social Democratic movement and the formation of trade unions in Russia, the Populists' idea of a people's revolution based on the peasantry made way for the Marxist conception of revolution by the industrial proletariat. This meant, of course, the revolution's postponement, as it presupposed the further unfolding of the capitalist system of production. The approaching social revolution was thus almost generally anticipated as a bourgeois revolution, to be supported by the socialist movement and the industrialist proletariat. And it could be supported best by making demands of a more radical nature than those the liberal bourgeoisie was able to formulate, or even think of. The workers were to lead this revolution, even though it could reach no more than a capitalistic bourgeois democracy, that is, conditions such as prevailed in the West.

This seemed to be all the more necessary because the liberal bourgeoisie was itself very weak and, as Alexander Herzen remarked, preferred, "against its own convictions, to walk on a leash, if only the mob is not released from it."[5] Quite apart from the question as to whether or not it was capable of initiating a bourgeois revolution, it was not willing to do so, out of fear of the blind rage of the peasant masses, which might destroy not only the autocratic regime but the bourgeoisie as well. It seemed so much better to gain political power gradually through the social transformation induced by capitalist development under the auspices of a strong state such as was provided for by a modified tsarist regime. Capital accumulation itself would slowly change the nature of the regime and force it to adapt itself to the requirements of modern society. While it was clear that it was the Revolution of 1905 which had led to the first, though meager, reforms of tsarism, such as the establishment of the Duma, this revolution, released by the industrial working class, also had opened the Pandora's box of the capital-labor relation and revealed the threat of an anti-bourgeois revolution.

For the Social Democrats, the development of capitalism in Russia, whatever its course, would at the same time, through its creation of an industrial proletariat, be a development toward socialism. And because capitalist development accelerated rather rapidly at the turn of the century, involving both the capitalization of agriculture and the formation of a proprietory peasantry, the expected revolutionary changes were no longer thought of as based on the liberation of the peasantry and the preservation and utilization of the remaining communal forms of agricultural production, but as based on the extension of capitalist market relations and their political reflections in bourgeois democracy. With this, Marxism came to look toward a socialist revolution in the wake of a successful bourgeois revolution.

For all practical purposes, however, Western socialism had already jettisoned its Marxian heritage. In the revisionist-reformist point of view, the extension of bourgeois democracy eliminated not only the possibility but also the need for a socialist revolution to be replaced by evolutionary changes in the capitalist class and exploitation relations. But if socialist revolution had already become an anachronism in the Western world, there was no point in expecting its arrival in Russia. And as the steady capitalization of the Russian economy promised a reluctant but nonetheless necessary democratization of its political structure, there was, perhaps, not even room for a bourgeois revolution in the Western sense of the term. Marxist revisionism was adapted to Russian conditions, on the one hand in the "legal Marxism" of the liberal bourgeoisie —for whom it merely implied the capitalization of Russia and its integration into the world market, together with all the paraphernalia of bourgeois democracy, such as political parties and trade unions—and, on the other hand in the reformist Social Democratic conviction that the impending revolution in Russia could only issue into a bourgeois state, which would first provide the basis for a vast socialist movement striving to transform the capitalist into a socialist society through a constant struggle for social reforms.

In the latter view, meaningful reforms in Russia presupposed a political revolution, and this revolution would, by force of circumstances, have a bourgeois character. This view was shared by the left wing of Russian Social Democracy, as represented since 1903 by its Bolshevik faction, but with the difference that this wing believed that such a revolution would have to be brought about by a political party based on the working class and the poor peasantry, for the liberal bourgeoisie itself, even apart from the question of its practical capabilities, was only too ready to stop short at some compromise with the tsarist regime. The impending revolution would be a worker-peasant revolution, or perhaps even a purely working-class revolution, even though it could accomplish no more within the Russian context than the creation of a modern state and the full release of the capitalist forces of production.

But, the left argued, even such a revolution might conceivably induce a revolution in Western Europe and through its internationalization alter the character of the Russian revolution. After all, such a possibility had entered the minds of Marx and Engels and still had an ideological basis in the West, thanks to the defense of "Marxian orthodoxy" by Karl Kautsky and his followers. This concept of "orthodoxy" was therefore based on a false apprehension of the nature of Western socialism, which mistook its ideology for reality, and on an incomprehension of the transformation this movement had undergone around the turn of the century. These illusions were lost at one stroke with the war of 1914, which revealed that not even Kautsky himself cared much for "Marxian orthodoxy," for which he had been the symbol within the Second International. The "trustee of revolutionary Marxism" overnight became the "renegade" Kautsky for the Bolsheviks in general and for his most devoted pupil, Lenin, in particular.

Prior to this revelation, the Russian socialists had paid far more attention to the conditions of the tsarist regime than to the actual state of international socialism. The latter, at least in an ideological sense, seemed to foreordain the course of the impending Russian revolution, just as Western capitalism prefigured the development of Russian capitalism. "Marxian orthodoxy," as Kautsky interpreted it, in opposition to the pure reformism of the revisionists, provided the ideology of Bolshevism, in opposition to the Menshevik, or reformist, wing of Russian Social Democracy. Whereas the latter did not expect more from the hoped-for Russian revolution than the undiluted rule of the bourgeoisie, the Bolsheviks envisioned the transcendence of this revolution through its internationalization, culminating in the rule of the proletariat. Of course, this was not a certainty, which may explain the ambiguities on the part of the Bolshevik Party as regards the character of the Russian revolution. While admitting its bourgeois nature, they employed at the same time a terminology referring to a socialist revolution, as if these could be one and the same thing.

These ambiguities had their origin in the prevailing Russian conditions, which seemed to rule out either a consistently bourgeois or a proletarian revolution, because of the unresolved quasi-feudal agricultural system and its dependence on the autocratic state. Any revolution must involve the great mass of the population; in this case that meant the peasantry, which, however, could not be expected to subordinate its own interests to those of the bourgeoisie or the industrial proletariat. These three classes would have to partake in the revolution, but could do so only with different ideas and different goals, which could hardly be brought under one hat. While their combined efforts were needed to end the tsarist regime, this could only lead to a reassertion of their particular class interests in the postrevolutionary situation. One class would have to dominate to hold the class-divided society together. Logically, and to judge by historical precedent, the bourgeoisie would have to be the ruling class.

However, as soon as the revolution was seen in an international context, the "historical precedents" and the "logical" rule of ascendance were no longer convincing. While two different social revolutions cannot occur together in a particular nation, they may occur simultaneously in an international setting, which may change the international class structure in such a way as to lead to the dominance of the proletariat over the whole of the revolutionary process, just as the diversity of the developmental stages of the various national entities does not prevent capitalism's over-all rule over the world economy. In view of this possibility, it made some sense to change the "rule" of historical ascendance and to try to base the Russian revolution on the political dominance of the working class, especially since the Russian bourgeoisie was itself an ineffective minority. The peasantry would have to be "neutralized," in one way or another, no matter which class, the bourgeoisie or the proletariat, should come in possession of the Russian state.

A social revolution cannot be organized, as it depends on conditions which escape conscious control. It can only be awaited, as the result of an observable intensification of the class contradictions existing within the given social relations of production. What can be organized in advance is the leadership required to give the expected revolution a definite direction and a particular goal. Any political party that thinks in terms of revolution concerns itself not with its preparation but with the organization of its leadership, the only thing that is organizable. This involves, of course, a continuous assessment and reassessment of the changing political and economic conditions, so as to make its control of the awaited revolution as effective as possible. Propaganda and agitation serve the formation of organizations aspiring to revolutionary leadership, but once these organizations exist, they see themselves as the irreplaceable presupposition of a successful revolution.

But how to lead a revolution that lacked any sort of homogeneity of interests within its revolutionary forces, as exemplified by the variety of organizations opposed to the social *status quo*? The situation in Russia at large, with its different specific class interests, was repeated within the revolutionary camp. All its organizations—the right and the left wing of the Social Revolutionaries,[6] the reformists and the revolutionaries of Russian Social Democracy, and the various ideological groupings between these major organizations—had their own ideas with respect to procedures and the desired outcome of the revolutionary process, thus precluding a unified revolutionary policy. Just as one class had to dominate the revolution itself, so one of the competing revolu-

tionary organizations had to strive for supremacy if it was to realize its own program.

As Lenin and the Bolsheviks had opted for the industrial proletariat as the leading element of the revolution, it followed that
the party of the proletariat, that is, the Bolshevik Party, must
strive to monopolize political power, if only to safeguard the proletarian character of the revolution. Quite apart from Lenin's assumption that the working class is unable to evolve a political
revolutionary consciousness on its own accord, the fact was that
the minority position of this class, together with the existence
and aspirations of other classes and their organizations, precluded
a democratic revolutionary development with an outcome favorable to the working class and socialism. Only a dictatorship, as
Lenin saw it, could maintain the proletarian impetus of the revolution and create preconditions for a socialist development in conjunction with the expected socialist revolutions in the developed
nations of the West. However, the very existence of the tsarist regime demonstrated that it was possible to hold political power in
spite of the existence of the most varied political and economic interests that in one way or another opposed the anachronistic autocratic government. If a backward and decaying political regime
had been able to keep itself in power, this should be even more
possible for a dictatorial regime geared to a progressive social development in harmony with the global course of evolution. Russia,
Lenin once said, "was accustomed to being ruled by 150,000 landowners. Why can 240,000 Bolsheviks not take over the task?"[7]
In any case, establishing such a dictatorship would mean having at
least a foot in the door leading to world revolution.

Already before the Menshevik-Bolshevik split of Russian Social Democracy in 1903, Lenin had shifted the question of the
Russian revolution away from purely theoretical considerations toward its practical problems, that is, the organization of its leadership. In his book *What Is to Be Done?*[8] however, he presented his
concern with organization as a theoretical problem, for, in his
view, "there can be no revolutionary movement without a revolutionary theory." By this he did not mean that men conceptualize
their activities, but referred to the social division of labor, as a division between mental and manual work, as it prevails in capitalist
society. Like all theory, the theory of socialism, according to
Lenin, "grew out of the philosophical, historical and economic

theories that were elaborated by the educated representatives of the propertied classes, the intellectuals."⁹ Due to its subordinate position in society, the working class may spontaneously evolve a trade-union consciousness, but not a revolutionary theory able to lead to a change of society. The revolutionary theory is not an outgrowth of the social production relations, but a result of science and philosophy and their practitioners' own dissatisfaction with these relations and the privileges bound up with them. It is, then, the conscience, the moral scruples, the idealistic disposition, and the knowledge of the intellectuals that provide the proletariat with the revolutionary consciousness it is unable to develop by itself. Thus the unhappiness of the intellectuals with the realities of capitalist society yields the revolutionary theory on which all revolutionary practice is based.

Lenin did not, as is often assumed, derive this strange inversion of Marxian theory from the peculiar conditions prevailing in Russia, but from a general principle, as is obvious in his application of this analysis to Western socialism. Here too, in Lenin's view, the labor movement restricted itself to purely reformist forms of class struggle because their intellectual leaders had "betrayed" their comrades and the ideas of revolution by leaving the path of revolutionary Marxism. Although the revolutionary intelligentsia is a necessary presupposition of any revolutionary activity, apparently it can lose its revolutionary inclinations and cease being the ferment of revolutionary theory. To avoid such "betrayals," it would be necessary to forge a type of revolutionary organization that allowed only the most steadfast revolutionaries into its ranks. In Lenin's view, this was made possible through the creation of the "professional revolutionary," whose whole existence depends on his revolutionary activity—in other words, someone like himself, who knows of no distinction between his individual and his organizational life and whose sole function is the promotion of revolution. It is true that Lenin also pointed to the requirement of illegality within the Russian setting, but as an additional argument, not as the basic rationale for his organizational concept. For him, the organizations of revolutionists are not identical with working-class organizations but are necessarily separated from the latter precisely because of their professional character. The effectiveness of such an organization, representing the "vanguard" of the revolution, depends on centralized leadership, endorsed by all its members, thus combining intraparty democracy with centralization, or, in brief, embodying to the principle of "democratic centralism." What all this amounted to was the formation of a party operating as a kind of state machinery, long before the question of the actual capture of state power arose. The party was to be built up as a counter-state to the existing state, ready to displace the latter at the first opportunity. The construction of this type of party was thus the practical preparation for its assumption of the power of the state. Here theory and practice fell together.

Because of the apparent remoteness of the Russian, or any other, revolution, Lenin's concept of the party-state was not grasped in its full meaning by the Social Democratic movement, but only as a rather queer idea of the relationship between spontaneity and organization, party and class, democratic and centralized leadership, and was largely adjudged as an aberration from a truly Marxian position. Western Social Democracy was itself highly centralized, as are all organizations in the capitalist system. Lenin's quest for an even more stringent centralization could hardly be understood, except as an argument for authoritarian control and one-man rule. Everyone knew from his own experience that "democratic centralism" is a contradiction in terms, as it is a practical impossibility to reach a real consensus in a centralized organization wherein the power of persuasion is also vested in the organized leadership. It made in particular no sense from Lenin's own point of view, which denied the "plain and simple" worker the ability to form his own revolutionary opinions and thus condemned him in advance to accept whatever the educated leadership proposed. Moreover, the many thousands of paid organizers and functionaries in the socialist parties and trade unions could see not much difference between themselves and the "professional revolutionaries" of Lenin's organization. The organization was also their livelihood, but it did not follow that this determined their revolutionary or anti-revolutionary attitudes. In the face of this opposition, from the right as well as the left wing of international socialism, Lenin and the Bolsheviks did not overstress their organizational principles but followed them nonetheless in the building up of the Bolshevik faction of Russian Social Democracy—a process that also assured Lenin's unique position within this organization.

The pyramidal structure of organizations is not simply the

way they are formed but also a means to their control. The higher one climbs up the organizational ladder, the greater the influence he can exert and the more difficult it becomes to be replaced by those occupying the lower rungs. This is not automatically so, but is deliberately built into the organization, so as to assure its control by those who are near, or have reached, its top. Although not totally foolproof the system works well, for which the whole of capitalism bears witness as well as its manifold separate organizations, which include those of the labor movement. Control of the organization once gained, this domination is rarely, if ever, relinquished through pressures from below. Unless the organization is itself destroyed, in most cases, only death can part it from its established leadership. According to Lenin, this is as it should be, for if the leadership *is* the correct one, it would be silly to replace it with a new and untried one. Observe, he wrote, how in Germany

> this vast crowd of millions values its "dozen" tried political leaders, how firmly it clings to them. Members of the hostile parties in parliament often tease the socialists by exclaiming: "Fine democrats you are indeed! Your movement is a working-class movement only in name; as a matter of fact it is the same clique of leaders that is always in evidence, Bebel and Liebknecht, year in year out, and that goes on for decades. Your deputies are supposed to be elected from among the workers, but they are more permanent than the officials appointed by the Emperor."
>
> But the Germans only smile with contempt at these demagogic attempts to set the "crowd" against the "leaders," to arouse turbid and vain instincts in the former, and to rob the movement of its solidity and stability by undermining the confidence of the masses in the "dozen of wise men." The political ideas of the Germans have already developed sufficiently, and they have acquired enough political experience to enable them to understand that without the "dozen" of tried and talented leaders, professionally trained, schooled by long experience and working in perfect harmony, no class in modern society is capable of conducting a determined struggle. . . . Our (Russian) wise-acres, however, at the very moment when Russian Social Democracy is passing through a crisis entirely due to our lack of a sufficient number of trained, developed and experienced leaders to guide the spontaneous ferment of the masses, cry out with the profundity of fools, it is a bad business when the movement does not proceed from the rank and file.[10]

It would of course be unfair to point to Lenin's early and rather silly ruminations on the question of organization, as presented in *What Is to Be Done?* were it not for the fact that they continued to motivate him throughout his life and guided the activities of the Bolshevik Party. On this point, which formed the starting point of the Leninist type of organization, and which occasioned the split within Russian Social Democracy, Lenin never wavered, bringing it to its full realization in the strictly centralized structure of his party and the latter's dictatorship over the working class in the name of socialism. However strange these ruminations may have sounded in the ears of socialists, for whom the labor movement implied the self-determination of the working class, they were at the same time devoid of all originality, as they merely copied the prevalent political procedures within the capitalist system and tried to utilize them for its overthrow. What Lenin proposed appeared to him to be a realistic approach to the practical needs of the revolution, the effectiveness of which could be questioned only by those who merely talked about revolution but did nothing to bring it about. As the bourgeois ideology had to be countered by a socialist ideology, so the centralism of bourgeois political rule had to be combatted by the centralized determination of the revolutionary party. Although within the general setting of the capital-labor relations, the revolutionary struggle which could yield practical results was, according to Lenin, mainly a fight between the existing state machinery and the party determined to destroy it. The latter was thus the precondition for the anticipated new state and the guarantee that the revolution would not dissipate into formless upheavals but would issue into the dictatorship of the party as a presupposition for the dictatorship of the proletariat. The means and methods of this struggle were determined by the previous structure of bourgeois society itself, but could be turned against it, if used intelligently by a truly revolutionary party and a truly revolutionary leadership, such as Lenin and the Bolsheviks endeavored to construct.

There was of course a wide gap between the Bolsheviks' intentions and their actual achievements. If statistics can be trusted, around 1905 there were about 8,400 organized Bolsheviks and most probably the same number of Mensheviks. By 1906, membership had grown to 13,000 for the Bolsheviks and 18,000 for the Mensheviks—"one may fairly safely conclude that both factions comprised about 40,000 members in 1907. [Thus] one ought not to view Russian Social Democracy as something centered

on the cafes of Geneva and composed of an 'élite mostly in ex-
ile.' "[11] But it is still astonishing that this small number, spread over
the whole of Russia, should be considered the "vanguard" of the
impending revolution. Of course, a rapid growth in numbers could
be expected with increasing industrialization, capitalization, and
radicalization, but even so this growth was limited by the general
backwardness of Russian society.

As to the social composition of Russian Social Democracy, it
could be considered a working-class movement, even if top-heavy
with elements from the middle class. But Lenin's concern was not
so much with what he called the "plain and simple" workers, but
with the "wise men," designated to lead those workers away from
the reformist into the revolutionary path of activity. Apart from
the impossibility of transforming all party members into "professional revolutionaries," which would release them from their
working-class status, and which was anyway precluded for financial reasons, the principle of centralization itself excluded more
than concentration upon the leadership. Lenin trusted in the rise
of revolutionary situations, brought about through society's contradictory development, but he mistrusted the idea that the objective conditions would also bring forth a subjective readiness for
revolutionary change. By and large, the working class was for him
a part of the objective conditions, not of the subjective requirements of the revolution. However necessary the aroused masses
were, their want of proper knowledge and ideological consistency
could easily lead to a failure to recognize their "historic mission,"
or to the submission to and betrayal by misleaders of the working
class, who either consciously or unconsciously put themselves at
the service of the bourgeoisie.

In the prerevolutionary phase of Bolshevism, Lenin's organizational concepts must have had a rather comical tinge, because of
the enormous distance the party would still have to travel to reach
its revolutionary goal. Although actually it functioned not much
differently from any other socialist organization, it presented itself
from its very beginning as the party that would actually lead the
revolution, because it was the only one in possession of the theory
that assured its success. This claim already implied a relentless
struggle against all other organizations and the demand for sole
control of the revolution. The party's authoritarianism can thus
not be blamed on unexpected difficulties that arose during the rev-

olution, for it constituted the principle of Bolshevism from the day of its initiation.

At the top of the organizational ladder there is only room for one. But this may have only ornamental meaning and need not imply an ultimate center of decision-making power. In noticeable contrast to other socialist organizations of the time, the Bolshevik Party was from the very outset under Lenin's complete and undivided control. It was not thinkable under any other leadership. Most theoreticians leave the practical execution of their ideas to others, but in Lenin the theoretical and the practical were combined in his own person. He watched over both with equal fervor, as if incapable of delegating any degree of responsibility to other people. There was of course dissension in the party, but it was always resolved to Lenin's satisfaction. An alternative solution could only split the party, as Lenin seemed to be unable to admit to errors detected by others than himself. He was capable of self-criticism and sudden reversals but not of accepting corrections by other people. But even so, A. N. Potresov,

> who had known Lenin since 1894, and organized and edited *Iskra* together with him, but later on, during the first and second revolutions, came to detest him, and was thrown into prison under Lenin's dictatorship, was impartial enough to write the following words about him . . . :
> "No one could sweep people away so much by his plans, impress them by his strength of will, and win them over by his personality as this man, who at first sight seemed so unprepossessing and crude, and, on the face of it, had none of the things that make for personal charm." Neither Plekhanov nor Martov, nor anyone else had the secret of that hypnotic influence on or rather ascendancy over people, which Lenin radiated. Only Lenin was followed unquestionably as the indisputable leader, as it was only Lenin who was that rare phenomenon, particularly in Russia—a man of iron will and indomitable energy, capable of instilling fanatical faith in the movement and the cause, and possessed of equal faith in himself."[12]

There are such men, fortunately not always at the head of a movement. The competitive-aggressive character of Lenin cannot be denied; it comes to the fore not only in his total rule over his own organization, but in all his writings, which—no matter what the subject matter—were always of a polemical nature, designed to destroy real or imaginary enemies of the revolution. Most probably he suffered from some form of paranoia, for his self-confidence was as excessive as his fear of political rivals. But this is neither here nor there, as it is quite possible to share his attitudes and convictions without being obsessed by them to the same degree. The world is swarming with "charismatic" people, sane or insane, who would like to head a social movement and to symbolize it in their own person. But each movement can have only one supreme leader, who must claw his way to the top and must command the necessary qualifications. Thus men with dispositions totally different from those characteristic of Lenin, such as Trotsky or Stalin, Hitler or Mussolini, may do as well in reaching and holding supreme power and in winning the admiration of the multitude as well as that of their underlings.

There must of course also be people who accept their subordination willingly and are ready to "follow the line" drawn by their leadership. But in a party that expects to become the ruling party, even subordination may appear as a good thing, to assure concerted actions leading to the desired goal. After all, this is how business is done and is the principle upon which state power rests, a situation to which most people have been habituated and which they regard as unavoidable. Just as the world of business competition leads to monopolization, the struggle for political leadership engenders a political monopoly, which must then be defended through the exclusion of any further opposition. In other words, the political monopoly must be organized, and thus while the struggle for power may issue into one-man rule, the latter must be retained by ending all serious contention within the organization. In this respect, the Leninist organization was a full success, for it was able to reach a consensus of its membership despite its high centralization dominated by a singular will. More than that, the situation was idealized by a ritual adulation of Lenin that was both earnestly felt and deliberately fostered as an expedient way to maintain internal cohesion. What seemed abnormal for a socialist movement became the norm, foreshadowing the future terror of Stalin's "personality cult," and was adopted by all the Marxist-Leninist organizations formed after the Bolshevik Revolution.

It is the Bolshevik type of organization that explains Lenin's extraordinary personal role in the determination of Bolshevik policy after the February Revolution of 1917. Lenin's uncontested leadership implied of course political paralysis on the part of those

Bolsheviks accustomed to follow the cherished "old man's" advice and bound to it by party discipline. There can be little doubt that there would not have been the *coup d'état* of October without Lenin's determination to grasp political power, which, he thought, was there for the asking, and in which he was proven right. The events of October must be credited to Lenin's leadership, although executed by Trotsky, the party, and its many sympathizers. After that, as the saying goes, nothing succeeds like success.

The will to assume political power by revolutionary means may always be present but has to await a historical opportunity to be exercised. What makes a revolutionary is of course his impatience with the slow course of social development and his desire to hasten its pace. He will therefore often endow his anticipations in regard to the existing social conflicts with a greater revolutionary potentiality than they actually possess. Although Lenin and his colleagues did not object to the policies adopted by Western socialism, which, for the time being, consisted in the utilization of bourgeois democracy and the labor market for purposes of fostering proletarian class consciousness and building up an independent labor movement, they saw this as a time-conditioned endeavor which did not exhaust the possibilities for working-class action. Although vaguely, Lenin recognized after the experience of 1905 that just as it seemed not impossible to take power in the context of a bourgeois revolution, and in conjunction with a Western revolution to annul the bourgeois character of such a revolution, so it would also be possible to set aside the traditional activities of Western socialism and to replace bourgeois democracy with a socialist dictatorship, which would turn the nominal into a real democracy. This view was also shared, with greater consistency, by people outside the Bolshevik Party, such as for instance, A. I. Helphand (Parvus) and L. Trotsky in their concept of the "permanent revolution."

As pointed out before, Russian Social Democracy around 1905 was too small an organized force to have more than a marginal effect upon the social upheavals of that year. There were about 3 million industrial workers, more than 2 million of whom participated in a wave of strikes which soon took on a political character as they took place within general crisis conditions aggravated by the Russian defeat in the Russo-Japanese war. Although the revolution involved nonproletarian layers of the population, as well as segments of the peasantry, the army, and the navy, it found in the striking workers in the big cities, particularly St. Petersburg and Moscow, its most decisive element. The strikes were spontaneous in the sense that they were not called by political organizations or trade unions but in the main were launched by unorganized workers who had no choice but to look upon their workplace as the springboard of their actions and the center of their organizational efforts. The local coordination of the activities demanded representation through city-wide soviets, workers' councils, or workers' deputies, to formulate policies and to negotiate with the authorities. Of all the soviets formed in Russia during the revolutionary events, the St. Petersburg Soviet, which lasted from October to December 1905, was perhaps the most representative. It found its first historian in Leon Trotsky—himself one of its leading members—who saw the soviets

> as a response to an objective need—a need born of the course of events. It was an organization which was authoritative and yet had no tradition, which could immediately involve a scattered mass of hundreds of thousands of people while having virtually no organizational machinery; which united the revolutionary currents within the proletariat; which was capable of initiative and spontaneous self-control—and most important of all, which could be brought out from underground within twenty-four hours.[13]

The soviets attracted the most articulate and therefore, generally, the most politically alert of the laboring population, and they found support in the socialist organizations and incipient trade unions.[14] The city-wide soviets comprised delegates of various factories, forming a kind of "workers' parliament" with an elected executive committee. The delegates could at any time be recalled. The soviets were impartial with respect to socialist organizations, allowing them to send delegates who could advise but had no voting rights. The difference between these traditional organizations and the soviets was summed up in Trotsky's remark, that while the socialist parties were organizations *within the proletariat*, and their immediate aim was to achieve influence over the masses, the soviet was, from the start, "the organization *of the proletariat*, and its aim was the struggle for revolutionary power."[15]

For Lenin, the soviets of 1905 were *"organs of direct mass struggle.* They originated as organs of the *strike* struggle. By force of circumstances they very quickly became the organs of the *general revolutionary* struggle against the government. . . . It was not some theory, not appeals on the part of someone, or tactics invented by someone, not party doctrine, but the force of circumstances that led these nonparty mass organs to realize the need for an uprising and transformed them into organs of an uprising."[16] Lenin saw the soviets as "the embryos of a provisional government" because "power would *inevitably* have passed to them had the uprising been victorious," and spoke of the need to shift the center of attention "to studying these embryonic organs of a new government that history has brought into being, to studying the conditions for their work and *their success.*"[17] But he still insisted on the undivided revolutionary leadership of the Social Democratic Party. The soviets were for Lenin "not an organ of proletarian self-government, nor an organ of self-government at all, but a fighting organization for the achievement of definite aims."[18] Although the party "has never renounced its intention of using nonparty organizations, such as the soviets," he said, it should do so in order to strengthen its own influence in the working class and to increase its own power.[19]

From this position Lenin never deviated even when he proclaimed the slogan "All power to the soviets" in order to break up the dual power of the soviets and the liberal Provisional Government established by the February Revolution of 1917. The soviets were, in Lenin's view, to be induced to eliminate the provisional government, but only to form a new government, based on the soviets instead of on the contemplated Constituent Assembly. This would exclude the nonworking population from direct or indirect participation in state activities and thus realize the dictatorship of the proletariat. The new government would be subject to the control of the soviets, not to that of any particular party. But at the same time, while asking for a soviet government, Lenin was still thinking in terms of a Bolshevik government, with or without the consent of the soviets. At the First Congress of Soviets on June 3, 1917, Tseretelli, a Menshevik Minister in the Provisional Government, made the remark that in Russia at that time there existed not one political party that would say, give us the power into our hands. "I answer there is," Lenin retorted. "No party can decline to do that, and our party does not decline. It is ready at any minute to take the whole power."[20]

At this time the situation was still in flux; the war was continuing despite the progressive dissolution of the army; counter-revolutionary plots were being hatched; the economy was disintegrating with increasing speed; and the Bolshevik faction in the soviets was still a small minority, unable to turn the situation to its own account. It was not possible to tell, from the existing political constellation, which way the wheel would turn. Would the coalition of the soviets with the Provisional Government last until the calling of the Constituent Assembly—to which all parties had committed themselves—and lead to the formation of a bourgeois government and the completion of the bourgeois revolution? Or would a change in the external situation, or in the composition of the soviets, end the coalition and issue into a renewal of the civil war? Or would the provisional government, with the aid of loyal parts of the army, subdue the soviets to its own will through some form of dictatorship? The many parties operating within the soviets and their widely diverging political and economic programs, as well as frictions within the government itself, made for a chaotic political situation in which everything and nothing seemed possible. Under these conditions, the Bolsheviks could come to power either by gaining the majority in the soviets and then trying to dislodge the Provisional Government, or by risking a military uprising with their own limited forces, without counting on the soviets' support. Either way was feasible and the best solution would be to prepare for both. This involved a certain ambivalence toward the soviets, which Lenin thus at times found indispensable and at other times saw as a hindrance to the execution of a second revolution. But no matter what role the soviets would come to play, it was power for the party that determined Lenin's policy, as may easily be surmised from all the subsequent developments. This was of course only consistent with both his general philosophy and his conception of the party as the determining element of the socialist revolution.

Because in February 1917 soldiers went over to the revolution, the first soviets were composed of soldiers' and workers' councils with the former in the great majority. The Petrograd Soviet in the second part of March 1917, for instance, had 3,000 delegates, 2,000 of whom were soldiers. The influence of the revolutionary intelligentsia was far greater in 1917 than in 1905, as may be seen from the fact that of the 42 members of the Petro-

grad Soviet's Executive Committee only seven were factory workers. Mensheviks and Social Revolutionaries were at first predominant. The Bolshevik fraction in the Petrograd Soviet consisted of
40 out of the 3,000 delegates. By September 1917, however, the
Bolsheviks had gained the majority. Their growing strength within
the revolutionary development was due to their own unconditional adaptation to the real goals of the rebellious masses. Apart
from the latter's narrower demands for the relief of immediate
miseries, their wider demands embraced the ending of the war and
the expropriation and distribution of the landed estates. The February Revolution was at once a bourgeois, a proletarian, and a
peasant revolution, but it was its peasant aspect that assured its
success. Of Russia's 174 million population only 24 million lived
in cities, and it was the terrible plight of the peasantry that allied
it to the industrial proletariat. Although the Provisional Government was ready to institute a series of agricultural reforms, it was
not willing to assent to the expropriation of the big landowners
without compensation, for this would violate the principle of
private property on which the rule of the bourgeoisie is based.
Neither was it willing to sue for peace, for it still hoped for an allied victory and participation in the spoils of war. The Bolsheviks,
however, were for the immediate ending of the war and for the
distribution of land to the peasantry. Because the majority of the
soldiers came from the peasantry, the soldiers' councils no less
than the workers' councils shifted their allegiance from the bourgeoisie and social reformist parties to the Bolsheviks.

It was not the Marxist agrarian program that attracted the
peasants but that of the Social Revolutionaries, which demanded
the nationalization of all land under the control of democratically
organized village communes on the basis of equal land holdings.
From a Marxian point of view such a program was utopian. Marxism favors large-scale production that does away with individual
peasant farming. Because it envisioned socialism as the successor
to capitalism, and because in its view capitalism itself is doing
away with small-scale peasant farming, it expected that the peasant
question would largely be solved within capitalism so as not to
constitute a major problem for socialism. Lenin's early opposition
to Narodnism and its Social Revolutionary heirs was based on the
belief that an equal distribution of land to the peasants was not
only highly unrealistic but in contradiction to a socialist mode of

production. He also favored the breaking up of the semifeudal estates but only to hasten the development of capitalistic agriculture, which would restore the concentration of landownership under more progressive conditions. At any rate, this was a problem of the future, of further capitalistic development. The peasantry, Lenin said, "can free itself from the yoke of capital by associating itself with the working-class movement, by helping the workers in their struggle for the socialist system, for transforming the land, as well as the other means of production (factories, works, machines, etc.) into social property. Trying to save the peasantry by protecting small-scale farming and small holding from the onslaught of capitalism would be a useless retarding of social development."[21]

Apart from all programs, however, soon after the February Revolution the peasants began to expropriate and divide the land on their own accord. Until then, the Provisional Government had paid little attention to the peasant question. It only began to consider it seriously in the face of upheavals in the countryside. But even so, it only brought forth vague suggestions regarding the expropriation and distribution of the land, the enactment of which into law was left to the forthcoming Constituent Assembly. Because Mensheviks and Social Revolutionaries were now represented in the Provisional Government, the latter's ambiguous attitude and inactivity regarding the land problem cost these parties the active support of the peasants. "We were victorious in Russia, and with such ease," Lenin pointed out at a later date,

> because we prepared our revolution during the imperialist war. . . . Ten million workers and peasants in Russia were armed, and our slogan was: an immediate peace at all costs. We were victorious because the vast masses of the peasants were revolutionarily disposed against the landowners. The Social Revolutionaries . . . demanded revolutionary methods, . . . but lacked the courage to act in a revolutionary way. We were victorious . . . not only because the undisputed majority of the working class was on our side . . . but also because half the army, immediately after our seizure of power, and nine-tenths of the peasants, in the course of some weeks, came over to our side; we were victorious because we adopted the agrarian programme of the Social Revolutionaries instead of our own.[22]

In the quest for state power, it was clear to Lenin that it was absolutely essential to win the peasants' support, even if only their passive support. The Marxist agrarian program had been developed in opposition to that of the Social Revolutionaries, but at a time when the practical questions of the revolution were not yet acute. Under Russian conditions this program was totally unrealistic. All abstract considerations of the agrarian problem became meaningless when the peasants simply seized what was seizable. It was not because "the Bolsheviks availed themselves of the agrarian program of the Social Revolutionaries that they were victorious," but because they merely sanctioned what was taking place anyway. It is true, of course, that in this way they won the "good will" of the peasants and thus had an easier time of gaining and holding state power. But Lenin's presentation makes it appear as if a timely opportunistic move, a part of a general strategy, led to the Bolsheviks' triumph, thus justifying opportunism as a weapon of revolution. The acquiescence in the peasants' seizure of land, though recognized as a violation of Marxian principles, was nonetheless seen as a clever ruse to help the "Marxist" revolution along. Although relentlessly denouncing the opportunism of their political adversaries, Lenin and the Bolsheviks prided themselves on their general willingness to resort to all kinds of temporary concessions and compromises, sacrificing their own principles to gain a greater advantage in the long run.

Although Lenin was the deadly enemy of the bourgeois revolution, his politics were those of the bourgeois mind; that is, he saw the struggle between classes and nations as dependent upon the strategies and tactics of political leaders and statesmen, who determine the movements of the populations. It was a question of outmaneuvering and outwitting one's adversaries, a game to be won by those most adept in the manipulation of events. Politics and revolution were an "art," which would give the palm of victory to the most versatile and most knowledgeable of the competing contestants—not an "art" in contrast to the rigidities of science, or the dullness of the commonplace, but as a matching of talents that would bring the best man to the top. To be sure, the game had to be played under the varying handicaps set by the prevailing objective social conditions, but even so, within these conditions it was still a question of "who was going to destroy whom" in the struggle for political power. It was this that Lenin meant by the preponderance of theory over practice, or that of the leaders over the more or less uneducated masses, who could only react blindly to situations beyond their comprehension.

Not denying the objective limitations set for the history-making social process by class relations and the level of economic development, Lenin succeeded in convincing himself that though history is made by men, it is actually made by only a few of them, who, by identifying themselves with particular class interests, alter the course of events through their powers of persuasion and their exceptional abilities. But every bourgeois knows that sheer arbitrariness is an impossibility, even though he may insist upon the history-making capacity of individuals and credit historical developments to the existence of great men. He overlooks the fact that the great man is such only because the apex of the pyramidical social structure demands his existence, no matter what his particular qualifications (although competition may on occasion bring some outstanding personality to the top of the pyramid). In a class-ridden society the role of the great man is not only filled automatically, it must be insisted upon to keep the social fabric together. No class society can exist without its great men, for this is only the other side of the same coin. By the same token, however, the great men are limited in their reach by the general socioeconomic conditions which they come to symbolize. Their interference in events is circumscribed by what is historically possible. But what is historically possible is not determined by what may be *politically possible*, but by the actual level of the social forces of production and the social relations associated with them.

It was political events that favored the Bolsheviks. At the First All-Russian Soviet Congress, in June 1917, the Bolsheviks controlled 13 percent of the 790 delegates; at the second congress, in October 1917, they controlled 51 percent of the 675 delegates. However, though the Bolsheviks had the majority in the soviets of Petrograd and Moscow as early as September 1917, Lenin would have been ready to take power even if it had been otherwise. "It would be naive," he wrote, "to wait for a 'formal' majority for the Bolsheviks. No revolution ever waits for *that*."[23] Despite opposition within his own party, he demanded an armed insurrection prior to the convocation of the Second All-Russian Congress of Soviets. A *fait accompli* would make it easier to get the congress's support for the elimination of the Provisional Government. To that end, the Petrograd Soviet organized a military-revolutionary committee under the leadership of Trotsky, which went into action on the twenty-fifth of October. Within a few hours of the *coup d'état*, Lenin was able to claim victory for the workers' and peasants' revolution, and, later in the day, to win the approval of the All-Russian Congress of Soviets. This was the easier because the right Social Revolutionaries and the Mensheviks had left the congress in protest against the *coup d'état*. On the following day the first Workers' and Peasants' Government was formed.

Lenin's timing of the insurrection proved to be correct. It found the Provisional Government defenseless and assured an almost bloodless transfer of power to the Soviet government. Supposedly, it also changed the hitherto bourgeois into a proletarian revolution, even though this was brought about not by a spontaneous rising of the working class but by a conspiratorily organized military force of armed Bolshevik workers and military detachments siding with the Bolsheviks. Although a party affair, it undoubtedly coincided with the real demands of the workers, as expressed in the shift of political allegiances within the soviets and in the general attitude of the working population. Lenin had actually succeeded in making the proletarian revolution *for* the workers, thus substantiating his own revolutionary concepts. However, when he demanded the preparation for the insurrection, he did not speak of the exercise of state power by the soviets but of that by the party. With the majority of the soviet deputies being Bolshevik, or supporting the Bolsheviks, he took for granted that the new government would be a Bolshevik government. And that was the case of course, even though some left Social Revolutionaries and left Socialists obtained positions in the new government.

At first, however, the Bolsheviks proceeded rather cautiously, emphasizing the democratic nature of their new regime and their willingness to accept the decisions of the popular masses even if not in agreement with then. They did not at once repudiate the election of the Constituent Assembly, which, as it turned out, gave a large majority to the Social Revolutionaries and put the Bolsheviks in the minority. But despite their election success, due to their traditional empathy with the peasants, the Social Revolutionaries were not a unified party, particularly with regard to the question of the continuation of war. The left Social Revolutionaries were in closer accord with the Bolsheviks than with the right wing of their own party. While the elections for the Constituent Assembly were being held, an All-Russian Congress of Peasant Deputies was also in progress. The congress split the Social Revolutionaries, and the left wing entered a coalition with the Bolsheviks. The election results had made clear that the Constituent Assembly would destroy the Bolshevik Party's political dominance and the accomplishments of the revolution as well. With the consent of the left Social Revolutionaries and some left Socialists, the Bolsheviks simply drove the assembly away.

The will of the majority of the population, workers and peasants, to reach for peace, land, bread, and liberty, found a complete counterpart in the political program of the Bolshevik Party. The early bourgeois democratic aspiration for a Constituent Assembly had lost its apparent importance, not only for the Bolsheviks, but for the broad masses as well. Not only in Russia but internationally revolutionaries hailed soviet rule as an accomplishment of historical significance. Even such a skeptical socialist as Rosa Luxemburg stated that by seizing power, the Bolsheviks had "for the first time proclaimed the final aim of socialism as the direct program of practical policies."[24] They had done so by solving "the famous problem of winning a majority of the people" by revolutionary tactics that led to a majority, instead of waiting for the latter to evolve a revolutionary tactic.[25] In her view, at least as far as the urban masses were concerned, Lenin's party had grasped their true interests by playing all power into the hands of the soviets.

From his own point of view, however, Lenin equated soviet power with the power of the Bolshevik Party; he saw in the latter's monopoly of the state the realization of the rule of the soviets. After all, there was only the choice between a capitalist government and a workers' and peasants' government able to prevent the return of the bourgeois rule. But to continue Bolshevik domination of the government and its state apparatus, the workers and peasants would have to continue to elect Bolsheviks to the soviets. For that there was no guarantee. Just as the Mensheviks and Social Revolutionaries, once in the majority, now found themselves in a minority position, so things could change again for the Bolsheviks. It was thus necessary to prevent a reemergence of the soviets, which might favor a return to bourgeois political institutions. Left to themselves, the soviets were quite capable of abdicating their power position for the promises of the liberal bourgeoisie and their social reformist allies. To secure the socialist character of the revolution demanded, then, the suppression of all anti-Bolshevik forces within and outside the soviet system. In a short time the soviet regime became the dictatorship of the Bolshevik Party. The emasculated soviets were retained, though only formally, to hide this fact.

Quite apart from the tactical participation in the elections to the Constituent Assembly, and the occasional lip service paid to this bourgeois institution, Lenin had already, in the so-called "April Theses" proposed to his organization after his return to Russia, argued that a parliamentary republic was unnecessary *because* of the existence of the soviets, which in his view would allow for a type of state such as had been brought about by the Paris Commune. In accordance with this idea, he did not think that socialism was the immediate task, but that the "transition to the control of production and the distribution of products by the soviet of workers' deputies" sufficed to serve the immediate needs of the revolution. What was of foremost importance was the nature of the state, of political power, from which everything else would flow in the direction of socialism. "All power to the soviets," did not include possession of the means of production, or the abolition of wage labor. The workers were not expected to administer but merely to oversee the industrial enterprises. The first decree of Workers' Control extended it

> over the production, storing, buying and selling of raw materials and finished goods as well as over the finances of the enterprises. The workers exercise this control through their elected organizations, such as factory and shop committees, soviet elders, etc. The office employees and the technical personnel are also to have representation in these committees. . . . The organs of workers' control have the right to supervise production. Commercial secrets are abolished. The owners have to show to the organs of workers' control all their books and statements for the current year and for the past year.[26]

However, capitalist production and workers' control are incompatible and this makeshift affair, whereby the Bolsheviks hoped to retain the aid of the capitalist organizers of production and yet satisfy the yearnings of the workers to take possession of industry, could not last for long. "We did not decree socialism all at once throughout the whole of industry," Lenin explained a year later, because socialism can take shape and become finally established only when the working class has learned to run the economy. . . . That is why we introduced workers' control, knowing that it was a contradictory and partial measure. But we consider it most important and valuable that the workers have themselves tackled the job, that from workers' control, which in the principal industries was bound to be chaotic, amateurish and partial, we have passed to workers' administration of industry on a nation-wide scale.[27]

The change from "control" to "administration" turned out to entail the abolition of both. To be sure, just as the emasculation of the soviets took some time, for it required the formation and consolidation of the Bolshevik state apparatus, so the workers' direct influence in factories and workshops was only gradually eliminated through such methods as shifting the controlling rights from the factory committees to the trade unions and then transforming the latter into agencies of the state. In fact, workers' control by factory councils or shop stewards preceded the governmental decree. These committees arose spontaneously during the February Revolution, as the only possible form of workers' representation, due to the destruction of the trade unions during the war. The latter had been, of course, the counterpart of Russian Social Democracy and were a stronghold of its Menshevik wing. They were rapidly revived after the February Revolution but found now a strong opposition in the factory committees, which held the trade unions to be superfluous under the changed conditions. Generally, the factory councils sided with the Bolsheviks and considered themselves a more adequate form of organization, not only in the fight for immediate demands, for workers' control, but also as a newly founded system for the administration of production in the enterprise and in the economy as a whole.

With the overthrow of the Provisional Government, and even before, serious attempts were made to integrate the factory councils into a centralized network so as to secure both the existence of the national economy and the undivided control of production and distribution by the producers themselves, which would practically mean the abolition of wage labor. But even as a mere tendency, and a rather weak one, considering the Russian conditions, this project was at once outlawed by the Bolshevik regime under the subterfuge that it would impair economic revival and reduce the productivity of labor. Although the factory committees had been one of the conditions of the Bolshevik assumption of power, their contemplated self-determination now endangered and contradicted the dictatorial rule of the Bolshevik government. With the Mensheviks' loss of power went also their control of the trade unions, which were taken over by the Bolsheviks. The factory councils were induced to subordinate themselves to the trade unions, in fact, to turn themselves into a trade-union instrument for the assertion of the latter's will in the factories. The trade unions, with their bureaucratic centralization, were less susceptible to independent actions and could more easily be integrated into the emerging Bolshevik state. And, as it was pointed out at the time, "the objective course of the revolution demanded the transition to government control and regulation of industry."[28]

In this way, workers' control reversed itself, becoming control over the workers and their production. The basic need was for greater production and, because mere exhortation could not induce the workers to exploit themselves more than had been customary, the Bolshevik state extended itself into the economic sphere, insisting all the while that economic control by the state actually meant control by the proletariat. This did not hinder Lenin from declaring that it was absolutely essential that the technical and organizational direction of production must be the exclusive right of the state-appointed managers and directors, for

> the foundation of socialism calls for absolute and strict *unity of will*, which directs the joint labors of hundreds, thousands, and tens of thousands of people . . . How can strict unity of will be assured? By thousands subordinating their wills to the will of one. Given ideal class-consciousness and discipline on the part of those taking part in the common work, this subordination would be quite like the mild leadership of a conductor of an orchestra. It may assume the sharp form of dictatorship if ideal discipline and class consciousness are lacking. But be that as it may, *unquestioning subordination* to a single will is absolutely necessary for the success of processes organized on the pattern of large-scale industry.[29]

If this statement is taken seriously, class consciousness must have been totally lacking in Russia, for control of production, and of social life in general, took on dictatorial forms exceeding anything experienced in capitalist nations and excluding any measure of self-determination on the part of the workers down to the present day.

The Idea
of the
Commune

The workers' failure to maintain control over their own destiny was due mainly to Russia's general objective unreadiness for a socialist development, but also to the fact that neither the soviets, nor the socialist parties, knew how to go about organizing a socialist society. There was no historical precedent and Marxist theory had not seriously concerned itself with the problem of the socialist reconstruction of society. However, past revolutionary occurrences had some relevance, particularly as regards Russia, because of her general backwardness. Following Marx and Engels, Russian Marxists were apt to point to the Paris Commune as an example of a working-class revolution under similarly unfavorable conditions. Trotsky wrote, for instance, that

> it is not excluded that in a backward country with a lesser degree of capitalist development, the proletariat should sooner reach political supremacy than in a highly developed capitalist state. Thus, in middle-class Paris, the proletariat consciously took into its hands the administration of public affairs in 1871. True it is that the reign of the proletariat lasted only for two months; it is remarkable, however, that in the far more advanced centers of England and the United States, the proletariat never was in power even for the duration of one day.[1]

Lenin, too, found in the Paris Commune a justification for his own attitude with respect to the Russian Revolution and the Soviet dictatorship. Quoting Marx, he cited as the great lesson of the Paris Commune that the bourgeois state cannot simply be taken over by the proletariat but must be destroyed and replaced by a proletarian state, or semistate, which would begin to wither away as soon as majority rule had replaced the minority rule of bourgeois society. "Overthrow the capitalists," he wrote, "crush with the iron hand of the armed workers the resistance of these exploiters, break the bureaucratic machine of the modern state— and you have before you a mechanism of the highest technical equipment, freed of 'parasites', capable of being set in motion by the united workers themselves who hire their own technicians, managers, bookkeepers, and pay them *all*, as, indeed, every 'state' official, with the usual workers' wages. Here is a concrete, practical task, immediately realizable in relation to all trusts, a task that frees the workers of exploitation and makes use of the experiences (especially in the realm of the construction of the state) which the Commune began to reveal in practice."[2]

The practice of the proletarian state as revealed by the Commune was a rather limited one, however, not so much "consciously" introduced, as Trotsky asserted, as spontaneously released by the particular conditions of the Franco-Prussian war, the siege of Paris, and the great patriotism of the Parisian population. But whatever the circumstances, the incorporation of the workers into the National Guard, which they came to dominate, gave them the weapons to express their opposition to the newly established bourgeois government that was trying to come to terms with the Prussian invaders. Their great suffering during the siege of Paris had not diminished the proletariat's patriotic ardor but merely intensified their hatred for the bourgeoisie, which was willing to accept the consequences of the defeat in order to secure its own rule through the disarming of the working class. In view of the increasingly revolutionary situation in Paris, the bourgeois government established itself in Versailles, preparing for the reconquest of the capital. The Paris municipal elections of March 26, 1871, gave the republican left opposition a majority of four to one and led to the proclamation of the *Commune de Paris*. The Commune shared the rule of the city with the Central Committee of the National Guard, responsible for its defense.

Although the Communal Revolution saw itself as inaugurating "a new political era" and as marking the "end of the old governmental and clerical world, of militarism, of monopolism, of privileges to which the proletariat owes its servitude, the Nation its miseries and disasters,"[3] the force of circumstances, as well as the variety of opinions which agitated the Communards, precluded a far-reaching or consistent socialist program. There were, however, the decrees that abolished the Army in favor of the National

Guard, the limitation of government salaries to the equivalent of workers' wages, the expropriation of Church property, the elimination of fines imposed upon workers by their employers, the abolition of nightwork in bakeries, the nationalization of workshops abandoned by their bourgeois owners, and so forth. But these measures did not as yet point to a radical social transformation. In the Executive Council of the Commune, moreover, workers were still in a minority. Of its 90 members, only 21 belonged to the working class, while the rest were middle-class people such as small tradesmen, clerks, journalists, writers, painters, and intellectuals. Only a few of the leading members of the Commune were adherents of the First International. The majority was divided between Proudhonists, Blanquists, and Jacobins of various descriptions, who were interested mainly in political liberties and the preservation of small property owners in a decentralized society. The Commune was thus open to different interpretations by a variety of interests operating within it.

All the shortcomings of the Commune, particularly in the light of Marx's own position, could not erase the fact that it was basically an anti-bourgeois government, one in which some workers actually exercised governmental functions and expressed their willingness to dominate society. This intrinsic fact weighed far heavier in Marx's estimation of the Commune than all its other aspects, which ran counter to his own concept of socialism.

The Commune was not initiated by the International and had no socialist character in the Marxian sense. That Marx nonetheless identified himself and the International with the Commune was seen by his political adversaries as an opportunist attempt to annex the glory of the Commune to Marxism.[4] There is no need to question Marx's motivations in making the cause of the Commune his own. The very passions released by the Paris Commune among the workers as well as the bourgeoisie indicate that the social class division can come to overrule and dominate the ideological and even material differentiations within each separate class. It was not the particular program adopted by the Commune that mattered— whether it was of a centralist or a federalist nature, whether it actually or only potentially implied the expropriation of the bourgeoisie—but the fact alone that segments of the working class had momentarily freed themselves from bourgeois rule, had arms at their disposal, and occupied the institutions of government. In the brutal answer of the bourgeoisie to this rather feeble first attempt at self-government on the part of the Parisian workers, all class-conscious workers recognized the ferocity and irreconcilability of the class enemy, not only in Paris but throughout the world. Instinctively as well as consciously, they stood at the side of the French workers, quite independently of all the theoretical and practical issues which otherwise divided the working-class movement. For this reason Marx described the Commune as "essentially a working-class government" and as "the political form, at last discovered, under which to achieve the economic emancipation of labor," for, as he argued, "the political rule of the producer cannot coexist with the perpetuation of his social slavery. The Commune was therefore to serve as the lever for uprooting the economic foundations upon which rests the existence of classes, and therefore of class rule."[5]

The destruction of the bourgeois state and the capture of political power made sense only on the assumption that it would be used to eliminate the capital-labor relation as well. One cannot have a workers' state in a capitalist society. Marx seemed convinced that, had the Commune survived, its own necessities would have forced it to shed its many inadequacies. "The multiplicity of interpretations to which the Commune has been subjected, and the multiplicity of interests which construed it in their favor," he wrote, "show that it was a thoroughly expansive political form, while all previous forms of government had been emphatically repressive."[6] The fall of the Commune precluded further speculation about its expansive quality and the direction it would take. But Marx saw no need to emphasize his own differences with the Commune, instead stressing those of its aspects that could serve the future struggles of the proletariat.

For this purpose, Marx simply side-stepped the problem of federalism and centralism, which, among others, divided the Marxists from the Proudhonists whose ideas dominated the Commune. He described the latter and its autonomy as instrumental in breaking the bourgeois state and realizing the producers' self-government. The Paris Commune, he wrote,

> was to serve as a model to all the great industrial centers in France. The communal regime once established in Paris and the secondary centers, the old centralized government would in the provinces, too, have to give way to the self-government of the producers. In a rough sketch of

national organization which the Commune had no time to develop it states clearly that the commune was to be the political form of even the smallest country hamlet, and that in the rural districts the standing army was to be replaced by a national militia, with an extremely short term of service. The rural communes of every district were to administer their common affairs by an assembly of delegates in the central town, and these district assemblies were again to send deputies to the National Delegation in Paris, each delegate to be at any time revocable and bound by the instructions of his constituents. The few but important functions which still would remain for a central government were not to be suppressed, as has been intentionally misstated, but were to be discharged by communal and, therefore, strictly responsible agents. The unity of the nation was not to be broken, but, on the contrary, to be organized by the Communal Constitution, and to become a reality by the destruction of the State power which claimed to be the embodiment of that unity independent of, and superior to, the nation itself, from which it was but a parasitic excrescence.[7]

By merely relating the theoretically contemplated national federation of the autonomous communes, Marx gave the impression of general agreement with the plan and its workability. But the whole of Marx's work speaks against this conclusion, for he had never been able to envision the return of political forms which had already been superseded by more advanced ones. He thus found it necessary to state that

It is generally the fate of completely new historical creations to be mistaken for the counterpart of older and even defunct forms of social life, to which they may bear a certain likeness. Thus, this new Commune, which breaks the modern State power, has been mistaken for a reproduction of the medieval communes, which first preceded, and afterwards became the substratum of, that very State power. The communal constitution has been mistaken for an attempt to break up into a federation of small states, as dreamt of by Montesquieu and the Girondins, that unity of great nations which, if originally brought about by political force, has now become a powerful coefficient of social production. The antagonism of the Commune against the State power has been mistaken for an exaggerated form of the ancient struggle against overcentralization.[8]

In Marx's opinion, then, the federal character of the Communal Constitution was not in opposition to a centralized social organization but merely realized the centralist requirements in ways different from those of the capitalist state, in ways that assured the self-rule of the producers. In short, as Lenin later insisted, Marx considered "the possibility of voluntary centralization, of a voluntary union of the communes into a nation, a voluntary fusion of the proletarian communes in the process of destroying bourgeois supremacy and the bourgeois state machinery."[9]

However, the truth of the matter seems to be that on this point Marx did not strive for great precision in the formulation of his ideas. Written in great haste and in commemoration of the defeated Commune, his address on the civil war was not really designed as a lesson on and solution to the problems of the proletarian revolution and the formation of a socialist society, especially as before, during, and after the Commune, Marx did not believe in the possibility of its success, which alone would have lent some reality to the problems posed in his address. Ten years after the Commune he described it as an "uprising of a single city under very special conditions, with a population which neither was nor could be socialistic."[10] Though the struggle had been hopeless, it was still instructive by pointing to the necessity of a proletarian dictatorship to break the power of the bourgeois state. But this did not make the Commune, as Lenin claimed, a model for the construction of the communist state. It is not a communist state, at any rate, that the proletariat has to build, but a communist society. Its real goal is not another state, whether federalist or centralist, democratic or dictatorial, but a classless society and abolition of the state.

The labor movement is no less prone to mythologize its own history than is the bourgeoisie. Historic events appear different from what they actually were and their descriptions are directed more to the emotional receptivity of people than to their need for accuracy. The class struggle, like any other, precludes objectivity. Marx and Engels were not above myth-making, even if covered up by a great amount of sophistry. When Lenin conceived of the Russian revolution as an emulation of the Paris Commune, he was appealing to a mythological Commune, not to its actual character. The Commune was of so great an interest to Lenin not because of what it actually implied, but because of what had been said about it by Marx and Engels. Representing a wing within the Marxist movement, he felt the need to justify his own position in terms of Marxian ideology. While hiding in Finland he wrote his pamphlet *State and Revolution* on a problem he had pondered many years before but which now, after the February Revolution, seemed to him no longer merely of theoretical but also of practical importance.

Despite his great respect for theory, Lenin was preeminently a practical politician. While there could be no practice without theory, only that theory out of many was acceptable which suited his particular practice—that is, the capture of political power under the given conditions. At the same time—as an excuse as well as a support—the acceptance of a theory must be based on authority; even an Emperor is there by the grace of God. For Lenin, the unquestioned authorities were Marx and Engels. In this respect he was fortunate because both were dead and unable to talk back, and also because during their lives they had commented on a great number of historical events, and had suggested measures to deal with them, in accordance with their own time-conditioned apprehension of these events. A dogmatic acceptance of Marxism will thus allow the faithful Marxist to find support for his own convictions by merely picking one or another statement out of the founding fathers' wide-ranging, though often erroneous, pronouncements on issues that, due to changed economic and political conditions, have long lost their meaning. Although Lenin wrote a great deal, he did not contribute, and had no intention to contribute, to the main body of Marxian doctrine—not because of a lack of ability to do so, but because, for him, Marx and Engels (and even Kautsky, up to 1914) had said all that needed to be said for the comprehension of history, capitalism, and the proletarian revolution.

Although there is really nothing positive to be learned from the Paris Commune except the obvious—that the proletariat cannot utilize but must overthrow the capitalist state—what attracted Lenin to Marx's comments on the Commune was the statement that "the political rule of the producers is incompatible with the eternalization of their social servitude"; that is, that this political rule, if maintainable, will lead to a socialist society. For Lenin, this political rule was of course embodied in the new state, emerging out of the revolution, which would then serve as the vehicle of the socialization process. Perhaps, carried away by his own revolutionary ardor—and quite in contrast to his own doctrine, which denied the proletariat the independent capacity to make a revolution, not to speak of building socialism—Lenin affirmed in *State and Revolution* the proletariat's ability to construct a really democratic society and to manage its own production under an egalitarian system of distribution. "Capitalist culture," he wrote now,

> has created large-scale production, factories, the postal services, telephones, etc., and *on this* basis the great majority of functions of the "old state power" has become simplified and can be reduced to such simple operations of registration, filing and checking, that they will be quite within the reach of every literate person, and it will be possible to perform them for "workingmen's wages," which circumstances can (and must) strip those functions of every shadow of privilege, of every appearance of "official grandeur." All officials, without exception, elected and subject to recall *at any time*, their salaries reduced to "workingmen's wages"—these simple and self-evident democratic measures, while completely uniting the interests of the workers and the majority of the peasants, at the same time serve as a bridge leading from capitalism to socialism.[11]

But, as we have seen before, in Lenin's view "workers' management" finds its actual realization through the political and economic power of the state. It is the latter that manages the relations of production and distribution; only this state is now equated with the working class itself. It is necessary, Lenin wrote,

> to organize the *whole* national economy like the postal system, in such a way that the technicians, managers, bookkeepers as well as *all* officials, should receive no higher wages than "workingmen's wages"; all under the control and leadership of the armed proletariat—this is our immediate aim. This is the kind of state and economic basis we need. *All* citizens are transformed into hired employees of the state, which is made up of armed workers. . . . The whole society becomes one office and one factory with equal pay and equal work.[12]

Of course, Lenin was too well versed in Marxian theory to leave the matter at this point. He knew that socialism excludes state rule, and he even quoted Engels's remark that "the first act in which the state really comes forward as the representative of society as a whole—the seizure of the means of production in the name of society—is at the same time its last independent act as a state."[13] It should follow that the socialist organization of production is a function not of the state, but of social institutions that progressively eliminate the functions of the state, finally to end them altogether. But Lenin saw the "withering away" of the state in a quite different light. "From the moment," he wrote, "when all members of society, or even only the overwhelming majority, have learned to govern the state *themselves*, have taken this business into their own hands, have established control over the insignificant minority of capitalists, over the gentry with capitalistic leanings, and the workers thoroughly demoralized by capitalism—from this moment the need for government begins to disappear."[14] Instead of dissolving the state, i.e., the "dictatorship of the proletariat," within the socialization process, it is the proletarian state itself, in Lenin's view, that actualizes the socialization process. The state has to govern in order for the great majority to learn how to govern the state.

Behind this reasoning, if such it is, hides Lenin's recognition of the objective difficulties in the way of the socialist reconstruction of Russian society. All that could be accomplished was the capture of state power and the state's intervention in the economy. Lenin was convinced that Russia's "modernization" could be more effectively realized through the agency of the state than by private-enterprise initiative, and he seems to have convinced himself of the possibility of imbuing the workers with the same idea, so that they might identify themselves with the Bolshevik state as the latter identified itself with the proletariat. However, when Lenin was writing *State and Revolution*, the Bolshevik state was only a mere possibility that might or might not become a reality. The existing Provisional Government had first to be overthrown, and the workers had to be encouraged to undertake this task, or at least not to interfere with those who would. They had to be convinced that there was no need to leave the organization of society to the bourgeoisie, but that they were quite capable, by themselves, of handling the matter. The very language of *State and Revolution*, as well as the rather primitive suggestions on how to go about building the new society, indicate that this pamphlet was not conceived as a serious discussion of the relations between the state and revolution, but as a propaganda instrument to induce Lenin's followers and the workers generally to make an end of the existing state. As such it came too late to affect the seizure of power, though it could still serve as a "Marxist" justification for the Bolshevik initiative.

Everything Lenin wrote prior to *State and Revolution*, and

every step taken after the seizure of power, turns the apparent radicalism displayed in this pamphlet into a mere opportunistic move to support the immediate aim of gaining power for the Bolshevik Party. It is quite possible that Lenin's identification with the proletariat was subjectively honest, in that he actually believed that the latter must come to see in his conception of the revolutionary process their own true interests and their real convictions. On the other hand, the ambiguities within his revolutionary proposals indicate that, while trusting his own revolutionary principles, Lenin did not trust those of the working class, which would first have to be educated to continue to do for themselves what, meanwhile, would be done for them by the Bolshevik state. What he allows the workers with his left hand, he takes away again with his right. It was then not a momentary emotional aberration on the part of Lenin that induced him to grant so much revolutionary self-determination to the workers, but a pragmatic move in the manipulation of the revolution in accordance with his own party concept of the socialist state.

State
and
Counter-Revolution

Lenin's state was to be a Bolshevik state supported by workers and peasants. As the privileged classes could not be expected to support it, it was necessary to disfranchise them and thus end bourgeois democracy. Once in power, the Bolsheviks restricted political freedoms—freedom of speech, press, assembly, and association, and the right to vote and to be elected to the soviets—to the laboring population, that is, to all people "who have acquired the means of living through labor that is productive and useful to society, that is, the laborers and employees of all classes who are employed in industry, trade, agriculture, etc., and to peasants and Cossack agricultural laborers who employ no help for purposes of making profits."[1] However, the peasants could not be integrated into the envisioned "one great factory," which transformed "all citizens into the hired employees of the state," for they had made their revolution for "private property," for land of their own, disregarding the fact that nominally all land belonged to the nation as a whole. The concessions made to the peasants were the price the Bolsheviks had to pay for their support. "The Russian peasantry," wrote Trotsky, "will be interested in upholding proletarian rule at least in the first, most difficult, period, no less than were the French peasants interested in upholding the military role of Napoleon Bonaparte, who by force guaranteed to the new owners the integrity of their land shares."[2]

But the peasants' political support of the Bolsheviks was one thing and their economic interests another. Disorganization through war and civil war reduced industrial and agricultural production. The large landed estates had been broken up to provide millions of agricultural laborers with small holdings. Subsistence farming largely displaced commercial farming. But even the market-oriented peasantry refused to turn its surpluses over to the state, as the latter had little or nothing to offer in return. The internal policies of the Bolshevik state were mainly determined by its relation to the peasantry, which did not fit into the evolving state-capitalist economy. To placate the peasants was possible only at the expense of the proletariat, and to favor the latter, only at the expense of the peasantry. To stay in power, the Bolsheviks were constantly forced to alter their positions regarding either one or the other class. Ultimately, in order to make themselves independent of both, they resorted to terroristic measures which subjected the whole of the population to their dictatorial rule.

The Bolshevik dilemma with regard to the peasants was quite generally recognized. Despite her sympathies for the Bolshevik Revolution, Rosa Luxemburg, for example, could not desist from criticizing their agricultural policies as detrimental to the quest for socialism. Property rights, in her view, must be turned over to the nation, or the state, for only then is it possible to organize agricultural production on a socialistic basis. The Bolshevik slogan "immediate seizure and distribution of the land to the peasants" was not a socialist measure but one that, by creating a new form of private property, cut off the way to such measures. The Leninist agrarian reform, she wrote, "has created a new and powerful layer of popular enemies of socialism in the countryside, enemies whose resistance will be much more dangerous and stubborn than that of the noble large landowners."[3] This criticism, however, did no more than restate the unavoidable dilemma. While she favored the taking of power by the Bolsheviks, Luxemburg recoiled before the conditions under which alone this was possible. Lenin, however, expected the peasants' continuing support not only because the Bolsheviks had ratified their seizure of land, but also because the Soviet state intended to be a "cheap government," in order to ease the peasants' tax burden.

It is partly with this "cheap government" in mind that Lenin spoke so repetitiously of the necessity of "workingmen's wages" for all the administrative and technical functionaries. "Cheap government" was to cement together the "workers' and peasants' alliance." During the first period of Bolshevik rule, moreover, the egalitarian principles enunciated in *State and Revolution* became largely a reality, due to the difficulties in the way of providing the urban population with the bare necessities of life. The government saw itself forced to take from the peasantry all their surplus grain, and often more than that, in the form of "loans,"' or in exchange for valueless paper money. Their violent reactions induced the Bolsheviks to replace the system of confiscation with a tax in kind, which failed to still the peasants' opposition. Finally, in 1921 the government was forced into a New Economic Policy (NEP), involving a partial return to capitalist market relations and an attempt to attract capital from abroad.

The invitation to invest in Russian industry was largely ignored by Western capitalism. The problem remained how to capitalize the country without ending up with a private-enterprise system—the logical outcome of a development of peasant farming under free market relations. The New Economic Policy could be regarded either as a mere interval in the "socialization process" or as a more permanent policy entailing the risk that the newly generating private capitalist forces would overtake the state-controlled sector of the economy and even destroy it. In such an eventuality, the Bolshevik intervention would have been in vain—a mere incident in a bourgeois revolution. Lenin felt sure, however, that a partial return to market relations could be politically mastered, i.e., that the Bolshevik Party could hold state power and secure enough economic weight by maintaining control of key positions, such as large-scale industry, banking, and foreign trade, thus neutralizing the emerging private property relations in agriculture, small-scale industry, and the retail trade. In time, the real social power would shift from the peasantry to state-controlled industry by virtue of the latter's growth.

In the end, however, the problems of the "mixed economy" of the NEP period were resolved by the forced collectivization of agriculture, the centrally planned economy, and the terroristic regime of Stalinism. The fears of Rosa Luxemburg with respect to Bolshevik peasant policy proved to be unwarranted. However, the destruction of peasant property by way of collectivization did not lead to socialism but merely secured the continuance of state capitalism. By itself, the collectivized form of agriculture has no socialist character. It is merely the transformation of small-scale into large-scale agricultural production by political means in distinction to the concentration and centralization process brought about, though imperfectly, in the capitalist market economy. Collectivization was to make possible a more effective extraction of surplus labor from the peasant population. It required a "revolution from above," a veritable war between the government and the peasantry,[4] wherein the government falsely claimed to act on behalf of and to be aided by the poor peasants, in wiping out the kulaks, or rich peasants, who were blocking the road to socialism.

Unless for higher wages, implying better living standards, wage workers see no point in exerting themselves beyond that unavoidable measure demanded by their bosses. Supervision, too, demands incentives. The new controllers of labor showed little interest in the improvement of production at "workingmen's wages." The negative incentive, implied in the need for employment in order to live at all, was not enough to spur the supervisory and technical personnel to greater efforts. It was therefore soon supplemented with the positive incentives of wage and salary differentials between and within the various occupations and professions, and with special privileges for particularly effective performances. These differentials were progressively increased until they came to resemble those prevalent in private-enterprise economies.

But to return to the Bolshevik government: Elected by the soviets, it was in theory subordinated to, and subject to recall by, the All-Russian Congress of Soviets, and merely empowered to carry on within the framework of its directives. In practice, it played an independent role in coping with the changing political and economic needs and the everyday business of government. The Congress of Soviets was not a permanent body, but met at intervals of shorter or longer duration, delegating legislative and executive powers to the organs of the state. With the "carrying of the class struggle into the rural districts," i.e., with the state-organized expropriatory expeditions in the countryside and the installation of Bolshevik "committees of the poor" in the villages, the "workers' and peasants' alliance" that had brought the Bolsheviks to power promised to deteriorate and to endanger the Bolshevik majority in the congress as well as its partnership with the left Social Revolutionaries. To be sure, the Bolshevik government, controlling the state apparatus, could have ignored the congress, or driven it away, as it had driven away the Constituent Assembly. But the Bolsheviks preferred to work within the framework of the soviet system, and to work toward a Congress of Soviets obedient to the party. To this end, it was necessary to control the elections of deputies to the soviets and to outlaw other political parties, most of all the traditional party of peasants, the Social Revolutionaries.

As the Mensheviks and the right Social Revolutionaries had withdrawn from the congress and opposed the government elected by it, they could easily be disfranchised, and were outlawed by order of the Central Committee of the Congress of Soviets in June 1918. The occasion to put an end to the left Social Revolutionaries arose soon, not only because of the widespread peasant discontent but also because of political differences, among which was the Social Revolutionaries' rejection of the Brest-Litovsk Peace Treaty. After the signing of the treaty, the left Social Revolutionaries withdrew from the Central Committee. The Fifth Congress of Soviets, in July 1918, expelled the left Social Revolutionaries. Both the Central Committee and the Council of People's Commissars were now exclusively in Bolshevik hands. The latter secured their majority in the soviets not only because their popularity was still in the ascendancy, but also because they had learned how to make it increasingly more difficult for non-Bolsheviks to enter the soviets. In time, the All-Russian Congress of Soviets became a manipulated body, automatically ratifying the actions of the government. The abdication of soviet power in favor of governmental rule, which Lenin had denounced with the slogan "All power to the soviets," was now for the first time actually realized in the Bolshevik one-party government.

With the soviets no longer thought of as the organizational instrument for a socialist production system, they became a kind of substitute parliament. The soviet state, it was proclaimed programmatically,

> while affording the toiling masses incomparably greater opportunities than those enjoyed under bourgeois democracy and parliamentary government, to elect and recall deputies in the manner easiest and most accessible to the workers and peasants, . . . at the same time abolishes the negative aspects of parliamentary government, especially the separation of the legislature and the executive, the isolation of the representative institutions from the masses. . . . The Soviet government draws the state apparatus closer to the masses by the fact that the electoral constituency and the basic unit for the state is no longer a territorial district, but an industrial unit (workshop, factory).[5]

The soviet system was seen by the Bolsheviks as a "transmission belt" connecting the state authorities at the top with the broad masses at the bottom. Orders issuing from above would be carried out below, and complaints and suggestions from the workers would reach the government through their deputies to the Congress of Soviets. Meanwhile, Bolshevik party cells and Bolshevik domination of the trade unions assured a more direct control within the enterprises and provided a link between the cadres in the factories and the govermental institutions. If so inclined, of course, the workers could assume that there was a connection between them and the government through the soviets, and that the latter could, via the electoral system, actually determine government policy and even change governments. This illusory assumption pervades more or less all electoral systems and could also be held for that of the soviets. By shifting the electoral constituency from the territorial district to the place of production, the Bolsheviks did deprive the nonworking layers of society of partaking in the parliamentary game,[6] without, however, changing the game itself. In the name of revolutionary necessity, the government made itself increasingly more independent of the soviets in order to achieve that centralization of power needed for the domination of society by a single political party. Even with Bolshevik domination of the soviets, general control was to be administered by the party and there, according to Trotsky,

> the last word belongs to the Central Committee. . . . This affords extreme economy of time and energy, and in the most difficult and complicated circumstances gives a guarantee for the necessary unity of action. Such a regime is possible only in the presence of the unquestioned authority of the party, and the faultlessness of its discipline. . . . The exclusive role of the Communist Party under the conditions of a victorious revolution is quite comprehensible. . . . The revolutionary supremacy of the proletariat presupposes within the proletariat itself the political supremacy of the party, with a clear programme of action. . . . We have more than once been accused of having substituted for the dictatorship of the Soviets the dictatorship of our party. Yet it can be said with complete justice that the dictatorship of the Soviets became possible only by means of the dictatorship of the party. It is thanks to the clarity of its theoretical vision and its strong revolutionary organization that the party has afforded to the Soviets the possibility of becoming transformed from shapeless parliaments of labor into the apparatus of the supremacy of labor. In this "substitution" of the power of the

party for the power of the working class there is nothing accidental, and in reality there is no substitution at all. The Communists express the fundamental interests of the working class. It is quite natural that, in the period in which history brings up those interests, . . . the Communists have become the recognized representatives of the working class as a whole.[7]

Whereas with regard to the soviets of 1905, Trotsky recognized that their "substance was their efforts to become organs of public authority," now, after the Bolshevik victory, it was no longer the soviets but the party and, more precisely, its central committee, that had to exercise all public authority.[8] The Bolsheviks, or at any rate their foremost spokesmen, Lenin and Trotsky, had no confidence whatever in the soviets, those "shapeless parliaments of labor," which, in their view, owed their very existence to the Bolshevik Party. Because there would be no soviet system at all without the party, to speak of a soviet dictatorship was to speak of the party dictatorship—the one implying the other. Actually, of course, it had been the other way around, for without the revolution made by the soviets the Bolshevik Party could never have seized power and Lenin would still have been in Switzerland. Yet to hold this power, the party now had to separate itself from the soviets and to control the latter instead of being controlled by them.

Notwithstanding the demagoguery displayed in *State and Revolution*, Lenin's and Trotsky's attitude regarding the capacities and incapacities of the working class were not at all surprising, for they were largely shared by the leading "elites" of all socialist movements and served, in fact, to justify their existence and privileges. The social and technical division of labor within the capitalist system did indeed deprive the proletariat of any control, and therewith understanding, of the complex production and distribution process that assures the reproduction of the social system. Although a socialist system of production will have a division of labor different from that prevalent in capitalism, the new arrangements involved will only be established in time and in connection with a total reorientation of the production process and its direction toward goals different from those characteristic of capitalism. It is therefore only to be expected that the production process will be disrupted in any revolutionary situation, especially when the productive apparatus is already in a state of decay, as was the case in the Russia of 1917. It is then also not surprising that workers should have put their hopes in the new government to accomplish for them what seemed extremely difficult for them to do.

The identification of soviets and party was clearly shared by the workers and the Bolsheviks, for otherwise the early dominance of the latter within the soviets would not be comprehensible. It was even strong enough to allow the Bolsheviks to monopolize the soviets by underhanded methods that kept non-Bolsheviks out of them. For the broad urban masses the Bolsheviks were indeed their party, which proved its revolutionary character precisely by its support of the soviets and by its insistence upon the dictatorship of the proletariat. There can also be no doubt that the Bolsheviks, who were, after all, convinced socialists, were deadly serious in their devotion to the workers' cause—so much, indeed, that they were ready to defend it even against the workers should they fail to recognize its necessary requirements.

According to the Bolsheviks, these necessary requirements, i.e., "work, discipline, order," could not be left to the self-enforcement of the soviets. The state, the Bolshevik Party in this case, would regulate all important economic matters by government ordinances having the force of law. The construction of the state served no other purpose than that of safeguarding the revolution and the construction of socialism. They spread this illusion among the workers with such great conviction because it was their own, for they were convinced that socialism could be instituted through state control and the selfless idealism of a revolutionary elite. They must have felt terribly disappointed when the workers did not properly respond to the urgency of the call for "work, discipline, and order" and to their revolutionary rhetoric. If the workers could not recognize their own interests, this recognition would have to be forced upon them, if necessary by terroristic means. The chance for socialism should not be lost by default. Sure only of their own revolutionary vocation, they insisted upon their exclusive right to determine the ways and means to the socialist reconstruction of society.

However, this exclusive right demanded unshared absolute power. The first thing to be organized, apart from party and soviets, was then the Cheka, the political police, to fight the counterrevolution in all its manifestations and all attempts to unseat the

Bolshevik government. Revolutionary tribunals assisted the work of the Cheka. Concentration camps were installed for the enemies of the regime. A Red Army, under Trotsky's command, took the place of the "armed proletariat." An effective army, obedient only to the government, could not be run by "soldiers' councils," which were thus at once eliminated. The army was to fight both external and internal foes and was led and organized by "specialists," by tsarist officers, that is, who had made their peace with the Bolshevik government. Because the army emerged victorious out of war and civil war, which lasted from 1918 to 1920, the Bolshevik government's prestige was enormously enhanced and assured the consolidation of its authoritarian rule.

Far from endangering the Bolshevik regime, war and civil war against foreign intervention and the White counter-revolution strengthened it. It united all who were bound to suffer by a return of the old authorities. Regardless of their attitude toward the Bolsheviks and their policies, the peasants were now defending their newly won land, the Mensheviks and Social Revolutionaries their very lives. The Bolsheviks, at first rent by internal dissension, united in the face of the common enemy and, if only for the duration of the civil war, gladly accepted the aid of the harrassed but still existing Mensheviks, Social Revolutionaries, and even Anarchists as that of a "loyal opposition." Finally, the interventionist character of the civil war gave the Bolshevik resistance the euphoria of nationalism as the government rallied the population to its side with the slogan "the fatherland is in danger."

In this connection it must be pointed out that Lenin's and so the Bolsheviks' nationalism and internationalism were of a peculiar kind, in that they could be used alternatively to advance the fortunes of the Russian revolution and those of the Bolshevik Party. In Trotsky's words, "Lenin's internationalism needs no recommendation. But at the same time Lenin himself is profoundly national. Lenin personifies the Russian proletariat, a young class, which politically is scarcely older than Lenin himself, but a class which is profoundly national, for recapitulated in it is the entire past development of Russia, in it lies Russia's entire future, with it the Russian nation rises and falls."[9] Perhaps, being so profoundly national, mere introspection may have led Lenin to appreciate the national needs and cultural peculiarities of oppressed peoples sufficiently to induce him to advocate their national liberation and self-determination, up to the point of secession, as one aspect of his anti-imperialism and as an application of the democratic principle to the question of nationalities. Since Marx and Engels had favored the liberation of Poland and home rule for Ireland, he found himself here in the best of company. But Lenin was a practical politician first of all, even though he could fulfill this role only at this late hour. As a practical politician he had realized that the many suppressed nationalities within the Russian Empire presented a constant threat to the tsarist regime, which could be utilized for its overthrow. To be sure, Lenin was also an internationalist and saw the socialist revolution as a world revolution. Still, this revolution had to begin somewhere and in the context of the Russian multinational state, the demand for national self-determination promised the winning of "allies" in the struggle against tsardom. This strategy was supported by the hope that, once free, the different nationalities would elect to remain within the Russian Commonwealth, either out of self-interest or through the urgings of their own socialist organizations, should they succeed in gaining governmental power. Analogous to the "voluntary union of communes into a nation," which Marx had seen as a possible outcome of the Paris Commune, national self-determination could lead to a unified socialist Russian Federation of Nations more cohesive than the old imperial regime.

Until the Russian Revolution, however, the problem of national self-determination remained purely academic. Even after the revolution, the granting of self-determination to the various nationalities within the Russian Empire was rather meaningless, for most of the territories involved were occupied by foreign powers. Self-determination had meanwhile become a policy instrument of the Entente powers, in order to hasten the break-up of the Austro-Hungarian Empire and an imperialistic redrawing of the map of Europe in accordance with the desires of the victor nations. But "even at the risk of playing into bourgeois hands, Lenin nevertheless continued to promote unqualified self-determination, precisely because he was convinced that the war would compel both the Dual Monarchy and the Russian Empire to surrender to the force of nationalism."[10] By sponsoring self-determination and thereby making the proletariat a supporter of nationalism, Lenin, as Rosa Luxemburg pointed out, was merely aiding the bourgeoisie to turn the principle of self-determination into an instrument of counter-revolution. Although this was actually the case, the Bolshevik regime continued to press for national self-determination by now projecting it to the international scene, in order to weaken other imperialist powers, in particular England, in an attempt to foster colonial revolutions against Western capitalism, which threatened to destroy the Bolshevik state.

Though Rosa Luxemburg's prediction, that the granting of self-determination to the various nationalities in Russia would merely surround the Bolshevik state with a cordon of reactionary counterrevolutionary countries, turned out to be correct, this was so only for the short run. Rosa Luxemburg failed to see that it was less the principle of self-determination that dictated Bolshevik policy than the force of circumstances over which they had no control. At the first opportunity they began whittling away at the self-determination of nations, finally to end up by incorporating all the lost independent nations in a restored Russian Empire and, in addition, forging for themselves spheres of interest in extra-Russian territories. On the strength of her own theory of imperialism, Rosa Luxemburg should have realized that Lenin's theory could not be applied in a world of competing imperialist powers, and would not need to be applied, should capitalism be brought down by an international revolution.

The civil war in Russia was waged mainly to arrest the centrifugal forces of nationalism, released by war and revolution, which threatened the integrity of Russia. Not only at her western borders, in Finland, Poland, and the Baltic nations, but also to the south, in Georgia, as well as in the eastern provinces of Asiatic Russia, new independent states established themselves outside of Bolshevik control. The February Revolution had broken the barriers that had held back the nationalist or regionalist movements in the non-Russian parts of the Empire. "When the Bolsheviks overthrew the Provisional Government in Petrograd and Moscow, nationalist or regionalist governments took over in the non–Great Russian areas of European Russia and in Siberia and Central Asia. The governing institutions of the Moslem peoples of the Transvolga (Tatars, Bashkirs), of Central Asia and Transcaspia (Kirghiz, Kazakhs, Uzbeks, Turkomans), and of Transcaucasia (Georgians, Armenians, Azerbaidzhanis, Tartars) favored autonomy in a Russian federation and opposed the Bolsheviks."[11] These peoples had to be reconquered in the ensuing civil war.

The nationalist aspect of the civil war was used for revolutionary and counter-revolutionary purposes. The White counter-revolution began its anti-Bolshevik struggle soon after the overthrow of the Provisional Government. Volunteer armies were formed to fight the Bolsheviks and were financed and equipped by the Entente powers in an effort to bring Russia back into the war against Germany. British, French, Japanese, and American troops landed in Murmansk, Archangel, and Vladivostok. The Czech Legion entered the conflict against the Bolsheviks. In these struggles, territories changed hands frequently but the counter-revolutionary forces, though aided by the Allied powers, proved no match for the newly organized Red Army. The foreign intervention continued even after the armistice between the Allied powers and Germany, and, with the consent of the Allies, the Germans fought in support of the counter-revolution in the Baltic nations, which led to the destruction of the revolutionary forces in these countries and the Soviet government's recognition of their independence. Poland regained its independence as an anti-Bolshevik state. However, the counter-revolutionary forces were highly scattered and disorganized. The Allied powers could not agree among themselves on the extent of their intervention and on the specific goals to be reached. Neither did they trust the willingness of their own troops to continue the war in Russia, nor in the acquiescence of their own population in a prolonged and large-scale war for the overthrow of the Bolshevik regime. The decisive military defeat of the various White armies induced the Allied powers to withdraw their troops in the autumn of 1918, thus opening the occupied parts of Russia to the Red Army. The French and British troops withdrew from the Ukraine and the Caucasus in the spring of 1919. American pressure led to the evacuation of the Japanese in 1922. But the Bolsheviks had definitely won the civil war by 1920. While the revolution had been a national affair, the counter-revolution had been truly international. But even so, it failed to dislodge the Bolshevik regime.

Lenin and Trotsky, not to speak of Marx and Engels, had been convinced that without a proletarian revolution in the West, a Russian revolution could not lead to socialism. Without direct political aid from the European proletariat, Trotsky said more than once, the working class of Russia would not be able to turn its temporary supremacy into a permanent socialist dictatorship.

The reasons for this he saw not only in the opposition on the part of the world reaction, but also in Russia's internal conditions, as the Russian working class, left to its own resources, would necessarily be crushed the moment it lost the support of the peasantry, a most likely occurrence should the revolution remain isolated. Lenin, too, set his hopes on a westward spreading of the revolution, which might otherwise be crushed by the capitalist powers. But he did not share Trotsky's view that an isolated Russia would succumb to its own internal contradictions. In an article written in 1915, concerned with the advisability of including in the socialist program the demand for a United States of Europe, he pointed out, first, that socialism is a question of world revolution and not one restricted to Europe and second, that such a slogan

> may be wrongly interpreted to mean that the victory of socialism in a single country is impossible, and it may also create misconceptions as to the relations of such a country to the others. Uneven economic and political development is an absolute law of capitalism. Hence, the victory of socialism is possible first in several or even in one capitalist country alone. After expropriating the capitalists and organizing their own socialist production, the victorious proletariat of that country will arise *against* the rest of the world—the capitalist world—attracting to its cause the oppressed classes of other countries, stirring uprisings in those countries against the capitalists, and in case of need using even armed force against the exploiting classes and their states.[12]

Obviously, Lenin was convinced—and all his decisions after the seizure of power attest to this—that even an isolated revolutionary Russia would be able to maintain itself unless directly overthrown by the capitalist powers. Eventually, of course, the struggle between socialism and capitalism would resume, but perhaps under conditions more favorable for the international working class. For the time being, however, it was essential to stay in power no matter what the future might hold in store.

The world revolution did not materialize, and the nation-state remained the field of operation for economic development as well as for the class struggle. After 1920 the Bolsheviks no longer expected an early resumption of the world revolutionary process and settled down for the consolidation of their own regime. The exigencies and privations of the civil war years are usually held responsible for the Bolshevik dictatorship and its particular harshness. While this is true, it is no less true that the civil war and its victorious outcome facilitated and assured the success of the dictatorship. The party dictatorship was not only the inevitable result of an emergency situation, but was already implied in the conception of "proletarian rule" as the rule of the Bolshevik Party. The end of the civil war led not to a relaxation of the dictatorship but to its intensification; it was now, after the crushing of the counterrevolution, directed exclusively against the "loyal opposition" and the working class itself. Already at the Eighth Congress of the Bolshevik Party, in March 1919, the demand was made to end the toleration of opposition parties. But it was not until the summer of 1921 that the Bolshevik government finally decided to destroy all independent political organizations and the oppositional groups within its own ranks as well.

In the spring of 1920 it seemed clear that the military balance in the civil war favored the Bolsheviks. This situation led to a resurgence of the opposition to the regime and to the draconian measures it had used during the war. Peasant unrest became so strong as to force the government to discontinue its expropriatory excursions into the countryside and to disband the "committees of the poor peasants." The workers objected to the famine conditions prevailing in the cities and to the relentless drive for more production through a wave of strikes and demonstrations that culminated in the Kronstadt uprising. As the expectations of the workers had once been based on the existence of the Bolshevik government, it was now this government that had to take the blame for all their miseries and disappointments. This government had become a repressive dictatorship and could no longer be influenced by democratic means via the soviet system. To free the soviets from their party yoke and turn them once again into instruments of proletarian self-rule required now a "third revolution." The Kronstadt rebellion was not directed against the soviet system but intended to restore it to its original form. The call for "free soviets" implied soviets freed from the one-party rule of Bolshevism; consequently, it implied political liberty for all proletarian and peasant organizations and tendencies that took part in the Russian Revolution.[13]

It was no accident that the widespread opposition to Bolshevik rule found its most outspoken expression at Kronstadt. It was here that the soviets had become the sole public authority long before this became a temporary reality in Petrograd, Moscow, and the nation as a whole. Already in May 1917 the Bolsheviks and left Social Revolutionaries held the majority in the Kronstadt Soviet and declared their independence vis-à-vis the Provisional Government. Although the latter succeeded in extracting some kind of formal recognition from the Kronstadt Soviet, the latter nonetheless remained the only public authority within its territory and thus helped to prepare the way for the Bolshevik seizure of power. It was the radical commitment to the soviet system, as the best form of proletarian democracy, that now set the Kronstadt workers and soldiers against the Bolshevik dictatorship in an attempt to regain their self-determination.

It could not be helped, of course, that the Kronstadt mutiny was lauded by all opponents of Bolshevism and thus also by reactionaries and bourgeois liberals, who in this way provided the Bolsheviks with a lame excuse for their vicious reaction to the rebellion. But this unsolicited opportunistic verbal "support" cannot alter the fact that the goal of the rebellion was the restoration of that soviet system which the Bolsheviks themselves had seen fit to propagandize in 1917. The Bolsheviks knew quite well that Kronstadt was not the work of "White generals," but they could not admit that, from the point of view of soviet power, they had themselves become a counter-revolutionary force in the very process of strengthening and defending their government. Therefore, they had not only to drown in blood this last attempt at a revival of the soviet system, but had to slander it as the work of the "White counter-revolution." Actually, even though the Mensheviks and Social Revolutionaries lent their "moral" support to the rebellion, the workers and sailors engaged in it had no intentions of resurrecting the Constituent Assembly, which they regarded as a stillborn affair of the irrevocable past. The time, they said, "has come to overthrow the commissarocracy. . . . Kronstadt has raised the banner of the uprising for a Third Revolution of the toilers. . . . The autocracy has fallen. The Constituent Assembly has departed to the region of the damned. The commissarocracy is crumbling."[14] The "third revolution" was to fulfill the broken promises of the preceding one.

With the Kronstadt rebellion the disaffection of workers and peasants had spread to the armed forces, and this combination made it particularly dangerous to the Bolshevik regime. But the rebellion held no realizable promise, not because it was crushed by the Bolsheviks but because, had it succeeded, it would not have been able to sustain and extend a libertarian socialism based on soviet rule. It was indeed condemned to be what it has been called: the Kronstadt Commune. Like its Paris counterpart, it remained isolated despite the general discontent, and its political objectives could not be reached under the prevailing Russian conditions. Yet it was able to hasten Lenin's "strategic retreat" to the New Economic Policy, which relaxed the Bolshevik economic dictatorship while simultaneously tightening its political authoritarian rule.

The workers' dissatisfaction with Lenin's dictatorship found some repercussion in his own party. Oppositional groups criticized not only specific party decisions, such as state control of trade unions, but also the general trend of Bolshevik policy. On the question of "one-man management," for instance, it was said that this was a matter not of a tactical problem but of two "historically irreconcilable points of view," for

> one-man management is a product of the individualistic conception of the bourgeois class. . . . This idea finds its reflection in all spheres of human endeavor—beginning with the appointment of a sovereign for the state and ending with a sovereign director in the factory. This is the supreme wisdom of bourgeois thought. The bourgeoisie do not believe in the power of a collective body. They like only to whip the masses into an obedient flock, and drive them wherever their unrestricted will desires. The basis of the controversy (in the Bolshevik Party) is mainly this: whether we shall realize communism through the workers or over their heads by the hand of the Soviet officials. And let us ponder whether it is possible to attain and build a communist economy by the hands and creative abilities of the scions from the other class, who are imbued with their routine of the past? If we begin to think as Marxians, as men of science, we shall answer categorically and explicitly—no. The administrative economic body in the labor republic during the present transitory period must be a body directly elected by the producers themselves. All the rest of the administrative economic Soviet institutions shall serve only as executive center of the economic policy of that all-important economic body of the labor republic. All else is goosestepping that manifests distrust toward all creative abilities of workers, distrust which is not compatible with the professed ideals of our party. . . . There can be no self-activity without freedom of thought and opinion, for self-activity manifests itself not only in initiative, action, and work, but in *independent thought* as well. We are afraid of action, we

have ceased to rely on the masses, hence we have bureaucracy with us. In order to do away with the bureaucracy that is finding its shelter in the Soviet institutions, we must first of all get *rid of all bureaucracy in the party itself.*[15]

Apparently, these oppositionists did not understand their own party or, in view of its actual practice, diverged from its principles as outlined by Lenin since 1903. Perhaps they had taken *State and Revolution* at face value, not noticing its ambivalence, and felt now betrayed, as Lenin's policy revealed the sheer demagoguery of its revolutionary declarations. It should have been evident from Lenin's concept of the party and its role in the revolutionary process that, once in power, this party could only function in a dictatorial way. Quite apart from the specific Russian conditions, the idea of the party as the consciousness of the socialist revolution clearly relegated all decision-making power to the Bolshevik state apparatus.

True to his own principles, Lenin put a quick end to the oppositionists by ordaining all factions to disband under threat of expulsion. With two resolutions, passed by the Tenth Congress of the Russian Communist Party, March 1921, "On Party Unity" and "On the Syndicalist and Anarchist Deviation in our Party," Lenin succeeded in completing what had hitherto only approximately been accomplished, namely, an end to all factionalism within the party and the securing of complete control over it through the Central Committee, which, in addition, was itself reorganized in such a fashion as to get rid of any opposition that might arise within the party leadership. With this was laid a groundwork on which nothing else could be built but the emerging omnipotence of the rising bureaucracy of party and state and the infinite power of the supreme leader presiding over both. The one-man rule of the party, which had been an informal fact due to the overriding "moral" authority of Lenin, turned into the unassailable fact of personal rule by whoever should manage to put himself at the top of the party hierarchy.

The bourgeois character of Bolshevik rule, as noted by its internal opposition, reflected the objectively nonsocialist nature of the Russian Revolution. It was a sort of "bourgeois revolution" without the bourgeoisie, as it was a proletarian revolution without a sufficiently large proletariat, a revolution in which the historical functions of the Western bourgeoisie were taken up by an apparently anti-bourgeois party by means of its assumption of political power. Under these conditions, the revolutionary content of Western Marxism was not applicable, not even in a modified form. Whatever one may think of Marx's declaration concerning the Paris Commune—that the "political rule of the proletariat is incompatible with the eternalization of their social servitude" (a situation quite difficult to conceive, except as a momentary possibility, that is, as the revolution itself)—Marx at least spoke of the "producers," not of a political party substituting for the producers, whereas the Bolshevik concept speaks of state rule alone as the necessary and sufficient prerequisite for the transformation of the capitalist into a socialist mode of production. The producers are controlled by the state, the state by the party, the party by the central committee, and the last by the supreme leader and his court. The destroyed autocracy is resurrected in the name of Marxism. In this way, moreover, ideologically as well as practically, the revolution and socialism depend finally on the history-making individual.

Indeed, it did not take long for the Russian Revolution and its consequences to be seen as the work of the geniuses Lenin, Trotsky, and Stalin; not only in the bourgeois view, to which this comes naturally, but also quite generally by socialists claiming adherence to the materialist conception of history, which finds its dynamic not in the exceptional abilities of individuals, but in the struggle of classes in the course of the developing social forces of production. Neither Marx nor any reasonable person would deny the role of the "hero" in history, whether for better or for worse; for, as previously pointed out, the "hero" is already implicit in class society and is himself, in his thoughts and actions, determined by the class contradictions that rend society. In his historical writings, for instance, Marx dealt extensively with such "heroes," like the little Napoleon, who brought ruin to his country, or, like Bismarck, who finished the goal of German unification, left undone by the stillborn bourgeois revolution. It is quite conceivable that without Napoleon III and without Bismarck the history of France and Germany would have been different from what it actually was, but this difference would have altered nothing in the socioeconomic development of both countries, determined as it was by the capitalist relations of production and the expansion of capital as an international phenomenon.

What is history anyway? The bourgeoisie has no theory of history, as it has no theory of social development. Since it merely describes what is observable or may be found in old records, history is everything and nothing at the same time and any of its surface manifestations may be emphasized in lieu of an explanation, which must always serve the social power relations existing at any particular time. Like economics, bourgeois history is pure ideology and gives no inkling of the reasons for social change. And, just as the market economy can only be understood through the understanding of its underlying class relations, so does this kind of history require another kind if its meaning is to be revealed. From a Marxian point of view, history implies changing social relations of production. That history which concerns itself exclusively with alterations in an otherwise static society, as interesting as it may be, concerns Marxism only insofar as these changes indicate the hidden process by which one mode of production releases social forces that point to the rise of another mode of production. From this point of view, the historical changes brought about by the Russian Revolution and the Bolshevik regime have their place within an otherwise unaltered mode of production, as its social relations remained capital-labor relations, even though capital—that is, control over the means of production—and with it wage labor were taken out of the hands of private entrepreneurs and placed in those of a state bureaucracy performing the exploitative functions of the former. The capitalist system was modified but not abolished. The history made by the Bolsheviks was still capitalist history in the ideological disguise of Marxism.

The existence of "great men" in history is a sure indication that history is being made within the hierarchical structure of class-ridden competitive societies. The Lenin cult, the Hitler cult, the Stalin cult, etc., represent attempts to deprive the mass of the population of any kind of self-determination and also to ensure their complete atomization, which makes this technically possible. Such cults have little to do with the "great men" themselves, as personalities, but reflect the need or desire for complete conformity to allow a particular class or a particular political movement sufficient control over broad masses for the realization of their specific objectives, such as war, or making a revolution. "Great men" require "great times," and both emerge in crisis situations that have their roots in the exaggeration of society's fundamental contradictions.

The helplessness of the atomized individual finds a sort of imaginary solace in the mere symbolization of his self-assertion in the leadership, or the leader, of a social movement claiming to do for him what he cannot do for himself. The impotence of the social individual is the potency of the individual who manages to represent one or another kind of historically given social aspiration. The anti-social character of the capitalist system accounts for its apparent social coherence in the symbolized form of the state, the government, the great leader. However, the symbolization must be constantly reinforced by the concrete forms of control executed by the ruling minority.

It is almost certain that without Lenin's arrival in Russia the Bolsheviks would not have seized governmental power, and in this sense the credit for the Bolshevik Revolution must be given to Lenin—or perhaps, to the German General Staff, or to Parvus, who made Lenin's entry into the Russian Revolution possible. But what would have happened in Russia without the "subjective factor" of Lenin's existence? The totally discredited tsarist regime had already been overthrown and would not have been resurrected by a counter-revolutionary coup in the face of the combined and general opposition of workers, peasants, the bourgeoisie, and even segments of the old autocratic regime. In addition, the Entente powers, relieved of the alliance with the anachronistic Russian autocratic regime, favored the new and ostensibly democratic government, if only in the hope of a more efficiently waged war against the Central European "anti-democratic" powers. Although attempts were made to resume the offensive in the west, they were not successful, and merely intensified the desire for an early peace, even a separate peace, in order to consolidate the new regime and to restore some modicum of order within the increasing social anarchy. A counter-revolution would have had as its object the forced continuation of the war and the elimination of the soviets and the Bolsheviks, to safeguard the private-property nature of the social production relations. In short, the "dictatorship of the proletariat" would most probably have been overthrown by a dictatorship of the bourgeoisie, enforced by a White terror and other fascist methods of rule. A different political system and different property relations would have evolved, but on the basis of the same production relations that sustained the Bolshevik state.

Similarly, there is little doubt that World War II was initiated by Adolf Hitler in an attempt to win World War I by a second try for German control of capitalist Europe. Without Hitler, the second war might not have broken loose at the time it actually did, but perhaps also not without the Stalin-Hitler Pact, or without the deepening of the worldwide depression, which set definite limits to the Nazis' internal economic policies, on which their political dominance depended. It is clear, however, that Hitler cannot be blamed for World War I or for the Great Depression preceding World War II. Governments are composed of individuals, representing definite ideologies and specific economic interests, for which reason it is always possible to give credit, or to put the blame, for any particular policy on individual politicians, and to assume that had they not been there, history would have run a different course. This might even be true, but the different course would in no way affect the general development insofar as it is determined by capitalist production relations.

In brief, it is not possible to make any reliable predictions with regard to historical development on the strength of political movements and the role of individuals within these movements as they are thrown up by the development of capitalism and its difficulties, so long as these occurrences do not concern the basic social production relations but only reflect changes within these relations. It is true that political and economic phenomena constitute an entity, but to speak of such an entity may be to refer to no more than erratic movements within the given social structure, and not to social contradictions destined to destroy the given political and economic entity by way of revolutionary changes that bring another society into existence. Just as there is no way to foresee economic development in its details, that is, at what point a crisis will be released or be overcome, there is also no way to account for political development in its details, that is, which social movement will succeed or fail, or what individual will come to dominate the political scene and whether or not this individual will appear as a "history-making" individual, quite apart from his personal qualifications. What cannot be comprehended cannot be taken into consideration, and political as well as economic events appear as a series of "accidents" or "shocks," seemingly from outside the system but actually produced by this system, which precludes the recognition of its inherent necessities. The very existence of political life attests to its fetishistic determination. Outside this fetishistic determination, this helpless and blind subjection to the capital-expansion process, the entity of politics and economics would not appear as such, but rather as the elimination of both in a consciously arranged organization of the social requirements of the reproduction process, freed of its economic and political aspects. Politics, and with it, that type of economy which is necessarily political economy, will cease with the establishment of a classless society.

That even Lenin was somehow aware of this may be surmised by his reluctance to use the term "wage labor" after the seizure of power. Only once, in deference to an international audience, at the founding Congress of the Third International in March 1919, did he speak of "mankind throwing off the last form of slavery: capitalist or wage slavery." Generally, however, he made it appear that the end of private capital implies the end of the wage system; although not automatically abolishing the wage system in a technical sense, it would free it from its exploitative connotations. In this respect, as in many others, Lenin merely harked back to Kautsky's position of 1902, which maintained that in the early stages of the construction of socialism wage labor, and therefore money, (or vice versa) must be retained in order to provide the workers with the necessary incentives to work. Trotsky, too, reiterated this idea, but with an exemplary shamelessness, stating that

> we still retain, and for a long time will retain, the system of wages. The farther we go, the more will its importance become simply to guarantee to all members of society all the necessaries of life; and thereby it will cease to be a system of wages. [But] in the present difficult period the system of wages is for us, first and foremost, not a method for guaranteeing the personal existence of any separate worker, but a method of estimating what the individual worker brings with his labor to the Labor Republic. . . . Finally, when it rewards some (through the wage system), the Labor State cannot but punish others—those who are clearly infringing labor solidarity, undermining the common work, and seriously impairing the Socialist renaissance of the country. Repression for the attainment of economic ends is a necessary weapon of the Socialist dictatorship.[16]

As the wage system is the basis of capitalist production, so it remains the basis of "socialist construction," which first allows people like Lenin and Trotsky, and their state apparatus, not only to assume the position but also to speak in the voice of the capitalists when dealing with the working class. As if the wage system had not always been the only guarantee for the workers to earn a livelihood, and as if it had not always been used to estimate the amount of surplus value to be extracted from their work!

As a theory of the proletarian revolution, Marxism does not recognize alterations within unchanged social production relations as historical changes in the sense of the materialist conception of history. It speaks of changes of social development from slavery to serfdom to wage labor, and of the abolition of the latter, and therewith all forms of labor exploitation, in a classless socialist society. Each type of class society will have its own political history, of course, but Marxism recognizes this as the politics of definite social formations, which will, however, come to an end with the abolition of classes, the last political revolution in the general social developmental process. Quite apart from its objective possibility or impossibility, the Bolshevik regime had no intention to abolish the wage system and was therefore not engaged in furthering a social revolution in the Marxian sense. It was satisfied with the abolition of private control over the accumulation of capital, on the assumption that this would suffice to proceed to a consciously planned economy and, eventually, to a more egalitarian system of distribution. It is true, of course, that the possibility of such an endeavor had not occurred to Marx, for whom the capitalist system, in its private-property form, would have to be replaced by a system in which the producers themselves would take collective and direct control of the means of production. From this point of view, the Bolshevik endeavor, through a historical novelty not contemplated by Marx, still falls within the history of the capitalist mode of production.

By adhering to the Marxist ideology evolved within the Second International, Lenin and the Bolsheviks succeeded in identifying their inversion of Marxian theory as the only possible form of its realization. While the Bolshevik concept implied no more than the formation of a state-capitalist system, this had been the way in which, at the turn of the century, socialism had been quite generally understood. It is therefore not possible to accuse the Bolsheviks of a "betrayal" of the then prevailing "Marxist" principles; on the contrary, they actualized the declared goals of the Social Democratic movement, which itself had lost all interest in acting upon its beliefs. What the Bolsheviks did was to realize the program of the Second International by revolutionary means. However, in doing so, that is, by turning the ideology into practice and giving it concrete substance, they identified revolutionary Marxism with the state-directed socialist society envisioned by the orthodox wing of international Social Democracy.

Prior to the Bolshevik Revolution, the bourgeoisie had looked upon Marxism as a meaningless utopia, contrary to the naturally given market relations and to human nature itself. There was of course the class struggle, but this, too, like competition in general, implied no more than the Darwinian struggle for existence, which justified its suppression or amelioration, as the case might be, in accordance with changing circumstances or opportunities. But the very fact of the existence of the bourgeoisie was proof enough that society could not prevail without class divisions, as its very complexity demanded its hierarchical structure. Socialism, in the Marxian sense of the self-determination of the working class, was not a practical possibility and its advocacy was not only stupid but also criminal, for its realization would destroy not only capitalist society but society itself. The adaptation of the reformist labor movement to the realities of social life and its successful integration into the capitalist system was additional proof that the capital-labor relations were the normal social relations, which could not be tampered with except at the price of social decay.

This argument was put aside by the Bolshevik demonstration that it is possible to have "socialism" on the basis of capital-labor relations and that a social hierarchy could be maintained without the bourgeoisie, simply by turning the latter into servants of the state, the sole proprietor of the social capital. Although Marx had said that capitalism presupposes the capitalist, this need not imply the capitalist as bourgeois, as owner of private capital, for the capital concentration and centralization process indicated the diminishing of their numbers and the increasing monopolization of capital. If there was an "end" to this process, it would be the end of private capital, as the property of many capitalists, and the end of market economy, which would issue into the complete monopoly of ownership of the means of production. This might as well be in the hands of the state, which would then become the organizer of social production in a system in which "market relations" were reduced to the exchange between labor and capital through the maintenance of wage labor in the state-controlled economy.

This concept might have made "socialism" comprehensible to the bourgeoisie, were it not for the fact that it involved their abolition as a ruling class. From the bourgeois point of view, it was quite immaterial whether they found themselves expropriated by a state, which was no longer their own, or by a proletarian revolution in the Marxian sense, that is, the appropriation of the means of production by the working class. The Bolshevik state-capitalist, or, what amounts to the same, state-socialist concept was consequently equated with the Marxian concept of socialism. When the bourgeoisie speaks of Marxism, it invariably refers to its Bolshevik interpretation, as this is the only one that has found concrete application. This identification of Marxism with the Leninist concept of socialism turned the latter into a synonym for Marxism, and as such it has dominated the character of all revolutionary and national-revolutionary movements down to the present day.

Whereas for the bourgeoisie Bolshevism and Marxism meant the same thing, Social Democracy could not possibly identify the Leninist regime as a socialist state, even though it had realized its own long-forgotten goal of reaching socialism via the capture of state power. Yet because Bolshevism had expropriated the bourgeoisie, it was equally impossible to refer to it as a capitalist system, without acknowledging that even legal conquest of the state by parliamentary means need not lead to a socialist system of production. Hilferding, for one, resolved the problem simply by announcing that Bolshevism was neither capitalism nor socialism, but a societal form best described as a "totalitarian state economy," a system based on an "unlimited personal dictatorship."[17] It was no longer determined by the character of its economy but by the personal notions of the omnipotent dictator. Denying his own long-held concept of "organized capitalism" as the inevitable result of the capital concentration process, and the consequent disappearance of the law of value as the regulator of the capitalist economy, Hilferding now insisted that from an economic point of view state-capitalism cannot exist. Once the state has become the sole owner of the means of production, he said, it renders impossible the functions of the capitalist economy because it abolishes the very mechanism which accounts for the economic circulation process by way of competition on which the law of value operates. But while this state of affairs had once been equated with the rise of socialism, it was now perceived as a totalitarian society equally removed from both capitalism and socialism. The one ingredient that excluded its transformation into socialism was the absence of political democracy. But if this were so, Hilferding was fundamentally in agreement with Lenin on the assumption that it is possible to institute socialism by political means, although there was no agreement as to the particular political means to be employed. In fact, Lenin was very much indebted to Hilferding, save in his rejection of the means of formal democracy as the criterion for the socialist nature of the state-controlled economy.

In this respect it is noteworthy that neither Lenin nor Hilferding had any concern for the social production relations as capital-labor relations, but merely for the character of the government presiding over the new society. In the opinion of both, it was the state that must control society, whether by democratic or dictatorial means; the working class was to be the obedient instrument of governmental policies. Just the same, it was Lenin's concept of "dictatorship" that carried the day, for the Bolsheviks had seized power, whereas Hilferding's "democracy" was slowly eroded by the authoritarian tendencies arising within the capitalist system. Besides, the "Marxism" of the Second International had lost its plausibility at the eve of World War I, whereas the success of the Bolshevik Revolution could be seen as a return to the revolutionary theory and practice of Marxism. This situation assured the rising prominence of the Leninist interpretation of Marxism, as dependent on the existence of a vanguard party not only for seizing power but also for securing the transition from capitalism to socialism. At any rate, in the course of time the Leninist conception of Marxism came to dominate that part of the international labor movement which saw itself as an anti-capitalist and anti–imperialist force.

We have dealt with Bolshevism and the Russian Revolution in some detail in order to bring out two specific points: first, that the policies of the Bolshevik regime subsequent to Lenin's death had their cause in the prevailing situation in Russia and the world at large as well as in the political concepts of the Leninist party; and second, that the result of this combination of factors implied a second and apparently "final" destruction of the labor movement as a Marxist movement. World War I and its support by the socialist parties of the Second International signified a defeat of Marxism as a potentially revolutionary workers' movement. The war and its aftermath led to a temporary revival of revolutionary activities for limited reformist goals, which indicated the workers' un-readiness to dislodge the capitalist system. Only in Russia did the revolutionary upheavals go beyond mere governmental changes, by playing the means of production—not at once, but gradually—into the hands of the Bolshevik party-state. But this apparent success implied a total inversion of Marxian theory and its willful transformation into the ideology of state-capitalism, which, by its very nature, restricts itself to the nation-state and its struggle for existence and expansion in a world of competing imperialist nations and power blocs.

The concept of world revolution as the expected result of the imperialist war, which seemingly prompted the Bolsheviks' seizure of power, was dependent upon Lenin's notion of the indispensable existence of a vanguard party, able to grasp the opportunity for the overthrow of the bourgeois state, and capable of avoiding, or correcting, the otherwise aimless squandering of spontaneously released revolutionary energies on the part of the rebellious masses. Aside from the Russian Bolsheviks, however, no vanguard party of the Leninist type existed anywhere, so that this first presupposition for a successful socialist revolution could not be met. In the light of Lenin's own theory, it was therefore logically inconsistent to await the extension of the Russian into an international revolution. But even if such vanguard parties could have been created overnight, so to speak, their goals would have been determined by the Leninist concept of the state and its functions in the social transformation process. If successful, there would have been more than one state-capitalist system but no international socialist revolution. In short, there would have been accomplished at an earlier time what actually came to pass after World War II without a revolution, namely the imperialistic division of the world into monopolistic and state-capitalistic national systems under the aegis of unstable power blocs.

Assuming for the sake of argument that revolutions in Western Europe had gone beyond purely political changes and had led to a dictatorship of the proletariat, exercised through a system of soviets controlling economic social relations, such a system would have found itself in opposition to the party-state in its Leninist incarnation. Most probably, it would have led to a revival of Russia's internal opposition to the Bolshevik power monopoly and to the dethroning of its leadership. A proletarian revolution in the Marxian sense would have endangered the Bolshevik regime even more than would a bourgeois and social democratic counter-revolution, because for the Bolsheviks the spreading of the revolution was conceivable only as the expansion of the Bolshevik Revolution and the maintenance of its specific characteristics on a global scale. This was one of the reasons why the Third International, as a "tool of world revolution," was turned into an international replica of the Leninist party.

This particular practice was based on Lenin's theory of imperialism. More polemical than theoretical in character, Lenin's *Imperialism: The Highest Stage of Capitalism* paid more attention to the fleeting political aspects of imperialism than to its underlying socioeconomic dynamics. It was intended to unmask the imperialist character of the first world war, seen as the general condition for social revolution. Lenin's arguments were substantiated by relevant data from various bourgeois sources, by a critical utilization of the theoretical findings of J. H. Hobson and Rudolf Hilferding, and by a rejection of Karl Kautsky's speculative theory of superimperialism as a way toward a peaceful capitalism. The data and the theories were bound up with a particular historical stage of capitalist development and contained no clues regarding its further course.

The compulsion to imperialism is inherent in capitalist production, but it is the development of the latter which accounts for its specific manifestations at any particular time. For Lenin, however, capitalism became imperialistic "only at a definite and very high stage of capitalistic development," a stage that implied the rule of national and international monopolies which, by agreement or force, divided the world's exploitable resources among themselves. In his view, this period is characterized not so much by the export of commodities as by that of capital, which allows the big imperialist powers, and a part of their laboring populations, an increasingly parasitical existence at the expense of the subjugated regions of the world. He perceived this situation as the "highest stage" of capitalism because he expected that its manifold contradictions would lead directly to social revolutions on an international scale.

However, although World War I led to the Russian Revolution, imperialism was not the "eve of the proletarian world revolution." What is noteworthy here nonetheless is the continuity between Lenin's early work on the development of Russian capitalism and his theory of imperialism and the impending world revolution. Against the Narodniks, as we saw, Lenin held that capitalism would be the next step in Russia's development and that, for that reason, the industrial proletariat would come to play the dominant role in the Russian revolution. But by involving not only the workers, but also the peasants and even layers of the bourgeoisie, the revolution would have the character of a "people's revolution." To realize all its potentialities, it would have to be led by an organization representing the socialism of the working class. Lenin's theory of imperialism as "the eve of world revolution" was thus a projection of his theory of the Russian revolution onto the world at large. Just as in Russia different classes and nationalities were to combine under proletarian leadership to overthrow the autocracy, so on an international scale whole nations, at various stages of development, are to combine under the leadership of the Third International to liberate themselves from both their imperialistic masters and their native ruling classes. The world revolution is thus one of subjugated classes and nations against a common enemy—monopolist imperialism. It was this theory that, in Stalin's view, made "Leninism the Marxism of the age of imperialism." However, based on the presupposition of successful socialist revolutions in the advanced capitalist nations, the theory could not be proven right or wrong, as the expected revolutions did not materialize.

This truly grandiose scheme, which puts Bolshevism in the center of the world revolutionary process and, to speak in Hegelian terms, made the *Weltgeist* manifest itself in Lenin and his party, remained a mere expression of Lenin's imaginary powers, for with every step he took the "greatest of *Realpolitiker*" found himself at odds with reality. Just as he had to jettison his own agrarian program in exchange for that of his Social Revolutionary opponents, to rid himself of the "natural economy" practiced with devastating results during the period of "war communism" and fall back to market relations in the New Economic Policy, and to wage war against the self-determination of oppressed nationalities at first so generously granted by the Bolshevik regime, so he saw himself forced to construct and utilize the Third International not for the extension of the international revolution but for no more than the defense of the Bolshevik state. His internationalism, like that of the bourgeoisie, could only serve national ends, camouflaged as general interests of the world revolution. But perhaps it was this total failure to further the declared goods of Bolshevism that really attests to Lenin's mastery of *Realpolitik*, if only in the sense that an unprincipled opportunism did indeed serve the purpose of maintaining the Bolsheviks in power.

Lenin's single-mindedness in gaining and keeping state power by way of compromises and opportunistic reversals, as dictated by circumstances outside his control, was not a practice demanded by Marxist theory but an empirical pragmatism such as characterizes bourgeois politics in general. The professional revolutionary turned into a statesman vying with other statesmen to defend the specific interests of the Bolshevik state as those of the Russian nation. Any further revolutionary development was now seen as depending on the protection of the first "workers' state," which thus became the foremost duty of the international proletariat. The Marxist ideology served not only internal but also external purposes by assuring working-class support for Bolshevik Russia. To be sure, this involved only part of the labor movement, but it was that part which could disrupt the anti-Bolshevik forces, which now included the old socialist parties and the trade unions. The Leninist interpretation of Marxism became the whole of Marxian theory, as a counter-ideology to all forms of anti-Bolshevism and all attempts to weaken or to destroy the Russian government. Simultaneously, however, attempts were also made to bring about a state of coexistence with the capitalist adversaries. Various concessions were proposed to demonstrate the mutual advantages to be gained through international trade and other means of collaboration. This two-faced policy served the single end of preserving the Bolshevik state by serving the national interests of Russia.

The German Revolution

Contrary to Bolshevik expectations, the Russian Revolution remained a national revolution. Its international repercussions involved no more than a growing demand for the ending of the war. The Bolsheviks' call for an immediate peace without annexations and reparations found a positive response among the soldiers and workers in the Western nations. But even so, and apart from short-lived mutinies in the French and British armed forces and a series of mass strikes in the Central European countries, it took another year before the military defeat of the German and Austrian armies and general war weariness led to the revolutionary upheavals that brought the war to a close.

The here decisive German Revolution of 1918 was a spontaneous political upheaval, initiated within the armed forces but embracing at once, either actively or passively, the majority of the population, to bring the war and therewith the monarchical regime to an end. It was not seriously opposed by either the bourgeoisie or the military, especially as it allowed them to place the onus of defeat upon the revolution. What was important was to prevent the political revolution from turning into a social revolution and to emerge from the war with the capitalist system intact.

At this time, neither the bourgeoisie nor the workers were able to differentiate between Marxism and Bolshevism, except in the political terms of democracy and dictatorship. Notwithstanding the military dictatorship in capitalist countries, it was the dictatorial nature of Bolshevism that the Social Democratic leadership used in order to defend the capitalist system in the name of democracy. Long before the November Revolution, the Social Democratic Party had been the spearhead in the struggle against Bolshevism, directly and indirectly opposing all working-class

actions that might impair the war effort or break up the class collaboration on which its continuation depended. But all these efforts failed to prevent the revolution from overthrowing the old
state and its war machine. So as not to lose all influence upon the
unfolding political events, the Social Democrats were compelled
to take part in them and to try to gain control of the revolutionary movement. To that end, the Social Democratic Party recognized the overthrow of the old regime and accepted the workers'
and soldiers' councils as a provisional social institution, which was
to lead to the formation of a republican democratic state in which
Social Democracy could continue to operate as of old.

The collapse of the German Army in the autumn of 1918 had
led to some constitutional and parliamentary reforms and the
bringing of Social Democrats into the government as a measure to
liquidate the war with the fewest internal troubles and, perhaps,
to gain better armistice conditions. While the workers' and soldiers' councils in Russia were already beginning to lose their independent powers to the emerging Bolshevik state apparatus, they
still inspired the spontaneous formation of similar organizations in
the German revolution and, to a lesser extent, the social upheavals
in England, France, Italy, and Hungary. In Germany, it was not
the lack of effective labor organizations but their class-collaborationist character and their social patriotism that induced the
workers to emulate the Russian example. Opposition to the continuation of the war, and preparations for the revolutionary overthrow of the existing systems had to be clandestinely organized,
outside the official labor movement, at the places of work, linked
with each other by means of committees of action. But before
these planned organizations could enter the revolutionary fray,
the spontaneously formed workers' and soldiers' councils had already put an end to the government by establishing their own political dominance.

The Social Democratic Party found itself forced to enter the
council movement, if only to dampen its possible revolutionary aspirations. This was not too difficult, since the workers' and soldiers' councils were composed not only of radical socialists, but
also of right-wing socialists, trade unionists, pacifists, nonpoliti-
cals, and even bourgeois elements. The radicals' slogan of the day,
"All power to the workers' and soldiers' councils," was therefore
self-defeating, unless, of course, events should take such a turn as

to alter the character and the composition of the councils. However, the great mass of the socialist workers mistook the political for a social revolution. The ideology and organizational strength of Social Democracy had left its mark; the socialization of production, if considered at all, was seen as a governmental concern, not as the task of the workers. "All power to the workers' councils" implied the dictatorship of the proletariat, for it would leave the nonworking layers of society without political representation. Democracy was still understood, however, as the general franchise. The mass of the workers demanded both workers' councils and a National Assembly. They got both—the councils as a meaningless part of the Weimar Constitution, and a parliamentary regime securing the continued existence of the capitalist system.

Whatever the differences between Bolshevism and Social Democracy, as political parties both thought themselves entitled to lead the working class and to determine its activities. Both assumed that it was the party through which the working class became aware of its class interests and was thus enabled to act upon them. While the Social Democratic Party was content with the control of working-class movements within bourgeois society, the Bolsheviks demanded the exclusive right to this control through the party state. But both these branches of Social Democracy saw themselves as the legitimate and indispensable representatives of the working class. A system of workers' and soldiers' councils, and new social institutions derived therefrom, was incomprehensible within the party concepts that had ruled the political labor movement prior to the revolution. And because opposition to capitalism had hitherto found its expression in the socialist parties, it is not surprising that they should have come to play a special and, as it turned out, the decisive role in the formulation of policy objectives for the emerging council movement.

In Russia too, as we have seen, the competition between the various socialist organizations within the soviets for control of the revolutionary movement excluded from the very beginning self-rule of the soviets, which, in fact, proclaimed as their political goal a democratic constitution and economic reforms compatible with the capitalist system. The Bolshevik *coup d'état* changed this situation by basing the rule of the party on the soviets, in which it had gained a majority, even though this majority was as accidental as that of 1903, which gave to Lenin's faction within Russian Social

Democracy the name "Bolshevik." This situation repeated itself in 1917 with the protesting departure of the right-wing socialists and Social Revolutionaries from the Second Congress of Soviets. The Bolshevik government emerged from the congress as the self-appointed "Soviet of Peoples' Commissars," although the congress went through the formality of ratifying the new government.

Similarly, at the German First Congress of Workers' and Soldiers' Councils, the Social Democratic leaders were able to appoint themselves to governmental positions because they controlled the voting majority of the hastily gathered delegates, mainly functionaries of the two socialist parties, the Majority Socialists and the Independent Socialists. This majority was retained also at the Second Congress of Workers' and Soldiers' Councils and assured that the political program adopted was that of the Social Democratic parties. The self-liquidation of the councils in favor of the National Assembly was a foregone conclusion, because of the continued hold of these parties on their members and their unbroken influence upon the unorganized mass of the working population. The revolution, insofar as it had a clear-cut political character, was thus a social democratic revolution, with an emphasis on democracy and a total neglect of the socialist aspect of the Social Democratic movement.

While in both Russia and Germany the workers' and soldiers' councils had been instrumental in making the revolution, they were unable to turn themselves into a means for the reorganization of the social production relations and thus left the reordering of society to the traditional labor movement. As far as Western Europe was concerned, this movement had long ceased to be a revolutionary movement, but it had not ceased to express specific class interests and their defense within bourgeois society. The socialist parties were still workers' organizations, despite their inconsistencies in class struggle situations and their violations of the socialist principles of the past. As institutions making their way within capitalism, their leaders and bureaucracies were no longer interested even in the programmatic "long-term" democratic transformation of capitalism, but concentrated upon the "short-term" enjoyments of their particular privileges within the *status quo*. Behind their effusive celebration of democracy as the "road to socialism" there stood no more than the desire to be fully integrated into the capitalist system, a desire shared by the bourgeoisie, which also favors social harmony.

It was then only to be expected that the class collaboration exercised throughout the war should be continued within and after the revolution. This was understood not only by the bourgeoisie but also by the military authorities, who accepted and supported the new "revolutionary government" even though its legitimation was still based on the workers' and soldiers' councils, seen as an unavoidable interregnum between the pre- and a postrevolutionary capitalist government. In order to proceed to the latter, the whole existing state apparatus was left undisturbed by the "socialist government" and continued to function in its usual ways. All that the revolution was supposed to accomplish was a change from the as yet imperfect to a more perfect bourgeois parliamentary regime, or the completion of the bourgeois revolution, so long delayed by the persistence of feudalistic elements within the rising capitalism. This was the immediate and only goal of German Social Democracy. Its reluctance to extend the revolution into the economic sphere was even more pronounced in the trade-union leadership, which set itself in opposition "to any socialist experiment and any form of socialization at a time when the population required work and food."[1] The close wartime cooperation between the trade unions and private industry was reinforced, in order to prevent and to break strikes and to combat the politicization of the workers via the factory councils in large-scale enterprises. In brief, the old labor movement in its entirety became an unabashed counter-revolutionary force within a revolution that had played political power into its hands.

Insofar as the November Revolution was a genuine revolutionary movement, it found its inspiration in the Bolshevik Revolution, seen as the usurpation of power by the soviets, and was therefore opposed to the convocation of a National Assembly and the restoration of bourgeois democracy. It stood thus in opposition both to the prerevolutionary labor movement and to the spontaneously formed workers' and soldiers' councils, which had made the Social Democratic policies their own. There was, however, the possibility that this immediately given situation might change, not only because of the generally unsettled conditions, but also because of the openly counter-revolutionary activity of the Social Democratic leadership, which might discredit it sufficiently to destroy its influence in its own organization and in the working class as a whole. This was not an unreasonable expectation, as the Social Democratic Party had been split on the issue of

war aims in 1917; this had led to the formation of the Independent Socialist Party (U.S.P.D.), as a first indication of the radicalization of the socialist movement. Until then, organizational fetishism, with its insistence upon unity and discipline, had been strong
enough to prevent an internal break. Even the Spartacus League,
which came to the fore in 1915, did not attempt to form a new
party, but contented itself with the position of a left opposition,
first in the old party and later within the framework of the Independent Socialists, so as not to lose contact with the organized
socialist workers. Although the leaderships of socialist parties were
considered to be beyond repair, this was held not to be true for
the rank and file, who might be won over to the revolution. However, the Independent Socialists themselves encompassed a right
wing, a center, and a left wing, reaching from E. Bernstein,
K. Kautsky, and R. Hilferding to K. Liebknecht, R. Luxemburg,
and F. Mehring, the latter three representing the Spartacus League.
As an opposition party to the social-patriotic Majority Socialists,
the U.S.P.D. was seen as the leading revolutionary organization
with the greatest influence upon the radical elements of the working class. But because of the divisive structure of the party it was
not able to play a consistently revolutionary role and left the determination of events to the social reformists. Only after these experiences, at the end of 1918, did the Spartacus League, together
with some other local radical groupings, constitute itself as the
Communist Party, calling for a soviet republic.

Just as little as the bourgeoisie and its Social Democratic
allies were able to assess their chances for survival during the first
weeks of the revolution, but could only try to prevent its radicalization through the immediate organization of all anti-revolutionary forces in a counter-revolution against the mere possibility of a
true socialist revolution, so the revolutionary minority could not
assess the probability of success or failure within a situation still
in flux and capable of going beyond its initial, limited, political
goals. For neither side, since both comprised social minorities insofar as their *conscious goals* were concerned, was there a way to
weigh its chances, except by trying to realize its objectives. Only by
probing the strength or weakness of the opponent was it possible
to influence events and to gain some insight into the otherwise unpredictable course of the revolution. But this was no longer a question of competing political programs on a purely ideological level,

but one of a confrontation of the armed revolution with the armed counter-revolution—a question of civil war. It was only in retrospect, after the defeat of the revolutionary minority, that it became clear that the revolutionary upheavals had been a cause lost in advance.

In organizing the defense of the capitalist system, the social reformists prepared for and provoked the civil war, all the while calling for its prevention, in order to arrest the rise of "Bolshevik anarchy" and to assure an orderly and bloodless transfer from the old to the new government. But civil war, Rosa Luxemburg wrote,

> is only another name for class struggle. The idea of reaching socialism without class struggle through the Parliament is a laughable petty-bourgeois illusion. The National Assembly belongs to the bourgeois revolution. Whoever wants to use it today throws the revolution back to the historical stage of the bourgeois revolution; he is merely a conscious agent of the bourgeoisie or an unconscious ideologist of the petty-bourgeoisie.[2]

But though this is true, it did not bother the majority of the socialist workers, who had shared for so long in this petit bourgeois ideology, and who had no desire to turn the revolution into civil war now that the war had actually ended. In distinction to the situation in Russia, where the revolution was to bring the war to an end, in the Central European nations the war was liquidated by the bourgeoisie itself and the revolution was a consequence of this liquidation. There was no longer a war to be turned into civil war. There was also no peasantry utilizing the breakdown of autocracy for the appropriation and division of the landed estates, but rather, except perhaps in Hungary, a capitalistic agriculture with a reactionary peasant population. For the revolution to succeed it would have to be one made by the industrial proletariat, set against all other classes in society, and would therefore require the participation of the working class as a whole. It could not succeed if carried out only by a minority.

In their revolutionary élan and audacity the minority of German revolutionaries were, in a sense, even more Bolshevik than the Bolsheviks in their attempts to set an example to the working class. But although they did not hesitate to react to the persistent provocations of the counter-revolution, and though they did initiate revolutionary actions on their own accord, it was not in order

to gain control over the revolution and to install their own dictatorship, but to bring about the class rule of the workers' councils.
While they did not want to make the revolution for the proletariat, they thought it possible that the sharpening of the class struggle would activate always greater masses of workers and draw
them into the fight against the counter-revolutionary forces masquerading as defenders of democracy. Although their efforts
ended in defeat, they had been inescapable, short of leaving the
field entirely uncontested to the counter-revolution whose main
stronghold, at this time, was German Social Democracy. Ironi-
cally, the Marxian aspect of the revolution was defeated in the
name of "Marxism" in its purely ideological social democratic
cast.

Ideology
and
Class Consciousness

In retrospect all lost causes appear as irrational endeavors, while those that succeed seem rational and justifiable. The goals of the defeated revolutionary minority have invariably been described as utopian and thus as indefensible. The term "utopian" does not apply, however, to objectively realizable projects, but to imaginary systems, which may or may not have concretely given material underpinnings that allow for their realization. There was nothing utopian in the attempt to gain control of society by way of workers' councils and to end the market economy, for in the developed capitalist system the industrial proletariat is the determining factor in the social reproduction process as a whole, which is not necessarily associated with labor as wage labor. Whether a society is capitalist or socialist, in either case it is the working class that enables it to exist. Production can be carried on without regard to its expansion in value terms and the requirements of capital accumulation. Distribution and the allocation of social labor are not dependent upon the indirect exchange relations of the market, but can be organized consciously through appropriate new social institutions under the open and direct control of the producers. Western capitalism in 1918 was not the necessary social production system but only the existing one, whose overthrow would merely have released it from its capitalist encumbrances.

What was missing was not the objective possibility for social change, but a subjective willingness on the part of the majority of the working class to take advantage of the opportunity to overthrow the ruling class and to take possession of the means of production. The labor movement had changed with changing capitalism, but in a direction contrary to Marxian expectations. Despite the pseudo-Marxist ideology, it tended toward the apolitical posi-

tion that characterizes labor movements in the Anglo-Saxon countries and toward their positive acceptance of the capitalist system.
The movement had become politically "neutral," so to speak, by
leaving political decisions to the accredited political parties of
bourgeois democracy, of which the Social Democratic Party was
one among others. The workers supported the party that promised,
or seemingly intended, to take care of their particular immediate
needs, which now comprised all their needs. They would not object to the nationalization of industries, were this the goal of their
favored party, but neither did they object to reneging on this principle in favor of the private-property system. They simply left
such decisions to their elected and more or less trusted leaders,
just as they awaited the managers' or entrepreneurs' orders in the
factories. They continued to deny themselves any kind of self-
determination by simply leaving things as they had been, which
seemed preferable to the turmoil and the uncertainties of a prolonged struggle against the traditional authorities. It is thus not
possible to say that Social Democracy "betrayed" the working
class; what its leaders "betrayed" was their own past, now that
they had become an appreciated part of the capitalist establishment.

The failure of the German Revolution seems to vindicate the
Bolshevik assertion that, left to itself, the working class is not able
to make a socialist revolution and therefore requires the leadership
of a revolutionary party ready to assume dictatorial powers. But
the German working class did not attempt to make a *socialist* revolution and thus its failure to do so cannot prove the validity of the
Bolshevik proposition. Moreover, there was a revolutionary "vanguard" that tried to change the purely political character of the
revolution. Although this revolutionary minority did not subscribe
to the Bolshevik party concept, it was no less ready to assume leadership, but as a part, not as the dominator, of the working class.
Under Western European conditions, a socialist revolution depended clearly on class and not on party actions, for here it is the
working class as a whole that has to take over political power and
the means of production. It is true of course—but true for all
classes, the bourgeoisie as well as the proletariat—that it is always
only a part of the whole that actually engages itself in social affairs, while another part remains inactive. But in either case, it is
the active part that is decisive as regards the outcome of the class

war. It is thus not a question of the whole of the working class literally partaking in the revolutionay process, but of a mass sufficient to match the forces mobilized by the bourgeoisie. This relative mass did not aggregate fast enough to offset the growing power of the counter-revolution.

The whole counter-revolutionary strategy consisted in forestalling a possible increase of the revolutionary minority. The great rush into the National Assembly, as the political goal of Social Democracy, was at the same time dictated by the fear that a prolonged existence of the workers' councils could lead to their radicalization in the direction of the revolutionary minority. With the demobilization of the army, the political diversity of the soldiers' councils would disappear, and the composition of the councils, based now exclusively in the factories, might take on a more consistently revolutionary character. That this fear was uncalled for came to light in the results of the election to the National Assembly, which gave the Majority Socialists 37.9 percent of the total vote, whereas the more radical Independent Socialists received only 7.6 percent. Social Democracy still had the confidence of the mass of the working class, despite, or perhaps because of, its anti-revolutionary program. Yet the fear persisted that the victory of bourgeois democracy might not be the last act of the revolution. With revolutionary Russia in the background, a new revolutionary upsurge remained a possibility—a situation calling for the systematic destruction of revolutionary forces that refused to accept the reconsolidation of the capitalist regime.

Although it demanded the end of the war, not the whole of the army joined the revolution. Nonetheless, so as to facilitate the orderly retreat from the frontlines and to avoid a large-scale civil war, the Military High Command accepted both the soldiers' councils and the provisional Social Democratic government. In close cooperation with the Military High Command, the newly established government began at once to select and to organize the more trustworthy elements from the dissolving army into voluntary formations (*Freikorps*) to challenge, disarm, and destroy the revolutionary minority. Under the command of the Social Democratic militarist Gustav Noske, these military forces succeeded in piecemeal fashion in eliminating the armed revolutionaries wherever they tried to drive the revolution beyond the confines of bourgeois democrary. The resort to White terror disturbed the complacency of the Social Democratic masses somewhat more than the revolutionary agitation of the Communists. However, this loss of confidence in the Social Democratic leadership did not benefit the Communists but merely increased the ranks of the divided oppositional Independent Socialists. Between the elections to the National Assembly in January 1919 and the election of the Reichstag in June 1920, the votes for the Majority Socialists declined from 37.9 percent to 21.6 percent, while those of the Independent Socialists increased from 7.6 percent to 18 percent.

Just as the Social Democratic Party utilized the council movement in order to sustain its own political influence, so it did not object to the nationalization of large-scale industry called for by the Second Congress of Workers' Councils. This was to be taken up by the National Assembly, which, of course, offered no guarantee that the demand would also be heeded. But this apparent commitment to the actualization of a program of nationalization—as a synonym for socialization—allowed the Provisional Government to camouflage its counter-revolutionary course with the promise to further the socialization process by peaceful, legal means, in contrast to the Communist endeavors to reach it by way of civil war. While the White terror ruled, this was only because "socialism was on the march" and found no other obstacle in its path than "Bolshevik anarchism." Wherever this promise was taken seriously, as for instance by the workers' and soldiers' councils in the Ruhr district, who made a first step toward socialization by assuming control over industries and mines in the expectation that the government would complete and ratify their actions, their independent initiative was quickly brought to an end by military means. In any case, the Social Democratic concept of nationalization did not include proletarian self-determination but merely, and at best, the taking over of industries by the state. It was in this sense only—that is, in the Bolshevik sense—that nationalization was debatable at all, and it was soon to be discarded as an object of discussion, together with the duly instituted parliamentary committee on socialization.

The November Revolution itself was thus its one and only result. Apart from the toppling of the monarchy, some changes in electoral procedures, the eight-hour day, and the transformation of the factory councils into nonpolitical shop stewards' committees under trade-union auspices, the liberal capitalist economy remained untouched and the state remained a bourgeois state. All the revolution had accomplished were some meager reforms that in any case could have been reached within the framework of capitalism's "normal" development. In the minds of the reformist Social Democrats social change had always been a purely evolutionary process of small progressive improvements which would eventually issue into a quantitatively different social system. They saw themselves, in 1914 and again in 1918, not as "counter-revolutionaries" or as "betrayers" of the working class but, on the contrary, as its true representatives, who cared for both the workers' most immediate needs and their final social emancipation. This is nothing to be wondered at, for, more often than not, even the capitalists see themselves as benefactors of the working class. With far more justification could the Social Democratic leadership imagine that its interventions in the revolutionary process would in the end be more beneficial to the working class than a radical overturn of all existing conditions, with its accompanying interruption of the routinely necessary social and productive functions. Gradualism seemed the only assurance that the social transformation could proceed with the least cost in human misery, and, of course, the least risk for the Social Democratic leadership. Moreover, the political revolution afforded, at least in theory, an opportunity to speed up the process of social reform by bridging the antagonism of labor and capital through a more democratic state and government.

In this view class conflict could be continuously softened through government-induced concessions made to the working class at the expense of the bourgeoisie. There could be an extension of political democracy into the economic sphere and "codetermination" of the social production and distribution process. There was no need for the dictatorship of a class, whether of the bourgeoisie or the proletariat. There could be a continuation of the class collaboration practiced during the war, now to serve peaceful ends, benefiting the whole of society. A condition was imagined, such as came to pass some decades later with the "welfare state" and the "social market economy," in which all conflicts could be arbitrated instead of being fought out, and a social harmony established that would be advantageous to all. The prewar confidence in the economic viability of the capitalist system was still alive: the setbacks of the war could be overcome through an increasing production, unhampered by time-consuming and dislocating social experiments. A bankrupt capitalism was not considered a proper base for socialism; as before, the latter would be a problem of the future, when the economy was once again in full flourish. If some workers did not see it this way, their folly should not be allowed to deprive the rest of society of the possibility to emerge from the shambles left by the war and to meet its more immediate needs in terms of bread and butter.

The reformists had no principles to "betray." They remained what they had been all along, but they were now obliged first of all to safeguard the system in which their cherished practice could continue. The revolution had to be reduced to a mere reform, so as to satisfy their deepest convictions and, incidentally, secure their political existence. The only thing to be wondered at was the great number of socialist workers for whom, at least ideologically, reforms were supposed to be only an intermediate stage in the march to the social revolution. Now that the opportunity was given to realize their "historical mission," they failed to take advantage of it, preferring instead the "easy way" of social reform and the liquidation of the revolution. Again, this is not a verification of the Kautsky-Lenin proposition that the working class is incapable of raising its class consciousness beyond mere trade unionism, for the German working class was a highly socialistically educated working class, quite able to conceive of a social revolution for the overthrow of capitalism. Moreover, it was not "revolutionary consciousness" that the middle-class intellectuals had carried into the working class, but only their own reformism and opportunism, which undermined whatever revolutionary consciousness evolved within the working class. Marxist revisionism did not originate in the working class but in its leadership, for which trade unionism and parliamentarism were the sufficient means for a progressive social development. They merely turned the historically restricted practice of the labor movement into a theory of socialism and, by monopolizing its ideology, were able to influence the workers in the same direction.

Still, the workers proved only too willing to share the leaders' reformist convictions. For Lenin, this was proof enough of their congenital incapacity to develop a revolutionary consciousness, which thus condemned them to follow the reformist lead. The solution was thus the replacement of reformist by revolutionary leaders, who would not "betray" the revolutionary potentialities of the laboring class. It was a question of the "right leadership," a struggle among intellectuals for the minds of the workers, a competition of ideologies for the allegiance of the proletariat. And thus it was the character of the party that was deemed the decisive element in the revolutionary process, even though this party would have to win the confidence of the masses through their intuitive recognition that it represented their own interests, which the masses themselves were not able to express in effective political action.

Simultaneously, the differentiation between class and party was seen as their identity, because the latter would compensate for the lack of political awareness on the part of the less-educated proletariat. Contrary to the Marxian theory that it is material conditions and social relations that account for the rise of a revolutionary consciousness within the proletariat, in the Social Democratic view (whether reformist or revolutionary) these very conditions prevent the workers from recognizing their true class interests and from finding ways and means to realize them. They are able to rebel, no doubt, but not to turn their wrath into successful revolutionary actions and meaningful social change. For this they need the aid of middle-class intellectuals who make the cause of the workers their own, even though, or because, they do not share in those deprivations of the working class which, in the Marxian view, would turn the workers into revolutionaries. This elitist notion implies, of course, that though ideas find their source in material social conditions, they are nonetheless the irreplacable and dominating element in the process of social change. But as ideas they are the privilege of that group in society which, with the given division of labor, attends to its ideological requirements.

But what is class consciousness anyway? Insofar as it merely refers to one's position in society it is immediately recognizable: the bourgeois knows that he belongs to the ruling class; the worker, that his place is among the ruled; and the social groups in between count themselves in neither of these basic classes. There is no problem so long as the different classes adhere to one and the same ideology, namely, the idea that these class relations are natural relations that will always prevail as a basic characteristic of the human condition. Actually, of course, the material interests of the various classes diverge and lead to social frictions that conflict with the common ideology. The latter is increasingly recognized as the ideology of the ruling class in support of the existing social arrangements and will be rejected as a statement of the inescapable destiny of human society. The ruling ideology is thus bound to succumb to the extension of class consciousness into the ideological sphere. The differences of material interests turn into ideological differences and then into political theories based on the concrete social contradictions. The political theories may be quite rudimentary, because of the complexities of the social issues involved, but they nonetheless constitute a change from mere class consciousness to a comprehension that social arrangements could be different from what they are. We are then on the road from mere class consciousness to a revolutionary class consciousness, which recognizes the ruling ideology as a confidence game and concerns itself with ways and means to alter the existing conditions. If this were not so, no labor movement would have arisen and social development would not be characterized by class struggles.

However, just as the presence of the ruling ideology does not suffice to maintain existing social relations, but must in turn be supported by the material forces of the state appratus, so a counter-ideology will remain just this unless it can produce material forces stronger than those reflected by the ruling ideology. If this is not the case, the quality of the counter-ideology, whether it is merely intuitive or based on scientific considerations, does not matter and neither the intellectual nor the worker can effect a change in the existing social relations. Revolutionaries may or may not be allowed to express their views, depending on the mentality that dominates the ruling class, but under whatever conditions they will not be able to dislodge the ruling class by ideological means. In this respect the ruling class has all the advantage, since with the means of production and the forces of the state it controls instrumentalities for the perpetuation and dissemination of its own ideology. As this condition persists until the actual overthrow of a given social system, revolutions must take place with insufficient ideological preparation. In short, the counter-ideology can triumph only through a revolution that plays the means of production and political power into the hands of the revolutionaries. Until then, revolutionary class consciousness will always be less effective than the ruling ideology.

MARXISM: YESTERDAY, TODAY, AND TOMORROW

Marxism: Yesterday, Today, and Tomorrow

In Marx's conception, changes in people's social and material conditions will alter their consciousness. This also holds for Marxism and its historical development. Marxism began as a theory of class struggle based on the specific social relations of capitalist production. But while its analysis of the social contradictions inherent in capitalist production has reference to the general trend of capitalist development, the class struggle is a day-to-day affair and adjusts itself to changing social conditions. These adjustments find their reflection in Marxian ideology. The history of capitalism is thus also the history of Marxism.

The labor movement preceded Marxian theory and provided the actual basis for its development. Marxism became the dominating theory of the socialist movement because it was able convincingly to reveal the exploitative structure of capitalist society and simultaneously to uncover the historical limitations of this particular mode of production. The secret of capitalism's vast development—that is, the constantly increasing exploitation of labor power—was also the secret of the various difficulties that pointed to its eventual demise. Marx's *Capital*, employing the methods of scientific analysis, was able to proffer a theory that synthesized the class struggle and the general contradictions of capitalist production.

Marx's critique of political economy was necessarily as abstract as political economy itself. It could deal only with the general trend of capitalist development, not with its manifold concrete manifestations at any particular time. Because the accumulation of capital is at once the cause of the system's unfolding and the reason for its decline, capitalist production proceeds as a cyclical process of expansion and contraction. These two situations imply different social conditions and therefore different reactions on the part of both labor and capital. To be sure, the general trend of capitalist development implies the increasing difficulty of escaping a period of contraction by a further expansion of capital, and thus a tendency toward the system's collapse. But it is not possible to say at what particular point of its development capital will disintegrate through the objective impossibility of continuing its accumulation process.

Capitalist production, implying the absence of any kind of conscious social regulation of production, finds some kind of blind regulation in the supply and demand mechanism of the market. The latter, in turn, adapts itself to the expansion requirements of capital as determined on the one hand by the changing exploitability of labor power and on the other hand by the alteration of the capital structure due to the accumulation of capital. The particular entities involved in this process are not empirically discernible, so that it is impossible to determine whether a particular crisis of capitalist production will be of longer or shorter duration, be more or less devastating as regards social conditions, or prove to be the final crisis of the capitalist system by provoking a revolutionary resolution through the action of an aroused working class.

In principle, any prolonged and deep-going crisis may release a revolutionary situation that may intensify the class struggle to the point of the overthrow of capitalism—provided, of course, that the objective conditions bring forth a subjective readiness to change the social relations of production. In the early Marxist movement, this was seen as a realistic possibility, due to the fact of a growing socialist movement and the extension of the class struggle within the capitalist system. The development of the latter was thought to be paralleled by the development of proletarian class consciousness, the rise of working-class organizations, and the spreading recognition that there was an alternative to capitalist society.

The theory and practice of the class struggle was seen as a unitary phenomenon, due to the self-expansion and the attendant self-limitation of capitalist development. It was thought that the increasing exploitation of labor and the progressive polarization of society into a small minority of exploiters and a vast mass of exploited would raise the workers' class consciousness and thus their revolutionary inclination to destroy the capitalist system. Indeed, the social conditions of that time allowed for no other perspective, as the unfolding of industrial capitalism was accompanied by increasing misery of the laboring classes and a noticeable sharpening of the class struggle. Still, this was merely a perspective afforded by these conditions, which did not as yet reveal the possibility of another course of events.

Although interrupted by periods of crisis and depression, capitalism has been able to maintain itself until now by a continuous expansion of capital and its extension into space through the acceleration of the increase in the productivity of labor. It proved possible not only to regain a temporarily lost profitability, but to increase it sufficiently to continue the accumulation process as well as to improve the living standards of the great bulk of the laboring population. The successful expansion of capital and the amelioration of the conditions of the workers led to a spreading doubt regarding the validity of Marx's abstract theory of capitalist development. Empirical reality in fact seemed to contradict Marx's expectations with regard to capitalism's future. Even where his theory was maintained, it was no longer associated with a practice ideologically aimed at the overthrow of capitalism. Revolutionary Marxism turned into an evolutionary theory, expressing the wish to transcend the capitalist system by way of constant reform of its political and economic institutions. Marxist revisionism, in both overt and covert form, led to a kind of synthesis of Marxism and bourgeois ideology, as a theoretical corollary to the practical integration of the labor movement into capitalist society.

Not too much should be made of this, however, for the organized labor movement has at all times comprised only the smaller portion of the laboring class. The great mass of workers acclimatizes itself to the ruling bourgeois ideology and—subject to the objective conditions of capitalism—constitutes a revolutionary class only potentially. It may become revolutionary by force of circumstances that overrule the limitations of its ideological awareness and thus offer its class-conscious part an opportunity to turn potentiality into actuality through its revolutionary example. This function of the class-conscious part of the working class was lost through its integration into the capitalist system. Marxism became an increasingly ambiguous doctrine, serving purposes different from those initially contemplated.

All this is history: specifically, the history of the Second

International, which revealed that its apparently Marxist orientation was merely the false ideology of a nonrevolutionary practice.
This had nothing to do with a "betrayal" of Marxism, but was the
result of capitalism's rapid ascendancy and increasing power,
which induced the labor movement to adapt itself to the changing
conditions of capitalist production. As an overthrow of the system
seemed impossible, the modifications of capitalism determined
those of the labor movement. As a reform movement, the latter
partook of the reforms of capitalism, based on the increasing productivity of labor and the competitive imperialistic expansion of
the nationally organized capitals. The class struggle turned into
class collaboration.

Under these changed conditions, Marxism, insofar as it was
not altogether rejected or reinterpreted into its opposite, took on
a purely ideological form that did not affect the pro-capitalist
practice of the labor movement. As such, it could exist side by
side with other ideologies competing for allegiance. It no longer
represented the consciousness of a workers' movement out to
overthrow the existing society, but a world-view supposedly based
on the social science of political economy. With this it became a
concern of the more critical elements of the middle class, allied
with, but not part of, the working class. This was merely the con-
cretization of the already accomplished division between the
Marxian theory and the actual practice of the labor movement.

It is of course true that socialist ideas were first and mainly
—though not only—propounded by members of the middle class
who had been disturbed by the inhuman social conditions of early
capitalism. It was these conditions, not the level of their intelli-
gence, that turned their attention to social change and therewith
to the working class. It is therefore not surprising that the capitalist improvements at the turn of the century should mellow their
critical acumen, and this all the more as the working class itself
had lost most of its oppositional fervor. Marxism became a preoccupation of intellectuals and took on an academic character. It was
no longer predominantly approached as a movement of workers
but as a scientific problem to be argued about. Yet the disputes
around the various issues raised by Marxism served to maintain the
illusion of the Marxian nature of the labor movement until it was
dispelled by the realities of World War I.

This war, which represented a gigantic crisis of capitalist production, led to a short-lived revival of radicalism in the labor movement and in the working class at large. To this extent it heralded a return to Marxian theory and practice. But it was only in Russia that the social upheavals led to the overthrow of the backward, semifeudal capitalist regime. Nonetheless, this was the first time that a capitalist regime had been ended through the actions of its oppressed population and the determination of a Marxist movement. The dead Marxism of the Second International seemed due for replacement by the living Marxism of the Third International. And because it was the Bolshevik Party, under Lenin's guidance, that turned the Russian into a social revolution, it was Lenin's particular interpretation of Marxism that became the Marxism of the new and "highest" stage of capitalism. This Marxism has quite justly been amended into the "Marxism-Leninism" that has dominated the postwar world.

This is not the place to reiterate the history of the Third International and the type of Marxism it brought forth. This story is well documented in countless publications, which either place the blame for its collapse upon Stalin's shoulders or trace it back to Lenin himself. The facts are that the concept of world revolution could not be realized and that the Russian Revolution remained a national revolution and therefore bound to the realities of its own socioeconomic conditions. In its isolation, it could not be adjudged a socialist revolution in the Marxian sense, for it lacked all the preconditions for a socialist transformation of society—that is, the dominance of the industrial proletariat, and a productive apparatus that, in the hands of the producers, could not only end exploitation but at the same time drive society beyond the confines of the capitalist system. As things were, Marxism could only provide the ideology supporting, even while contradicting, the reality of state-capitalism. In other words, as in the Second International, so also in its successor, subordinated as it was to the special interests of Bolshevik Russia, Marxism could only function as an ideology to cover up a nonrevolutionary and finally a counter-revolutionary practice.

In the absence of a revolutionary movement, the Great Depression, affecting the world at large, issued not into revolutionary upheavals but into fascism and World War II. This meant the total eclipse of Marxism. The aftermath of the new war initiated a fresh wave of capitalist expansion on an international scale. Not only did monopoly capital emerge strengthened from the conflict, there also arose new state-capitalistic systems by way of either national liberation or imperialistic conquest. This situation involved not a reemergence of revolutionary Marxism but a "cold war," that is, the confrontation of differently organized capitalist systems in a continuing struggle for spheres of interest and shares of exploitation. On the side of state capitalism, this confrontation was camouflaged as a Marxist movement against the capitalist monopolization of the world economy, while for its part, private-property capitalism was only too glad to identify its state-capitalist enemies as Marxists, or Communists, bent on destroying with the freedom to amass capital all the liberties of civilization. This attitude served to attach the label "Marxism" firmly to the state-capitalist ideology.

Thus the changes brought about by a series of depressions and wars led not to a confrontation between capitalism and socialism, but to a division of the world into more or less centrally controlled economic systems and to a widening of the gap between capitalistically developed and underdeveloped nations. It is true that this division is generally seen as one between capitalist, socialist, and "third world" countries, but this is a misleading simplification of rather more complex differentiations between these economic and political systems. "Socialism" is commonly understood as meaning a state-controlled economy within the national framework, in which planning replaces competition. Such a system is no longer capitalism in the traditional sense, but neither is it socialism in the Marxian sense of an association of free and equal producers. Functioning in a capitalist and therefore imperialist world, it cannot help partaking in the general competition for economic and political power and, like capitalism, must either expand or contract. It must grow stronger in every respect, in order to limit the expansion of monopoly capital by which it would otherwise be destroyed. The national form of so-called socialist or state-controlled regimes sets them in conflict not only with the traditional capitalist world, or particular capitalist nations, but also with each other; they must give first consideration to national interests, i.e., the interests of the newly emerging and privileged ruling strata whose existence and security are based on the nation-state. This leads to the spectacle of a "socialist" brand of imperialism and the threat of war between nominally socialist countries.

Such a situation was inconceivable in 1917. Leninism, or (in

Stalin's phrase) "the Marxism of the age of imperialism," expected a world revolution on the model of the Russian Revolution. Just as in Russia different classes had combined to overthrow the autocracy, so also on an international scale nations at various stages of development might fight against the common enemy, imperialist monopoly capital. And just as in Russia it was the working class, under the leadership of the Bolshevik Party, that transformed the bourgeois into a proletarian revolution, so the Communist International would be the instrument to transform the anti-imperialist struggles into socialist revolutions. Under these conditions, it was conceivable that the less-developed nations might bypass an otherwise inevitable capitalist development and be integrated into an emerging socialist world. Based on the presupposition of successful socialist revolutions in the advanced nations, this theory could be proven neither right nor wrong, as the expected revolutions did not materialize.

What is of interest in this context are the revolutionary inclinations of the Bolshevik movement prior to and shortly after its assumption of power in Russia. Its revolution was made in the name of revolutionary Marxism, as the political-military overthrow of the capitalist system and the establishment of a dictatorship to assure the transformation to a classless society. However, even at this stage, and not only because of the particular conditions prevailing in Russia, the Leninist concept of socialist reconstruction deviated from the notions of early Marxism and was based instead on those evolved within the Second International. For the latter, socialism was conceived as the automatic outgrowth of capitalist development itself. The concentration and centralization of capital implied the progressive elimination of capitalist competition and therewith of its private-property nature, until socialist government, emerging from the democratic parliamentary process, would transform monopoly capital into the monopoly of the state and thus initiate socialism by governmental decree. Although to Lenin and the Bolsheviks this seemed an unrealizable utopia as well as a foul excuse for abstaining from any kind of revolutionary activity, they too thought of the institution of socialism as a governmental concern, though to be carried out by way of revolution. They differed with the Social Democrats with regard to the means to reach an otherwise common goal—nationalization of capital by the state and centralized planning of the economy.

Lenin also agreed with Karl Kautsky's philistine and arrogant assertion that the working class by itself is unable to evolve a revolutionary consciousness, which has to be brought to it from the outside by the middle-class intelligentsia. The organizational form of this idea was the revolutionary party as the vanguard of the workers and as the necessary presupposition for a successful revolution. If, in this view, the working class is incapable of making its own revolution, it will be even less able to build up the new society, an undertaking reserved for the leading party as the possessor of the state apparatus. The dictatorship of the proletariat thus appears as that of the party organized as the state. And because the state has to have control over the whole society, it must also control the actions of the working class, even though this control is supposed to be exercised in its favor. In practice, this turned out to be the totalitarian rule of the Bolshevik government.

The nationalization of the means of production and the authoritarian rule of government certainly differentiated the Bolshevik system from that of Western capitalism. But this did not alter the social relations of production, which in both systems are based on the divorce of the workers from the means of production and the monopolization of political power in the hands of the state. It was no longer private capital but state-controlled capital that now opposed the working class and perpetuated the wage-labor form of productive activity, while allowing for the appropriation of surplus labor through the agency of the state. Though the system expropriated private capital, it did not abolish the capital-labor relationship upon which modern class rule rests. It was thus merely a question of time before the emergence of a new ruling class, whose privileges would depend precisely on the maintenance and reproduction of the state-controlled system of production and distribution as the only "realistic" form of Marxian socialism.

Marxism, however, as the critique of political economy and as the struggle for a nonexploitative classless society, has meaning only within the capitalist relations of production. An end of capitalism would imply the end of Marxism as well. For a socialist society, Marxism would be a fact of history like everything else in the past. Already the description of "socialism" as a Marxist system denies the self-proclaimed socialist nature of the state-capitalist system. Marxist ideology functions here as no more than an attempt to justify the new class relations as necessary requirements for the construction of socialism and thus to gain the acquiescence of the laboring classes. As in the capitalism of old, the special interests of the ruling class are made to appear as general interests.

But even so, in the beginning Marxism-Leninism was a revolutionary doctrine, for it was deadly serious about realizing its own concept of socialism by direct, practical means. While this concept implied no more than the formation of a state-capitalist system, this was the way in which, at the turn of the century, socialism had been quite generally understood. It is therefore not possible to speak of a Bolshevik "betrayal" of the prevailing Marxist principles; on the contrary, it realized the state-capitalist transformation of private-property capitalism, which had been the declared goal also of Marxist revisionists and reformists. The latter, however, had lost all interest in acting upon their apparent beliefs and preferred to accommodate themselves to the capitalist *status quo*. What the Bolsheviks did was to actualize the program of the Second International by way of revolution.

Once they were in power, however, the state-capitalist structure of Bolshevik Russia determined its further development, now generally described with the pejorative term "Stalinism." That it took on this particular character was explained by reference to the general backwardness of Russia and by her capitalist encirclement, which demanded the utmost centralization of power and inhuman sacrifices on the part of the working population. Under different conditions, such as prevailed in capitalistically more advanced nations and under politically more favorable international relations, it was said, Bolshevism would not require the particular harshness it had to exercise in the first socialist country. Those less favorably inclined toward this first "experiment in socialism" asserted that the party dictatorship was merely an expression of the still "half-Asiatic" nature of Bolshevism and could not be duplicated in the more advanced Western nations. The Russian example was utilized to justify reformist policies as the only way to improve the conditions of the working class in the West.

Soon, however, the fascist dictatorships in Western Europe demonstrated that one-party control of the state was not restricted to the Russian scene but was applicable in any capitalist system. It could be utilized just as well for the maintenance of existing social relations of production as for their transformation into state-capitalism. Of course, fascism and Bolshevism continued to differ with respect to economic structure, even as they became politically indistinguishable. But the concentration of political control in the totalitarian capitalist nations implied the central coordination of economic activity for the specific ends of fascist policies and therewith a closer approximation to the Russian system. For fascism this was not a goal but temporary measure, analogous to the "war socialism" of World War I. Nonetheless, it was a first indication that Western capitalism was not immune to state-capitalist tendencies.

With the hoped-for but rather unexpected consolidation of the Bolshevik regime and the relatively undisturbed coexistence of the opposing social systems until World War II, Russian interests required the Marxist ideology not only for internal but also for external purposes, to assure the support of the international labor movement in the defense of Russia's national existence. This involved only a part of the labor movement, to be sure, but that part could disrupt the anti-Bolshevik front, which now included the old socialist parties and the reformist trade unions. As these organizations had already jettisoned their Marxian heritage, the supposed Marxian orthodoxy of Bolshevism became practically the whole of Marxist theory as a counter-ideology to all forms of anti-Bolshevism and all attempts to weaken or destroy the Russian state. Simultaneously, however, attempts were made to secure the state of coexistence through various concessions to the capitalist adversary and to demonstrate the mutual advantages that could be gained through international trade and other means of collaboration. This two-faced policy served the single end of preserving the Bolshevik state and securing the national interests of Russia.

In this manner, Marxism was reduced to an ideological weapon exclusively serving the defensive needs of a particular state and a single country. No longer encompassing international revolutionary aspirations, it utilized the Communist International as a limited policy instrument for the special interests of Bolshevik Russia. But these interests now included, in increasing measure, the maintenance of the international *status quo* in order to secure that of the Russian system. If at first it had been the failure of world revolution that induced Russia's policy of entrenchment, it was now the stability of world capitalism that became a condition of Russian security, and which the Stalinist regime endeavored to enhance. The spread of fascism and the high probability of new attempts to find imperialist solutions to the world crisis endangered not only the state of coexistence but also Russia's internal conditions, which demanded some degree of international tranquility. Marxist propoganda ceased to concern itself with problems of capitalism and socialism but, in the form of anti-fascism, directed itself against a particular political form of capitalism that threatened to unleash a new world war. This implied, of course, the acceptance of anti-fascist capitalist powers as potential allies and thus the defense of bourgeois democracy against attacks from either the right or the left, as exemplified during the civil war in Spain.

Even prior to this historical juncture, Marxism-Leninism had assumed the same purely ideological function that characterized the Marxism of the Second International. It was no longer associated with a political practice whose final aim was the overthrow of capitalism, if only to bring about state-capitalism masquerading as socialism, but was now content with its existence within the capitalist system in the same sense in which the Social Democratic movement accepted the given conditions of society as inviolable. The sharing of power on an international scale presupposed the same on the national level, and Marxism-Leninism outside of Russia turned into a strictly reformist movement. Thus only the fascists were left as forces actually aspiring to complete control over the state. No serious attempt was made to forestall their rise to power. The labor movement, including its Bolshevik wing, relied exclusively upon traditional democratic processes to meet the fascist threat. This meant its total passivity and progressive demoralization and assured the victory of fascism as the only dynamic force operating within the world crisis.

It was of course not only Russia's political control of the international communist movement, via the Third International, that explains its capitulation to fascism, but also the movement's bureaucratization, which concentrated all decision-making power in the hands of professional politicians who did not share the social conditions of the impoverished proletariat. This bureaucracy found itself in the "ideal" position of being able to express its verbal opposition to the system and yet, at the same time, to partake of the privileges that the bourgeoisie bestows upon its political ideologists. They had no driving reason to oppose the general policies of the Communist International, which coincided with their own immediate needs as recognized leaders of the working class in a bourgeois democracy. Finally, however, it is the general apathy of the workers themselves, their unreadiness to look for their own independent solution of the social question, that explains this state of affairs together with its fascist outcome. A half-century of Marxist reformism under the leadership principle, and its accentuation in Marxism-Leninism, produced a labor movement unable to act upon its own interests and therefore incapable of inspiring the working class as a whole to attempt to prevent fascism and war through a proletarian revolution.

As in 1914, internationalism, and with it Marxism, was again drowned in the surging sea of nationalism and imperialism. Policies found their basis in the exigencies of the shifting imperialist power constellations, which led first to the Hitler-Stalin pact and then to the anti-Hitler alliance between the USSR and the democratic powers. The end of even the purely verbal aspirations of Marxism found a belated symbolization in the liquidation of the Third International. The outcome of the war, preordained by its imperialist character, divided the world into two power blocs, which soon resumed competition for world control. The anti-fascist nature of the war implied the restoration of democratic regimes in the defeated nations and thus the reemergence of political parties, including those with a Marxist connotation. In the East, Russia restored her empire and added to it spheres of interest as so much war booty. The breakdown of colonial rule created the "third world" nations, which adopted either the Russian system or a mixed economy of the Western type. A form of neocolonialism arose that subjected the "liberated" nations to more indirect but equally effective control by the great powers. But the spread of state-capitalist-oriented nations was commonly seen as the diffusion of Marxism over the globe, and the arrest of this tendency as a struggle against a Marxism that threatened the (undefined) freedoms of the capitalist world. This type of Marxism and anti-Marxism has no connection whatever with the struggle between labor and capital as envisioned by Marx and the early labor movement.

In its current form, Marxism has been more of a regional than an international movement, as may be surmised from its precarious hold in the Anglo-Saxon countries. The postwar revival of Marxist parties affected mainly nations that faced particular economic difficulties, such as France and Italy. The division and occupation of Germany precluded the reorganization of a mass communist party in the Western zone. The socialist parties finally repudiated their own past, still tinged with Marxist ideas, and turned themselves into bourgeois or "people's" parties defending democratic capitalism. Communist parties do continue to exist throughout the world, legally or illegally, but their chances of affecting political events are more or less nil for the present and the foreseeable future. Marxism, as a revolutionary workers' movement, finds itself today at its historically lowest ebb.

All the more astonishing is the unprecedented capitalist response to theoretical Marxism. This new interest in Marxism in general, and in "Marxist economics" in particular, pertains almost exclusively to the academic world, which is essentially the world of the middle class. There is an enormous outpouring of Marxian literature; "Marxology" has become a new profession, and there are Marxist branches of "radical" economics, history, philosophy, sociology, psychology, and so forth. All may prove to be no more than an intellectual fad. But even so this phenomenon bears witness to the present twilight state of capitalist society and its loss of confidence in its own future. Whereas in the past the progressive integration of the labor movement into the fabric of capitalism implied the accommodation of socialist theory to the realities of an unfolding capitalism, this process is now seemingly reversed through the many attempts to utilize the findings of Marxism for capitalist purposes. This two-pronged endeavor at reconciliation, at overcoming at least to some extent the antagonism between Marxian and bourgeois theory, reflects a crisis in both Marxism and bourgeois society.

Although Marxism encompasses society in all its aspects, it focuses upon the social relations of production as the foundation of the capitalist totality. In accordance with the materialist conception of history, it concentrates its interests on the economic and therefore the social conditions of capitalist development. Whereas the materialist conception of history has long since been quietly plagiarized by bourgeois social science, until quite recently its application to the capitalist system remained unexplored. It is the development of capitalism itself that has forced bourgeois economic theory to consider the dynamics of the capitalist system and thus to emulate, in some fashion, the Marxian theory of accumulation and its consequences.

Here we must recall that the shift of Marxism from a revolutionary to an evolutionary theory turned—with respect to theory —around the question as to whether or not Marx's accumulation theory was also a theory of the objective necessity of capitalism's collapse. The reformist wing of the labor movement asserted that there was no objective reason for the system's decline and destruction, while the revolutionary minority wing held on to the conviction that capitalism's immanent contradictions must lead to its inevitable end. Whether this conviction was based on contradictions in the sphere of production or in that of circulation, left-wing Marxism insisted upon the certainty of capitalism's eventual collapse, expressed by ever more devastating crises, which would bring forth a subjective readiness on the part of the proletariat to overthrow the system by revolutionary means.

The reformists' denial of objective limits to capitalism turned their attention from the sphere of production to that of distribution, and so from the social relations of production to market relations, which are the sole concern of bourgeois economic theory. Disturbances of the system were now seen as arising from supply and demand relations, which unnecessarily caused periods of overproduction through a lack of effective demand due to unjustifiably low wages. The economic problem was reduced to the question of a more equitable distribution of the social product, which would overcome the social frictions within the system. For all practical purposes, it was now held, bourgeois economic theory was of greater relevance than Marx's approach, and therefore Marxism should avail itself of the going market and price theory in order to be able to play a more effective role in the framing of social policies.

It was now said that there were economic laws that operated in all societies and were not subject to Marxian criticism. The critique of political economy had as its object merely the institutional forms under which the eternal economic laws assert themselves. Changing the system would not change the laws of economics. While there were differences between the bourgeois and the Marxian approach to the economy, there were also similarities which both had to recognize. The perpetuation of the capital-labor relation, i.e., the wage system, in the self-styled socialist societies, their accumulation of social capital, and their application of a so-called incentive system that divided the work force into various income categories—all these and more were now held to be unalterable necessities enforced by economic laws. These laws required the application of the analytical tools of bourgeois economics so as to allow for the rational consummation of a planned socialist economy.

This kind of Marxism, "enriched" by bourgeois theory, was soon to find its complement in the attempt to modernize bourgeois economic theory. This theory had been in crisis ever since the Great Depression in the wake of World War I. The theory of market equilibrium could neither explain nor justify the prolonged depression, and thus it lost its ideological value for the bourgeoisie. However, neoclassical theory found a sort of resurrection through its Keynesian modification. Although it had to be admitted that the hitherto assumed equilibrium mechanism of the market and price system was no longer operative, it was now asserted that it could be made to be so with a little governmental help. The disequilibrium of insufficient demand could be straightened out by government-induced production for "public consumption," not only on the assumption of static conditions but also under conditions of economic growth when balanced by appropriate monetary and fiscal means. The market economy, assisted by government planning, would then overcome capitalism's susceptibility to crisis and depression and would allow, in principle, for a steady growth of capitalist production.

The appeal to government and its conscious intervention in the economy, as well as the attention paid to the dynamics of the system, diminished the sharp opposition between the ideology of laissez-faire and that of the planned economies. This corresponded to a visible convergence of the two systems, one influencing the other, in a process leading perhaps to a combination of the favorable elements of both in a future synthesis able to overcome the difficulties of capitalist production. In fact, the long economic upswing after World War II seemed to substantiate these expectations. However, despite the continuing availability of governmental interventions, a new crisis has followed this period of capitalist expansion, as it always had in the past. The clever "fine-tuning" of the economy and the "trade-off" between inflation and unemployment did not prevent a new economic decline. The crisis and the means designed to cope with it have proved to be equally detrimental to capital. The current crisis is thus accompanied by the bankruptcy of neo-Keynesianism, just as the Great Depression spelled the end of neoclassical theory.

Apart from the fact that the actual crisis conditions brought the dilemma of bourgeois economic theory to a head, its long-standing impoverishment through its increasing formalization raised many doubts in the heads of academic economists. The current questioning of almost all the assumptions of neoclassical theory and its Keynesian offspring has led some economists—most forcefully represented by the so-called neo-Ricardians—to a half-hearted return to classical economics. Marx himself is looked upon as a Ricardian economist and as such finds increasing favor among bourgeois economists intent on integrating his "pioneer work" into their own specialty, the science of economics.

Marxism, however, signifies neither more nor less than the destruction of capitalism. Even as a scientific discipline it offers nothing to the bourgeoisie. And yet, as an alternative to the discredited bourgeois social theory, it may serve the latter by providing it with some ideas useful for its rejuvenation. After all, one learns from the opposition. Moreover, in its apparently "realized" form in the "socialist countries," Marxism points to practical solutions that may also be useful in the mixed economies, such as a further increase of stabilizing governmental regulations. An income and wage policy, for instance, comes quite close to the analogous arrangements in centrally controlled economic systems. Finally, in view of the absence of revolutionary movements, the academic type of Marxian inquiry is risk-free, inasmuch as it is restricted to the world of ideas. Strange as it may seem, it is the lack of such movements in a period of social turmoil that turns Marxism into a marketable commodity and a cultural phenomenon attesting to the tolerance and democratic fairness of bourgeois society.

The sudden popularity of Marxian theory nonetheless reflects an ideological as well as an economic crisis of capitalism. Above all it affects those responsible for the manufacture and distribution of ideologies—that is, middle-class intellectuals specializing in social theory. Their class as a whole may feel itself endangered by the course of capitalist development, with its visible social decay, and thus genuinely seek for alternatives to the social dilemma that is also their own. They may do so for motives that, however opportunistic, are necessarily bound up with a critical attitude toward the prevailing system. In this sense, the current "Marxian renaissance" may foreshadow a return of Marxism as a social movement of both theoretical and practical import.

Nonetheless, at present there is little evidence of a revolutionary reaction to the capitalist crisis. If one distinguishes between the "objective left" in society, that is, the proletariat as such, and the organized left, which is not strictly proletarian, then it is only in France and Italy that one can speak of organized forces that could conceivably challenge capitalist rule, provided they had such intentions. But the communist parties and trade unions of these countries have long since transformed themselves into purely reformist parties, at home within the capitalist system and ready to defend it. The very fact of their large working-class following indicates the workers' own unreadiness, or unwillingness, to overthrow the capitalist system, and indeed their immediate desire to find accommodation within it. Their illusions concerning the reformability of capitalism support the political opportunism of the communist parties.

With the aid of the self-contradictory term "Eurocommunism," these parties try to differentiate their present attitudes from past policies—that is, to make it clear that their traditional, albeit long forgotten, state-capitalist goal has been definitively given up in favor of the mixed economy and bourgeois democracy. This is the natural counterpart to the integration of the "socialist countries" into the capitalist world market. It is also a quest for the assumption of larger responsibilities within the capitalist countries and their governments and a promise not to disrupt that limited degree of cooperation reached by the European powers. It does not imply a radical break with the state-capitalist part of the world, but merely the recognition that this part too is presently not interested in further extension of the state-capitalist system by revolutionary means, but rather in its own security in an increasingly unstable world.

While socialist revolutions at this stage of development are more than just doubtful, all working-class activities in defense of the workers' own interests possess a potentially revolutionary character. In periods of relative economic stability the workers' struggle itself hastens the accumulation of capital, by forcing the bourgeoisie to adopt more efficient ways to increase the productivity of labor. Wages and profits may, as mentioned, rise together without disturbing the expansion of capital. A depression, however, brings the simultaneous (though unequal) rise of profits and wages to an end. The profitability of capital must be restored before the accumulation process can be resumed. The struggle between labor and capital now involves the system's very existence, bound up as it is with its continuous expansion. Objectively, ordinary economic struggles for higher wages take on revolutionary implications, and thus political forms, as one class can succeed only at the expense of the other.

Of course, the workers might be prepared to accept, within limits, a decreasing share of the social product, if only to avoid the miseries of drawn-out confrontations with the bourgeoisie and its state. Because of previous experiences, the ruling class expects revolutionary activities and has armed itself accordingly. But the political support of the large labor organizations is equally necessary to prevent large-scale social upheavals. As a prolonged depression threatens the capitalist system, it is essential for the communist parties as well as other reformist organizations to help the bourgeoisie to overcome its crisis conditions. They must try to prevent working-class activities that might delay a capitalist recovery. Their opportunistic policies take on an openly counter-revolutionary character as soon as the system finds itself endangered by working-class demands that cannot be satisfied within a crisis-ridden capitalism.

Although the mixed economies will not transform themselves into state-capitalist systems on their own accord, and though the left-wing parties have, for the time being, discarded their state-capitalist goals, this may not prevent social upheavals on a scale large enough to override the political controls of both the bourgeoisie and their allies in the labor movement. If such a situation should occur, the current identification of socialism with state-capitalism, and a forced rededication of communist parties to the early tactics of Bolshevism, could very well sidetrack any spontaneous rising of the workers into state-capitalist channels. Just as the traditions of Social Democracy in the Central European countries prevented the political revolutions of 1918 from becoming social revolutions, so the traditions of Leninism may prevent the realization of socialism in favor of state capitalism.

The introduction of state capitalism in capitalistically advanced countries as a result of World War II demonstrates that this system is not restricted to capitalistically undeveloped nations but may be applicable universally. Such a possibility was not envisioned by Marx. For him, capitalism would be replaced by socialism, not by a hybrid system containing elements of both within capitalist relations of production. The end of the competitive market economy is not necessarily the end of capitalist exploitation, which can also be realized within the state-planning system. This is a historically novel situation indicating the possibility of a development characterized generally by state monopoly over the means of production, not as a period of transition to socialism but as a new form of capitalist production.

Revolutionary actions presuppose a general disruption of society that escapes the control of the ruling class. Thus far such actions have occurred only in connection with social catastrophes, such as lost wars and the associated economic dislocations. This does not mean that such situations are an absolute precondition for revolution, but it points to the extent of social disintegration necessary to lead to social upheavals. Revolution must involve the rebellion of a majority of the active population, something that is not brought about by ideological indoctrination but is the result of sheer necessity. The resulting activities produce their own revolutionary consciousness, namely an understanding of what has to be done so as not to be destroyed by the capitalist enemy. But at present, the political and military power of the bourgeoisie is not threatened by internal dissension and the mechanisms for manipulatory economic actions are not as yet exhausted. And despite increasing international competition for the shrinking profits of the world economy, the ruling classes of the various nations will still support one another in the suppression of revolutionary movements.

The enormous difficulties in the way of social revolution and a communist reconstruction of society were frightfully underestimated by the early Marxist movement. Of course, capitalism's resiliency and adaptability to changing conditions could not be discovered short of trying to put an end to it. It should be clear by now, however, that the forms taken by the class struggle during the rise of capitalism are not adequate for its period of decline, which alone allows for its revolutionary overthrow. The existence of state-capitalist systems also demonstrates that socialism cannot be reached by means deemed sufficient in the past. Yet this proves not the failure of Marxism but merely the illusory character of many of its manifestations, as reflexes of illusions created by the development of capitalism itself.

Now as before, the Marxian analysis of capitalist production and its peculiar and contradictory evolution by way of accumulation is the only theory that has been empirically confirmed by capitalist development. To speak of the latter we must speak in Marxian terms or not at all. This is why Marxism cannot die but will last as long as capitalism exists. Although largely modified, the contradictions of capitalist production persist in the state-capitalist systems. As all economic relations are social relations, the continuing class relations in these systems imply the constancy of the class struggle, even if, at first, only in the one-sided form of authoritarian rule. The unavoidable and growing integration of the world economy affects all nations regardless of their particular socioeconomic structure and tends to internationalize the class struggle and thereby to undermine attempts to find national solutions for social problems. So long, then, as class exploitation prevails, it will bring forth a Marxist opposition, even if all Marxist theory should be suppressed or used as a false ideology in support of an anti-Marxian practice.

History, of course, has to be made by people, by way of the class struggle. The decline of capitalism—made visible on the one hand by the continual concentration of capital and centralization of political power, and on the other hand by the increasing anarchy of the system, despite, and because of, all attempts at more efficient social organization—may well be a long drawn-out affair. It will be so, unless cut short by revolutionary actions on the part of the working class and all those unable to secure their existence within the deteriorating social conditions. But at this point the future of Marxism remains extremely vague. The advantages of the ruling classes and their instruments of repression have to be matched by a power greater than that which the laboring classes have thus far been able to generate. It is not inconceivable that this situation will endure and thus condemn the proletariat to pay ever heavier penalties for its inability to act upon its own class interest. Further, it is not excluded that the perseverance of capitalism will lead to the destruction of society itself. Because capitalism remains susceptible to catastrophic crises, nations will tend, as they have in the past, to resort to war, to extricate themselves from difficulties at the expense of other capitalist powers. This tendency includes the possibility of nuclear war, and as matters stand today, war seems even more likely than an international socialist revolution. Although the ruling classes are fully aware of the consequences of nuclear warfare, they can only try to prevent it by mutual terror, that is, by the competitive expansion of the nuclear arsenal. As they have only very limited control over their economies, they also have no real control over their political affairs, and whatever intentions they may harbor to avoid mutual destruction do not greatly affect the probability of its occurrence. It is this terrible situation that precludes the confidence of an earlier period in the certainty and success of socialist revolution.

As the future remains open, even if determined by the past and the immediately given conditions, Marxists must proceed on the assumption that the road to socialism is not yet closed and that there is still a chance to overcome capitalism prior to its self-destruction. Socialism now appears not only as the goal of the revolutionary labor movement but as the only alternative to the partial or total destruction of the world. This requires, of course, the emergence of socialist movements that recognize the capitalist relations of production as the source of increasing social miseries and the threatening descent into a state of barbarism. However, after more than a hundred years of socialist agitation, this seems to be a forlorn hope. What one generation learns, another forgets, driven by forces beyond its control and therefore comprehension. The contradictions of capitalism, as a system of private interests determined by social necessities, are reflected not only in the capitalist mind but also in the consciousness of the proletariat. Both classes react to the results of their own activities as if they were due to unalterable natural laws. Subjected to the fetishism of commodity production they perceive the historically limited capitalist mode of production as an everlasting condition to which each and everyone has to adjust. Since this erroneous perception secures the exploitation of labor by capital, it is of course fostered by the capitalist as the ideology of bourgeois society and indoctrinated into the proletariat.

The capitalist conditions of social production force the working class to accept its exploitation as the only way to secure its livelihood. The immediate needs of the worker can only be satisfied by submitting to these conditions and their reflection in the ruling ideology. Generally, he will accept one with the other, as representative of the real world, which cannot be defied except by suicide. An escape from bourgeois ideology will not alter his actual position in society and is at best a luxury within the conditions of his dependence. No matter how much he may emancipate himself ideologically, for all practical purposes he must proceed as if he were still under the sway of bourgeois ideology. His thoughts and actions are of necessity discrepant. He may realize that his individual needs can only be assured by collective class actions, but he will still be forced to attend to his immediate needs as an individual. The twofold nature of capitalism as social production for private gain reappears in the ambiguity of the worker's position as both an individual and a member of a social class.

It is this situation, rather than some conditioned inability to transcend capitalist ideology, that makes the workers reluctant to express and to act upon their anti-capitalist attitudes, which complement their social position as wage workers. They are fully aware of their class status, even when they ignore or deny it, but they also recognize the enormous powers arrayed against them, which threaten their destruction should they dare to challenge the capitalist class relations. It is for this reason too that they choose a reformist rather than revolutionary mode of action when they attempt to wring concessions from the bourgeoisie. Their lack of revolutionary consciousness expresses no more than the actual social power relations, which indeed cannot be changed at will. A cautious "realism"—that is, a recognition of the limited range of activities open to them—determines their thoughts and actions and finds its justification in the power of capital.

Unless accompanied by revolutionary action on the part of the working class, Marxism, as the theoretical comprehension of capitalism, remains just that. It is not the theory of an actual social practice, intent and able to change the world, but functions as an ideology in anticipation of such a practice. Its interpretation of reality, however correct, does not affect the immediately given conditions to any important extent. It merely describes the actual conditions in which the proletariat finds itself, leaving their change to the future actions of the workers themselves. But the very conditions in which the workers find themselves subject them to the rule of capital and to an impotent, namely ideological, opposition at best. Their class struggle within ascending capitalism strengthens their adversary and weakens their own oppositional inclinations. Revolutionary Marxism is thus not a theory of class struggle as such, but a theory of class struggle under the specific conditions of capitalism's decline. It cannot operate effectively under "normal" conditions of capitalist production but has to await their breakdown. Only when the cautious "realism" of the workers turns into unrealism, and reformism into utopianism—that is, when the bourgeoisie is no longer able to maintain itself except through the continuous worsening of the living conditions of the proletariat— may spontaneous rebellions issue into revolutionary actions powerful enough to overthrow the capitalist regime.

Until now the history of revolutionary Marxism has been the history of its defeats, which include the apparent successes that culminated in the emergence of state-capitalist systems. It is clear that early Marxism not only underestimated the resiliency of capitalism, but in doing so also overestimated the power of Marxian ideology to affect the consciousness of the proletariat. The process of historical change, even if speeded up by the dynamics of capitalism, is exceedingly slow, particularly when measured against the lifespan of an individual. But the history of failure is also one of illusions shed and experience gained, if not for the individual, at least for the class. There is no reason to assume that the proletariat cannot learn from experience. Quite apart from such considerations, it will at any rate be forced by circumstances to find a way to secure its existence outside of capitalism, when this is no longer possible within it. Although the particularities of such a situation cannot be established in advance, one thing is clear: namely, that the liberation of the working class from capitalist domination can only be achieved through the workers' own initiative, and that socialism can be realized only through the abolition of class society through the ending of the capitalist relations of production. The realization of this goal will be at once the verification of Marxian theory and the end of Marxism.

1978

Notes

Foreword

1. *Marx and Keynes* (Boston: Porter Sargent, 1969).
2. "Marinus van der Lubbe: Proletarier oder Provokateur?" *Der Freidenker* 5/6 (4 January 1934), p. 7.

Marxism and Bourgeois Economics: Introduction

1. *Capital*, Vol. I (Chicago: Kerr, 1906), p. 20.
2. *Ibid.*, p. 19.
3. F. Engels in *Capital*, Vol. II (Chicago: Kerr, 1909), p. 27.
4. W. C. Mitchell, *Types of Economic Theory*, Vol. II (New York: Kelley, 1969), p. 117.
5. H. Meissner, *Burgerliche Ökonomie im Modernen Kapitalismus* (Berlin: Dietz, 1967), pp. 684-85.

Value and Price

1. P. Sraffa, ed., *The Works and Correspondence of David Ricardo*, Vol. I (Cambridge: Cambridge University Press, 1966), p. 13.
2. *Capital*, Vol. I, p. 71.
3. *Ibid.*, p. 84.
4. *Ibid.*, pp. 92-3.
5. One example among many: According to I. I. Rubin, "*the law of value is the law of equilibrium of the market economy.* . . . The aim of this (Marx's) theory is to discover the laws of equilibrium of labor allocation behind the regularity in the equalization of things in the process of exchange . . . . The subject-matter of the theory of value is the *interrelation of various forms of labor* in the process of distribution, which is established through the relations of exchange among things, i.e. products of labor." *Essays on Marx's Theory of Value* (Detroit: Black and Red, 1972), p. 67.
6. *Capital*, Vol. I, p. 86.

7. *Theories of Surplus-Value*, Vol. III (London: Lawrence and Wishart, 1972), p. 130.

8. The requirements of the capitalist reproduction process have been *illustrated* by Marx in the abstract reproduction diagrams in the second volume of *Capital* (Chapters XX-XXI). These diagrams divide total social production into two sectors: one producing means of production and the other means of consumption. Each sector is composed of constant and variable capital and produces surplus value. The transactions between the two sectors are *imagined* to be such as to reproduce the total social capital either on the same or on an enlarged scale. But what is a presupposition for the postulated reproduction diagrams—namely, that allocation of social labor required for the reproduction process—must in reality first be brought about blindly, through the uncoordinated strivings of the individual capitals that make up the total capital.

9. Ricardo, pp. 88-97.

10. *Ibid.*, p. 42.

11. *Capital*, Vol. III (Chicago: Kerr, 1906), p. 209.

12. F. Engels, *Ergänzung und Nachtrag zum 3. Band des Kapital*, Marx-Engels *Werke*, Vol. 25, p. 909.

13. *Grundrisse* (Harmondsworth: Penguin, 1973), p. 140.

14. Marx-Engels, *Selected Works*, Vol. II (Moscow: Foreign Languages Publishing House, 196?), p. 461.

15. *Theories*, Vol. III, p. 463.

16. *Capital*, Vol. III, p. 181.

17. *Ibid.*, p. 50.

18. *Theories of Surplus-Value*, Vol. II (London: Lawrence and Wishart, 1969), p. 211.

19. *Theories*, Vol. III, p. 463.

20. *Ibid.*, p. 190.

21. *Capital*, Vol. III, p. 246.

22. *Ibid.*, p. 969.

23. *Ibid.*, p. 187.

24. *Ibid.*, p. 199.

The Transformation Problem

1. In P. Sweezy, ed., *Karl Marx and the Close of His System* (New York: Kelley, 1949), p. 30.

2. *Ibid.*, p. 34.

3. *Ibid.*, p. 36.

4. L. V. Bortkiewicz, "On the correction of Marx's fundamental theoretical construction in the third volume of *Capital*," in Sweezy, ed., *op. cit.*

5. *Theoretische Grundlagen des Marxismus* (1905).

6. Bortkiewicz, p. 199.

7. *Cf. Capital* Vol. III, p. 185: "If we consider capitals I to V as one single total capital, it will be seen that the composition of the sum of the five

capitals amounts to 500, being 390 C + 110 V, so that the average composition is 78 C + 22 V.

Capitals	Rate of surplus value	Surplus value	Rate of profit	Used-up C	Values of commodities	Cost price
I. 80c + 20v		20	20%	50	90	70
II. 70c + 30v		30	30%	51	111	81
III. 60c + 40v	100%	40	40%	51	131	91
IV. 85c + 15v		15	15%	40	70	55
V. 95c + 5v		5	5%	10	20	15
390c + 110v		110	100%		Total	
78c + 22v		22	22%	Average		

If we allot this surplus-value uniformly to capitals I to V, we arrive at the following prices of commodities:

Capitals	Surplus value	Value	Cost prices of commodities	Price of commodities	Rate of profit	Deviation of price from value
I. 80c + 20v	20	90	70	98		+ 2
II. 70c + 30v	30	111	81	103		− 8
III. 60c + 40v	40	131	91	113	22%	−18
IV. 85c + 15v	15	70	55	77		+ 7
V. 95c + 5v	5	20	15	37		+17

Summing up, we find that the commodities are sold at 2 + 7 + 17 = 26 above, and 8 + 18 = 26 below their value, so that the deviations of prices from values mutually balance one another by the uniform distribution of the surplus value, or by the addition of the average profit of 22% per hundred of advanced capital to the respective cost-prices of the commodities of I to V."

8. Bortkiewicz, p. 201.

9. *Capital*, Vol. II, p. 532.

10. *Ibid.*, p. 578.

11. Bortkiewicz, p. 266.

12. Bortkiewicz, p. 206.

13. Meghnad Desai, *Marxian Economic Theory* (London: Gray-Mills, 1974), p. 3.

14. *Ibid.*, p. 55.

15. P. A. Samuelson, "Understanding the Marxian Notion of Exploita-

tion . . . ," in *Journal of Economic Literature* (June 1971), p. 422.

16. M. Morishima, "The Fundamental Marxian Theorem: A Reply to Samuelson," in *Journal of Economic Literature* (December 1971), p. 73.

17. In *Journal of Economic Literature* (December 1971), p. 58.

18. M. Morishima, *Marx's Economics* (Cambridge: Cambridge University Press, 1973), p. 86.

19. In *Journal of Economic Literature* (December 1971), p. 65.

20. P. Sraffa, *Production of Commodities by Means of Commodities* (Cambridge: Cambridge University Press, 1966).

21. P. Sraffa, *Introduction* to Ricardo, p. xxxi.

22. Cf. M. Cogoy, "Das Dilemma der neo-ricardianischen Theorie," in H. G. Backhaus *et al.*, eds., *Gesellschaft* (Frankfurt: Suhrkamp, 1974), pp. 205-263.

23. Sraffa, p. v.

24. Cogoy, pp. 252-3.

25. *Ibid.*, p. 218.

26. *Ibid.*, p. 255.

27. *Cf.* M. Cogoy, *Wertstruktur und Preisstruktur. Die Bedeutung der linearen Produktionstheorie für die Kritik der politischen Ökonomie* (Frankfurt: Suhrkamp, 1977).

28. Unfortunately, this further discussion of Cogoy's work was not written.

29. P. Sweezy, *The Theory of Capitalist Development* (New York: Monthly Review, 1942), p. 129.

30. *Ibid.*

31. R. Dorfman, *The Price System* (Engelewood Cliffs, N.J.: Prentice-Hall, 1964), p. 40.

32. *Capital*, Vol. III, p. 271.

Value and Capital

1. *Theories of Surplus-Value*, Vol. I (Moscow: FLPH, n.d.), p. 110.

2. *Capital*, Vol. III, p. 282.

3. *Ibid.*, p. 290.

4. *Ibid.*, p. 283.

5. *Ibid.*, p. 261.

6. *Capital*, Vol. I, p. 683.

7. *Ibid.*, p. 689.

8. *Capital*, Vol. III, p. 306.

9. S. Kuznets, *Capital in the American Economy* (National Bureau of Economic Research, 1961), p. 34.

10. *Ibid.*, p. 6.

11. *Ibid.*, p. 7.

12. *Ibid.*, p. 445.

13. *Ibid.*, p. 63.

14. *Ibid.*, p. 67.

15. *Ibid.*, p. 430.

16. O. Morgenstern, *On the Accuracy of Economic Observations* (Princeton: Princeton University Press, 1963), p. 286.

17. *Ibid.*, p. 303.

18. *Ibid.*, p. 305.

19. This is sometimes attempted, as for instance by J. M. Gillman in *The Falling Rate of Profit* (1958). Data with respect to national income, the value of production, the number of workers employed, their payrolls, and the value added by manufacture, as reported by the Bureau of Internal Revenue, the Census of Manufacturers, the Bureau of Labor Statistics, etc. are translated into the Marxian categories of constant capital, variable capital, and surplus value. Their interrelations within the rising organic composition of capital and the effect of this upon the rate of profit are calculated in these price terms, in the hope that this will resemble the Marxian categories. It stands to reason that Gillman's data, like the data derived from the technical composition of capital, will yield some trends—without, however, saying anything definite about a temporary or a tendential fall of the rate of profit. While Gillman's confidence in the available data is quite naive, his knowledge of Marxian theory is less than required to deal effectively with the problems he considers. He assumes, for instance, that the fall in the rate of profit is due to the "limitations of the consumer market potentials wherein alone profits can be realized." For him it is not the production but the realization process that leads to the fall of the profit rate, even though (and strangely enough) he explains a detected rise in the rate of profit by the cheapening of the constant part of capital. (*Cf.* P. Mattick's review, "Value theory and capital accumulation" in *Science & Society* 23 : 1 (Winter 1959), pp. 27-51.—Ed.)

Theory and Reality

1. *Capital*, Vol. I, p. 707.

2. *Cf.* J. Conyers, Jr. "Jobless Numbers," *The New York Times*, 1 January 1976: "How does the Labor Department slant the statistics? The method is fairly simple. It merely defines in very narrow terms who is unemployed and calls many people employed who are not, in any real sense. Amazingly, millions who searched for jobs so long that they stopped looking are not considered officially jobless, because they don't fit the department's 'unemployment' category (they must have looked for jobs within the four weeks preceding the monthly survey) . . . If we add 5.3 million discouraged workers and just half the part-time workers (1.8 million) to the official 7.7 million, the number of the unemployed soars to 14.8 million."

3. *The New York Times*, 30 November 1975.

4. I. L. Kellner, "Counting the Employed, Not the Unemployed," *The New York Times*, 26 October 1975.

5. As reported in *The New York Times*, 31 October 1976.

6. Marx, *Grundrisse*, p. 706.

7. J. Schmookler, *Invention and Economic Growth* (Cambridge, Mass.: Harvard University Press, 1966), p. 3.

8. For example: The Temporary National Economic Committee, Monograph 29, *The Distribution of Ownership in the 200 Largest Nonfinancial Corporations* (1940); D. Lynch, *The Concentration of Economic Power* (1946); G. C. Means, *The Corporate Revolution in America* (1962); F. Lundberg, *The Rich and the Super-Rich* (1968); M. Mintz and J. S. Cohen, *America Inc.* (1971); J. M. Blair, *Economic Concentration* (1972); A. D. Chandler, Jr., *The Visible Hand: The Managerial Revolution in American Business* (1977).

9. For comprehensive and detailed data see L. H. Kimmel, *Share Ownership in the United States* (Washington, D.C.: The Brookings Institution, 1952). See also J. Crockett and I. Friend, *Characteristics of Stock Ownership* (New York: The Ford Foundation, 1963).

10. As of 1966, General Motors, with sales of $20.2 billion, fell between the Netherlands' GNP of $20.8 billion and Argentina's GNP of $18.7 billion. With net sales of about $12.2 billion each, Ford and Standard Oil of New Jersey fell between the GNP of Czechoslovakia, $13.4 billion, and that of the Union of South Africa, $11.9 billion. The net sales figures for Royal Dutch Shell, General Electric, Chrysler, Unilever, and Mobil Oil fell within the range of the GNPs of Venezuela, Norway, Greece, Colombia, and New Zealand.

11. The effect on the distribution of surplus value of monopolistic price determination in only one branch of production—albeit an important one—was recently and dramatically demonstrated by the Organization of Petroleum Exporting Countries (OPEC), which, in collaboration with the International Oil Cartel, managed a sixfold increase of oil prices within a few years. Although in unequal measure, this affects both the developed and the underdeveloped nations by distorting the reproduction of their economies as well as all international trade and payments relations. Less dramatic, but even more devastating, are the self-serving price policies of the monopolies in general. With regard to the oil interests, J. M. Blair writes in *The Control of Oil* (New York: Pantheon, 1977): "It also seems clear that little consideration was given by either the OPEC countries or the major companies to the broad economic and social consequences of their actions, e.g. retarding the development of the world's poorer countries by draining away their limited foreign exchange balances, aggravating a serious worldwide recession, and imperiling the monetary basis of conducting world trade " (p. 320).

12. Marx, *Theories of Surplus-Value*, Vol. III, p. 447.

13. J. Hicks, *A Theory of Economic History* (New York: Oxford University Press, 1969), p. 158.

14. K. Boulding, *The Meaning of the Twentieth Century* (New York: Harper & Row, 1964), p. 171.

15. *Ibid.*, p. 170.

16. As reported in *The New York Times*, 15 April 1977.

17. As reported in *Time*, 5 February 1979, p. 127.

18. W. D. Nordhaus, *The Falling Share of Profits* (Brookings Paper on Economic Activity 1, 1974).

19. *Ibid.*, p. 169.

20. *Ibid.*, p. 170.

21. In accordance with the queer concept that profits are a reward for taking risks and are determined by the degree of the latter, Nordhaus assumes that the main reason for the declining rate of profit will be found in the greater or lesser, but continuous, fall in the "costs of capital," due to a change "in the general economic climate" induced by governmental interventions in the economy, which gradually "dissipated the fear of a new Great Depression." As the holders of securities "are risk-averse maximizers of capital utility," the fall of the "risk-premium" lowered the rate of return on capital and thus its share of the Gross National Product.

22. According to M. Feldstein, the most obvious of these special circumstances are "(1) price and wage controls, (2) the oil embargo and jump in energy prices, and (3) very rapid rate of inflation. Price controls not only limited profits directly but also contributed to shortages that cut profits even more. The oil embargo caused further shortages and the jump in energy costs meant that the existing capital was not optimal for current relative input prices. While this development may have raised the return on new equipment, it lowered that on old equipment valued at replacement cost. . . . The rapid rate of inflation led to a fall in economic profits because current accounting methods caused firms to overestimate accounting profits and therefore to set prices inappropriately." (*Is the Rate of Profit Falling?* Brookings Papers on Economic Activity 1: 1977, p. 221). All these items represent *reactions* to a prior fall of the rate of profit and thus cannot explain the latter. The results of the fall of the rate of profit are here taken for its causes.

23. F. M. Gottheil, *Marx's Economic Predictions* (Evanston, Ill.: Northwestern University Press, 1966), p. 96.

24. *Ibid.*, p. 97.

25. *Ibid.*, p. 98.

26. *Ibid.*, p. 97.

27. *Ibid.*, p. 98.

28. *Ibid.*, p. 103.

29. *Ibid.*, p. 105.

30. *Ibid.*, p. 116.

Revolution and Reform: Introduction

1. *Capital*, Vol. I, p. 836.

2. *A Contribution to the Critique of Political Economy* (Chicago: Kerr, 1904), p. 12.

3. Thomas Rutherford, *Institutes of Natural Law* (1754), quoted by P. Larkin in *Property in the Eighteenth Century* (London: Longmans, Green, 1930), p. 102.

4. *Contribution to the Critique of Political Economy*, p. 12.

Capitalism and Socialism

1. *Das Finanzkapital* (1909); English translation, *Finance Capital* (Lon-

Capitalism and Socialism

don: Routledge and Kegan Paul, 1981).

2. *Studien zur Theorie und Geschichte der Handelskrisen* (1901); *Theoretische Grundlagen des Marxismus* (1905).

3. Actually, Hilferding has no crisis theory; he merely describes the differences in market conditions that distinguish periods of prosperity from those of depression. Insofar as he attempts an explanation, it is clearly self-contradictory. On the one hand, he maintains with Marx that the cause of crisis must be looked for in the sphere of production, in the recurring difficulty of producing the surplus value necessary for a further profitable expansion of capital; on the other hand, he speaks of a lack of coordination between the expanding capital and the growing consumption, which disturbs the supply and demand relations in terms of prices, thereby impairing the realization of the produced surplus value. Besides this particular disproportionality, Hilferding mentions a number of others, such as may arise between fixed and circulating capital; between technical and value relations of production; between the functions of money as a hoard and as medium of exchange; between unequal changes in the turnover of the different capital entities, and so forth.

Although Hilferding refers to the law of the falling rate of profit in the course of the rising organic composition of capital, and for that reason rejects the popular underconsumption theories, he asserts nevertheless that the differences in the organic composition of the diverse capitals display themselves in discrepancies arising between production and consumption in terms of price relations. He forgets that it is the general, or average, rate of profit that regulates the prices of production, regardless of differences in the organic compositions of the individual capitals, and that it is the accumulation process itself that allocates social labor in favor of a more rapid growth of the constant capital. However, searching for the cause of crisis in the circulation process, Hilferding speaks of a difference between market prices and the prices of production. He says, in other words, that some capitalists realize profits beyond that contained in the price of production, while others realize correspondingly less than the profit implied in the price of production, as determined by the organic composition of the total social capital. This implies, of course, an impairment of the function of the average rate of profit as a result of the increasing monopolization of capital, which, however, does not alter the size of the total social profit, or surplus value, with respect to the accumulation requirements of the total social capital on which Marx's crisis theory is based. Whereas in Marx's theory the value relations regulate the price relations, in Hilferding's interpretation the actual price relations disrupt the regulatory force of the value relations, because prices do not register the value requirements for the equilibrium conditions of the expanded reproduction of capital.

4. In a speech delivered at the Social-Democratic Party Congress in Kiel, 1927. *Cf. Protokoll der Verhandlungen des sozialdemokratischen Parteitages 1927 in Kiel* (Berlin: 1927), pp. 165-224.

5. Karl Kautsky, *Am Tage nach der sozialen Revolution. (Die soziale Revolution*, part II) (Berlin, 1902); English translation, "The Day after the Social Revolution," in *The Social Revolution* (Chicago: Kerr, 1902).

6. Karl Kautsky, *Der Weg zur Macht* (1909): English translation, *The Road to Power* (Chicago: S. A. Bloch, 1909).

Reform and Revolution

1. Engels's position on this question has been passionately criticized by the Leninist and Ukrainian nationalist Roman Rosdolsky in his book *Friedrich Engels und das Problem der "Geschichtslosen Völker"* (Frankfurt: Archiv für Sozialgeschichte, Bd. 4, 1964).

2. F. Engels, *Briefe an Bebel (1879)* (Berlin: Dietz, 1958), p. 41.

3. Upton Sinclair, *My Lifetime in Letters* (Columbia, Mo.: University of Missouri Press, 1960), pp. 75-76.

4. W. T. Rodgers and B. Donoughue, *The People into Parliament* (New York: Viking, 1966), p. 73.

The Limits of Reform

1. In his book *In Place of Fear* (New York, 1952, pp. 21-23), Aneurin Bevan relates that in 1919—with the British trade unions threatening a nationwide strike—the then Prime Minister David Lloyd George told the labor leaders that they must be aware of the full consequences of such an action, for "if a force arises in the State which is stronger than the State itself, then it must be ready to take on the functions of the State, or withdraw and accept the authority of the State." From that moment on, one of the labor leaders said, "we were beaten and we knew we were." After this, Bevan continues, "the General Strike of 1926 was really an anticlimax. The leaders in 1926 . . . had never worked out the revolutionary implications of direct action on such a scale. Nor were they anxious to do so. . . . It was not so much the coercive power of the State that restrained the full use of the workers' industrial power. . . . The workers and their leaders paused even when their coercive power was greater than that of the State. . . . The opportunity for power is not enough when the will to seize it is absent, and that will is attendant upon the traditional attitude of the people toward the political institutions that form part of their historical heritage." This may be so, but actually, in this particular case, it was not the attitude of the workers with regard to their historical heritage, but merely their submission to their own organizations and their leaderships that allowed the latter to call off the General Strike, out of fear that it might lead to revolutionary upheavals because of the government's apparently intractable determination to break the strike by force.

Lenin's Revolution

1. *Cf.* Kautsky, *The Road to Power* (1909).

2. The individuals referred to here represent not only themselves but currents within the labor movement, in which they played outstanding roles through their contributions to the movement's theory and practice.

3. Lenin, *Collected Works*, Vol. 35 (Moscow: Progress, 1966), p. 76.

4. The literature and documentation of the Russian revolution is so im-

mense that hardly anything can or need be added to it apart from the work of professional historians, especially as this upheaval has been treated from every conceivable point of view, pro and contra, as well as with respect to its impact upon the world at large and the development of capitalism. We will therefore deal only with aspects of this revolution relevant to understanding its effect upon the labor movement in general and the theory and practice of Marxism in particular.

5. *My Past and Thoughts. The Memoirs of Alexander Herzen* (Berkeley: University of California Press, 1973), p. 500.

6. The Social-Revolutionary Party represented the interests of the peasantry in the Russian revolution. It was organized in 1905 through the unification of a number of Populist groups. Its program demanded a federated republic based on a general frachise, and stressed the "socialization" of all land, that is, its ownership and control by democratically organized communities on the basis of equal holdings and the abolition of hired labor. Although it included workers and intellectuals, the party did not concern itself with the nationalization of industry, on the assumption that the abolition of landownership would by itself prevent the further development of the capitalist relations of production. However, its left wing, the "Maximalists," advocated the inclusion in its program of the socialization of industry under the aegis of a Workers' Republic. It also differentiated itself from the pro-war right wing of the party by its internationalist stand on the war issue. Forming a political bloc with the Mensheviks, the Social-Revolutionaries dominated the Petrograd Soviet; by themselves they controlled the Soviet of Peasant Deputies. In the election for the All-Russian Constituent Assembly, in November 1917, they received 17 million out of 41,700,000 votes, and the party's chairman, V. M. Chernov, was elected President of the Assembly. Prior to this, the party was represented in the Provisional Government formed at the time of the February Revolution. Its left wing supported the Bolsheviks and took part in the first Bolshevik government, as well as in the dispersal of the Constituent Assembly.

7. Lenin, *Collected Works*, Vol. 21 (Moscow: Progress, 1964), p. 336.

8. *What is to be Done?* (New York, 1929), written in February 1902.

9. *Ibid.*, p. 33.

10. *Ibid.*, pp. 113-4.

11. David Lane, *The Roots of Russian Communism* (State College, Pa.: Pennsylvania State University Press, 1969), pp. 12-15. This is an extensive analysis—with respect to the country as a whole and to specific districts—of the social composition, structure, membership, and political activity of Russian social democratic groups from 1889 to 1907.

12. As quoted by N. Valentinov in his book *Encounters with Lenin* (1968) p. 42. See also A. Balabanoff, *My Life As a Rebel* (1968), and other memoirs.

13. L. Trotsky, *1905* (New York: Vintage, 1972), p. 104.

14. For a detailed history of the soviets see O. Anweiler, *The Soviets: The Russian Workers, Peasants, and Soldiers Councils, 1905-1921* (New York: Pantheon, 1974).

15. Trotsky, *1905*, p. 251.

16. Lenin, "The Dissolution of the Duma and the Tasks of the Proletariat" (1906) in *Collected Works*, Vol. 11 (Moscow: Progress, 1962), pp. 124-5.

17. *Ibid.*, pp. 128-9.

18. "Socialism and Anarchism" (1905), in *Collected Works*, Vol. 10 (Moscow: Progress, 1962), p. 72.

19. "Draft Resolutions for the Fifth Congress of the R.S.D.L.P." (1907), in *Collected Works*, Vol. 12 (Moscow: Progress, 1962), pp. 142-4.

20. Trotsky, *The History of the Russian Revolution*, Vol. I (Ann Arbor: University of Michigan Press, 1932), p. 479. *Cf.* M. Ferro, *The Russian Revolution of February 1917* (Englewood Cliffs, N.J.: Prentice-Hall, 1972), p. 308.

21. "The Workers' Party and the Peasantry" (1902) in *Collected Works* Vol. 4 (Moscow: Progress, 1960), p. 422.

22. "Speech in Defense of the Tactics of the Communist International" at the Third Congress of the Communist International (July 1921), *Against Dogmatism and Sectarianism in the Working-Class Movement* (Moscow, 1965), pp. 179-81.

23. "The Bolsheviks Must Assume Power" (Letter to the Central Committee of the Petrograd and Moscow Party Committees, September 1917) in *Collected Works*, Vol. 26 (Moscow: Progress, 1964), p. 21.

24. R. Luxemburg, *The Russian Revolution* (Ann Arbor: University of Michigan Press, 1961), p. 39.

25. *Ibid.*

26. J. Bunyan and H. H. Fisher, *The Bolshevik Revolution* (Stanford: Stanford University Press, 1934).

27. *Questions of the Socialist Organization of the Economy* (Moscow: p. 173).

28. A. M. Pankratova, *Fabrikräte in Russland* (Frankfurt: Fischer, 1976), p. 232. This important book, first published in Moscow in 1923, offers a comprehensive description—albeit from a Bolshevik point of view—of the rise, activities, and aspirations of the Russian factory councils, their relations to the trade unions, and their elimination by the Bolshevik state.

29. Lenin, *Questions of the Socialist Organization of the Economy*, p. 127.

The Idea of the Commune

1. L. Trotsky, *Our Revolution* (New York, 1918), p. 85.

2. Lenin, *State and Revolution* (New York: International, 1932), p. 44.

3. Quoted by A. Horne, *The Fall of Paris* (New York: Penguin, 1965), p. 33).

4. According to Bakunin, for instance, the impression made by the *Commune* was so powerful that "even Marxists, whose ideas were overthrown by the uprising, saw themselves forced to lift their hats before it. Not only that, in contradiction to all logic and their own true feelings, they adopted the program of the *Commune* as their own. It was a comical but unavoidable travesty, for otherwise they would have lost all their followers due to the mighty passion the revolution aroused all over the world." Quoted by F. Brupbacher, *Marx und Bakunin* (Munich: Die Aktion, 1922), pp. 101-102.

5. Marx, *The Civil War in France*, in *Political Writings*, Vol. 3 (Harmondsworth: Penguin, 1974), p. 212.
6. *Ibid.*
7. *Ibid.*, p. 210.
8. *Ibid.*, p. 211.
9. Lenin, *State and Revolution*, p. 46.
10. Marx to Domela Nienwenhuis, Marx-Engels *Werke*, Vol. 35, p. 160.
11. *State and Revolution*, pp. 38-40.
12. *Ibid.*, pp. 44, 83, 84.
13. *Ibid.*, p. 16.
14. *Ibid.*, p. 84.

State and Counter-Revolution

1. *Constitution of the Russian Socialist Federated Soviet Republic* (1918), Article 4, Chapter XIII.
2. Trotsky, *Our Revolution*, p. 98.
3. Luxemburg, *The Russian Revolution*, p. 46.
4. Lord Moran reports the following dialogue between Churchill and Stalin in Moscow in 1942: Churchill: "When I raised the question of the collective farms and the struggle with the *kulaks*, Stalin became very serious. I asked him if it was as bad as the war. 'Oh, yes,' he answered, 'Worse. Much worse. It went on for years. Most of them were liquidated by the peasants, who hated them. Ten millions of them. But we had to do it to mechanize agriculture. In the end, production from the land was doubled. What is a generation?' Stalin demanded as he paced up and down the length of the table." C .Moran, *Churchill: The Struggle for Survival, 1940-1965* (Boston: Houghton, 1966), p. 70.
5. Lenin, *Program of the CPSU (B)*, adopted 22 March 1919 at the Eighth Congress of the Party.
6. Stalin's Constitution of 1936 reestablished the universal right to vote, but combined it with a number of controls that preclude the election to state institutions of anyone not favored by the Communist Party, thus demonstrating that universal franchise and dictatorship can exist simultaneously.
7. Trotsky, *Dictatorship vs. Democracy* (New York, 1922), pp. 107-9.
8. Trotsky, undoubtedly as outstanding a revolutionary politician as Lenin, is nonetheless of no interest with respect to the Bolshevik Revolution, either as a theoretician or as a practical actor, because of his total submission to Lenin, which allowed him to play a great role in the seizure of power and the construction of the Bolshevik state. Prior to his unconditional deference to Lenin, Trotsky opposed both the Mensheviks and the Bolsheviks, the first because of their passive acceptance of the expected Russian Revolution as a bourgeois revolution in the traditional sense, and the second because of Lenin's insistence on a "peasant-worker alliance," which in Trotsky's view could not lead to a socialist revolution. According to Trotsky, moreover, the socialist revolution, dominated by the industrial proletariat, cannot be contemplated at all within the framework of a national revolution, but must from the start be approached as an international revolution, uniting the Russian revolution with revolutions in Western Europe, that is, as a "permanent

revolution" under the hegemony of the working class. Changing over to
Lenin's ideas and their apparent validity in the context of the Russian situation, Trotsky became the prisoner of a dogmatized Leninism and thus unable
to evolve a Marxist critique of the Bolshevik Revolution.

9. Trotsky, "Lenin on his 50th Birthday," in *Fourth International* (Jan-
uary-February 1951), pp. 28-9.

10. A. J. Mayer, *Wilson vs. Lenin* (1964), p. 301.

11. H. H. Fisher, "Soviet Policies in Asia," in *The Annals of the American
Academy of Political and Social Science* (May 1949), p. 190.

12. "On the Slogan for a United States of Europe" (1915), in *Collected
Works*, Vol. 21 (Moscow: Progress, 1964), p. 342.

13. This found its expression in the program adopted by the sailors, soldiers, and workers of Kronstadt: 1) Immediate new elections to the soviets.
The present soviets no longer express the wishes of the workers and peasants.
The new elections should be by secret ballot, and should be preceded by free
electorial propaganda. 2) Freedom of speech and of the press for workers and
peasants, for the Anarchists, and for the left socialist parties. 3) The right of
assembly, and freedom of trade union and peasant organizations. 4) The organization, at the latest on 10th March 1921, of a conference of non-party
workers, soldiers and sailors of Petrograd, Kronstadt and the Petrograd district. 5) The liberation of all political prisoners of the socialist parties, and of
all imprisoned workers, peasants, soldiers and sailors belonging to working
class and peasant organizations. 6) The election of a commission to look into
the dossiers of all those detained in prisons and concentration camps. 7) The
abolition of all political sections in the armed forces. No political party
should have privileges for the propagation of its ideas, or receive State sub-
sidies to this end. In the place of the political sections, various cultural groups
should be set up, deriving resources from the State. 8) The immediate abolition of the militia detachments set up between towns and countryside. 9) The
equalization of rations for all workers, except those engaged in dangerous or
unhealthy jobs. 10) The abolition of party combat detachments in all military
groups. The abolition of party guards in factories and enterprises. If guards
are required, they should be nominated, taking into account the views of the
workers. 11) The granting to the peasants of freedom of action on their own
soil and the right to own cattle, provided they look after them themselves and
do not employ hired labor. 12) We request that all military units and officer
trainee groups associate themselves with this resolution. 13) We demand the
press give proper publicity to this resolution. 14) We demand that handicraft
production be authorized provided it does not utilize wage labor. Quoted by
Ida Mett, *The Kronstadt Commune* (London: Solidarity, 1967), pp. 6-7. For
a detailed history of the Kronstadt rebellion, see Paul Avrich, *Kronstadt 1921*
(Princeton: Princeton University Press, 1970).

14. In *Izvestiya*, Journal of Kronstadt's Temporary Revolutionary Committee, 12 March 1921; quoted in *The Truth about Kronstadt* (Prague, 1921).

15. A. Kollontai, *The Workers' Opposition* (1921).

16. *Dictatorship vs. Democracy*, p. 149.

17. Article written for *Sotsialistichesky Viestnik*; English version in *Proletarian Outlook* 6:3 (1940).

The German Revolution

1. *Korrespondenzblatt der Generalkomission der Gewerkschaften* 28:46 (16 November 1918).

2. In *Rote Fahne*, 20 November 1918.

About
the
Author

Paul Mattick, born in Germany in 1904, was trained as a tool and die maker. Around the time of the first world war he became active in the revolutionary left in Berlin and Cologne, and began to write. After emigrating to the United States in 1926, he became involved in the Industrial Workers of the World (IWW) and later in the unemployed workers' movement of the depression years, and from 1934 until 1943 edited the journals *International Council Correspondence*, *Living Marxism*, and *New Essays*. His many books in English include *Marx and Keynes*, *Critique of Marcuse*, *Anti-Bolshevik Communism*, *Economics, Politics, and the Age of Inflation*, and *Economic Crisis and Crisis Theory*. *Marxism—Last Refuge of the Bourgeoisie?* is Paul Mattick's last book. He died in Cambridge, Massachusetts, in February 1981. Intended as the summing up of a lifetime's reflection on capitalist society and revolutionary opposition to it, this provocative work continues an important current in the history of Marxist theory.